SlideGuide

for

Gardner's Art through the Ages: The Western Perspective

Twelfth Edition

Volume I

Fred S. Kleiner

Christin J. Mamiya

THOMSON

WADSWORTH

Australia • Canada • Mexico • Singapore • Spain • United Kingdom • United States

Printed in the United States of America
3 4 5 6 7 09 08 07

Printer: Thomson West

ISBN-13: 978-0-495-00522-3
ISBN-10: 0-495-00522-3

Thomson Higher Education
10 Davis Drive
Belmont, CA 94002-3098
USA

Asia (including India)
Thomson Learning
5 Shenton Way
#01-01 UIC Building
Singapore 068808

Australia/New Zealand
Thomson Learning Australia
102 Dodds Street
Southbank, Victoria 3006
Australia

Canada
Thomson Nelson
1120 Birchmount Road
Toronto, Ontario M1K 5G4
Canada

UK/Europe/Middle East/Africa
Thomson Learning
High Holborn House
50–51 Bedford Road
London WC1R 4LR
United Kingdom

Latin America
Thomson Learning
Seneca, 53
Colonia Polanco
11560 Mexico
D.F. Mexico

Spain (including Portugal)
Thomson Paraninfo
Calle Magallanes, 25
28015 Madrid, Spain

Contents

Chapter 1

The Birth of Art:
Africa, Europe, and the Near East in the Stone Age

Goals

- Understand the origins of art in terms of time period, human development, and human activity. Explore origins of creativity, representation, and stylistic innovation in the Paleolithic Period.
- Describe the role of human and animal figures in Paleolithic art. Examine the materials and techniques of the earliest art making in the Paleolithic period.
- Illustrate differences between the Paleolithic and Neolithic art as a result of social and environmental changes.
- Understand and evaluate the types of art prevalent in the Neolithic period.

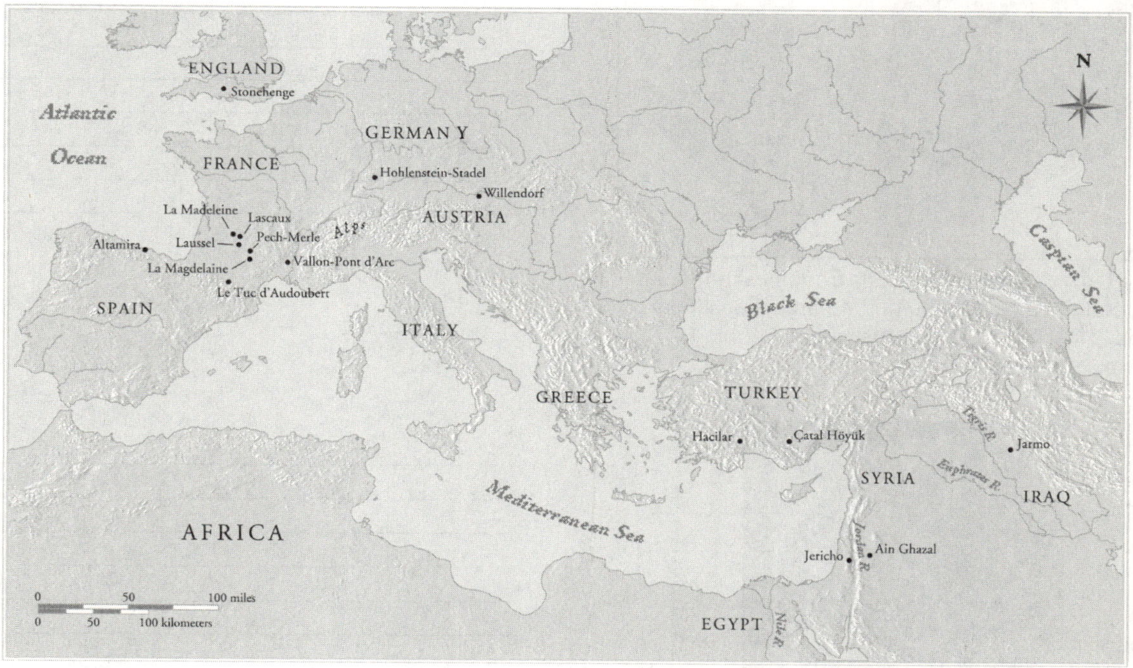

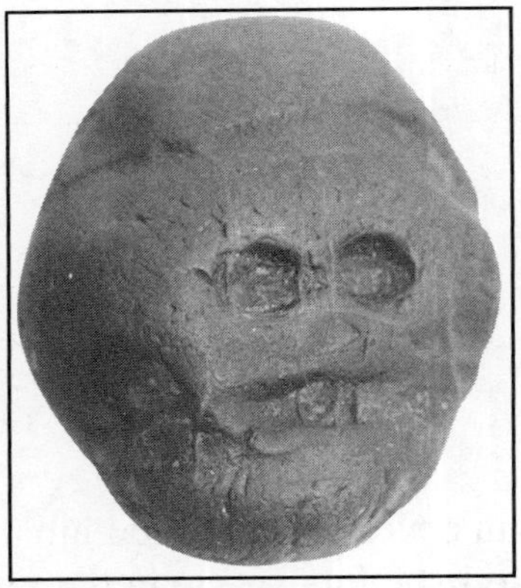

FIG. 01-01 Waterworn pebble resembling a human face, from Makapansgat, South Africa, ca. 3,000,000 BCE. Reddish brown jasperite, approx. 2 3/8″ wide. (page 2)

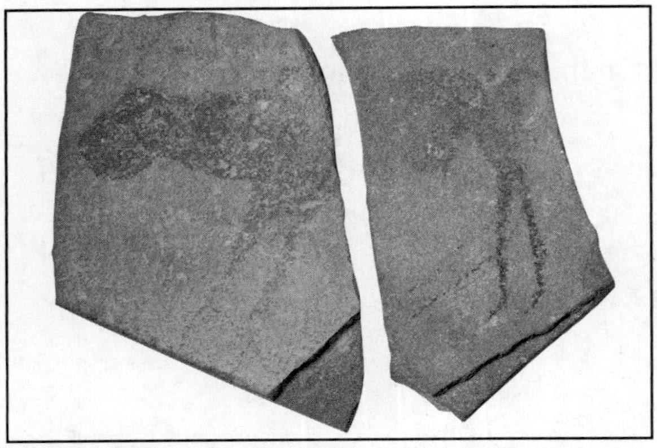

FIG. 01-02 Animal facing left, from the Apollo 11 Cave, Namibia, ca. 23,000 BCE. Charcoal on stone, approx. 5″ × 4 1/4″. State Museum of Namibia, Windhoek. (page 3)

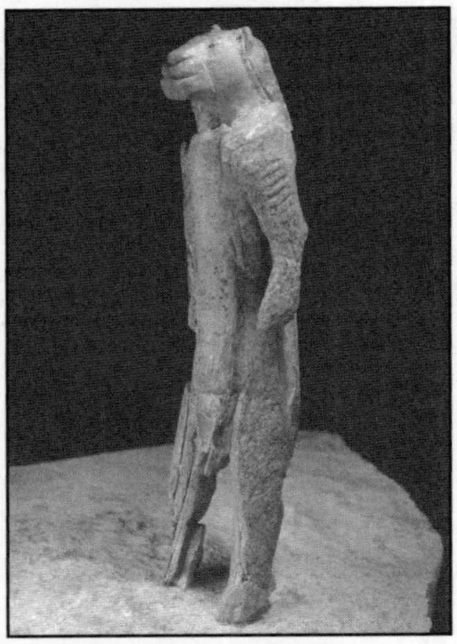

FIG. 01-03 Human with feline head, from Hohlenstein-Stadel, Germany, ca. 30,000–28,000 BCE. Mammoth ivory, 11 5/8″ high. Ulmer Museum, Ulm. (page 3)

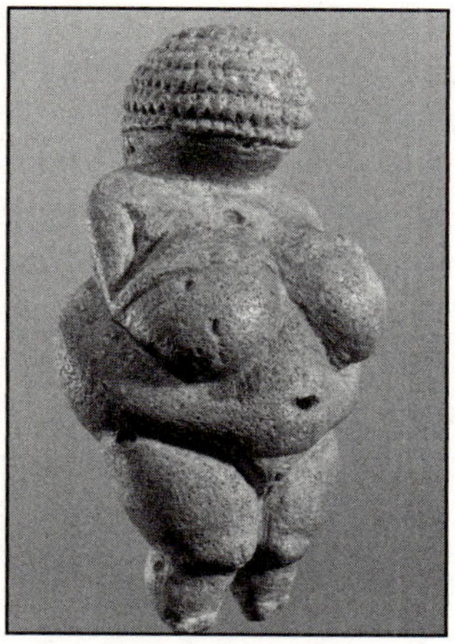

FIG. 01-04 Nude woman *(Venus of Willendorf),* from Willendorf, Austria, ca. 28,000–25,000 BCE. Limestone, approx. 4 1/4″ high. Naturhistorisches Museum, Vienna. (page 4)

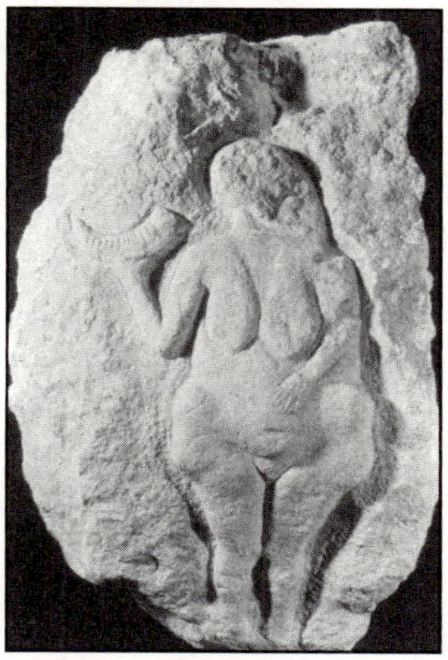

FIG. 01-05 Woman holding a bison horn, from Laussel, Dordogne, France, ca. 25,000–20,000 BCE. Painted limestone, approx. 1′ 6″ high. Musée d'Aquitaine, Bordeaux. (page 4)

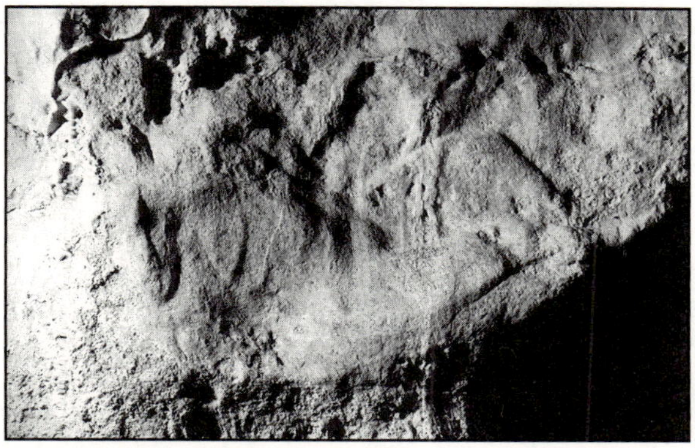

FIG. 01-06 Reclining woman, rock-cut relief, La Magdelaine cave, Tarn, France, ca. 12,000 BCE. Approx. half life-size. (page 5)

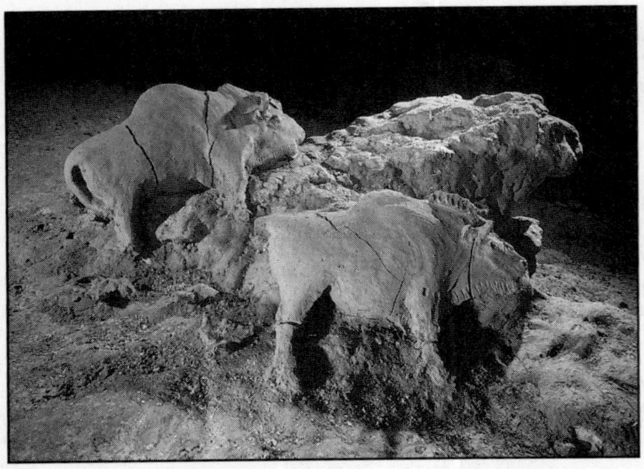

FIG. 01-07 Two bison, reliefs in cave at Le Tuc d'Audoubert, Ariège, France, ca. 15,000–10,000 BCE. Clay, each approx. 2′ long. (page 5)

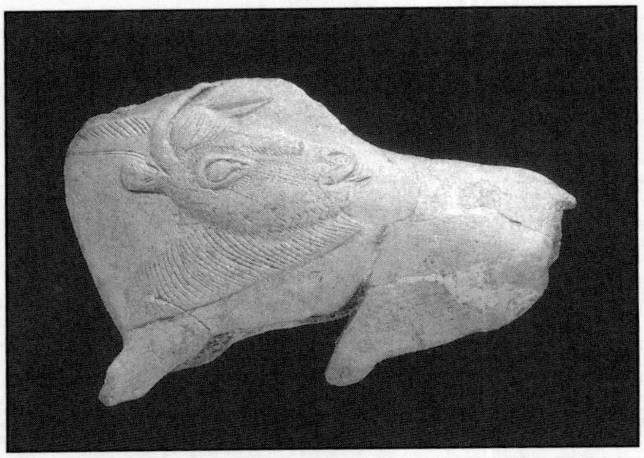

FIG. 01-08 Bison with turned head, fragmentary spearthrower, from La Madeleine, Dordogne, France, ca. 12,000 BCE. Reindeer horn, approx. 4″ long. Réunion des Musées Nationaux. (page 6)

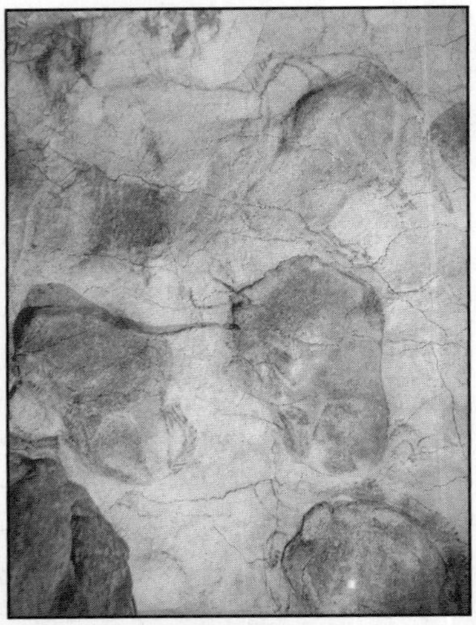

FIG. 01-09 Bison, detail of a painted ceiling in the Altamira cave, Santander, Spain, ca. 12,000–11,000 BCE. Each bison approx. 5′ long. (page 6)

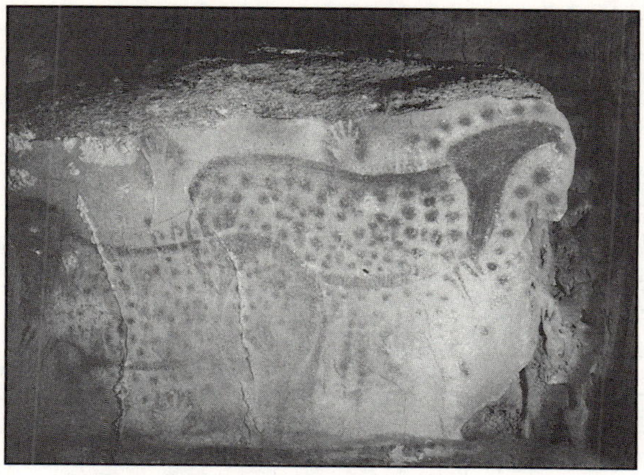

FIG. 01-10 Spotted horses and negative hand imprints, wall painting in the cave at Pech-Merle, Lot, France, ca. 22,000 BCE. Approx. 11′ 2″ long. (page 7)

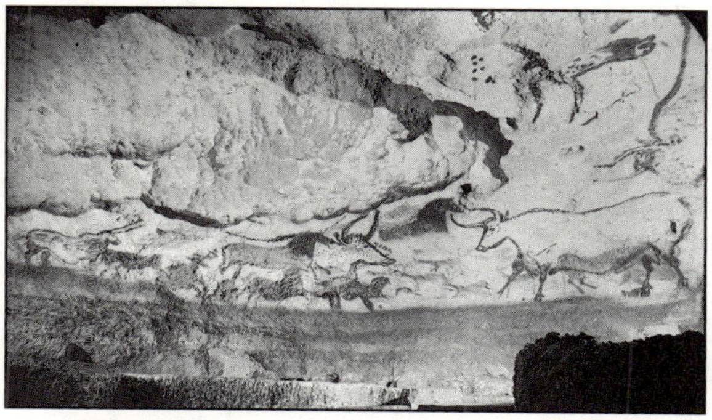

FIG. 01-11 Hall of the Bulls (left wall), Lascaux, Dordogne, France, ca. 15,000–13,000 BCE. Largest bull approx. 11′ 6″ long. (page 8)

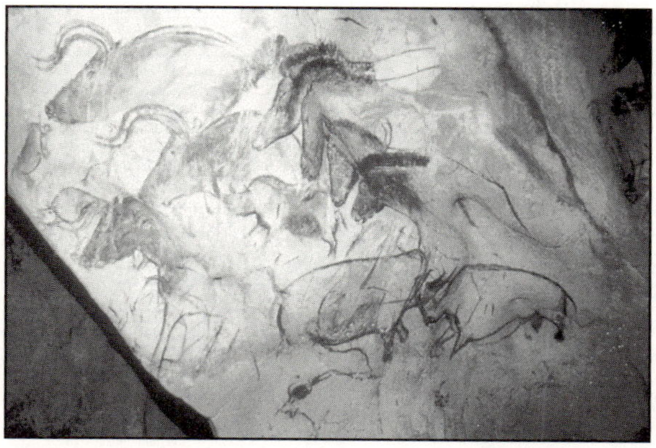

FIG. 01-12 Aurochs, horses, and rhinoceroses, wall painting in Chauvet Cave, Vallon-Pont-d'Arc, Ardèche, France, ca. 30,000–28,000 or ca. 15,000–13,000 BCE. Approx. half life-size. (page 9)

FIG. 01-13 Rhinoceros, wounded man, and disemboweled bison, painting in the well, Lascaux, Dordogne, France, ca. 15,000–13,000 BCE. Bison approx. 3′ 8″ long. (page 10)

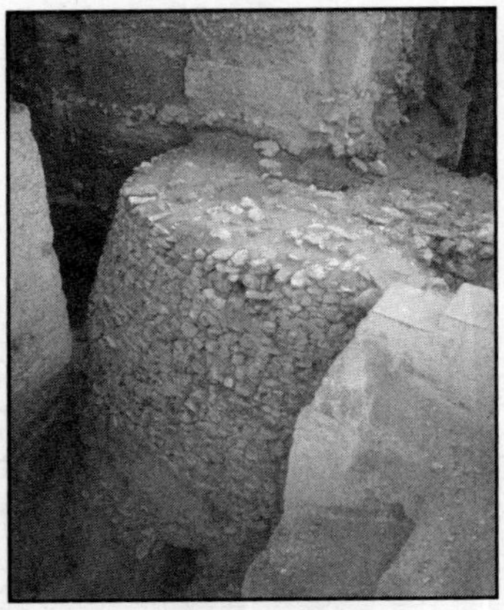

FIG. 01-14 Great stone tower built into the settlement wall, Jericho, ca. 8000–7000 BCE. (page 11)

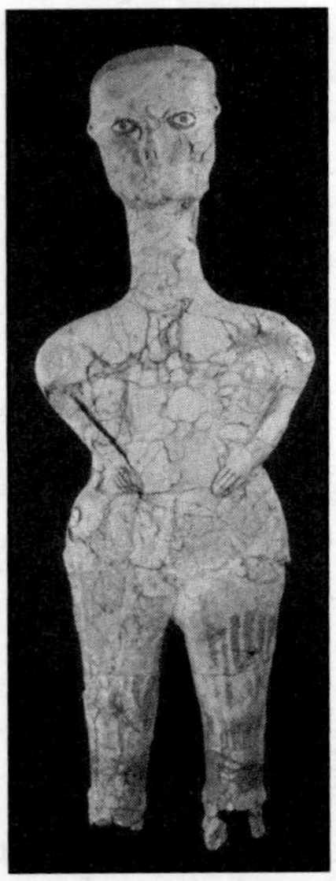

FIG. 01-15 Human figure, from Ain Ghazal, Jordan, ca. 6750–6250 BCE. Plaster, painted and inlaid with cowrie shell and bitumen, 3′ 5 3/8″ high. Louvre, Paris. (page 11)

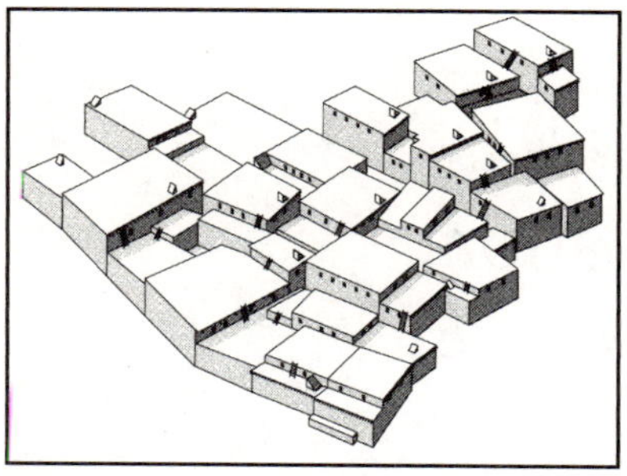

FIG. 01-16 Schematic reconstruction drawing of a section of Level VI, Çatal Höyük, Turkey, ca. 6000–5900 BCE (after J. Mellaart). (page 12)

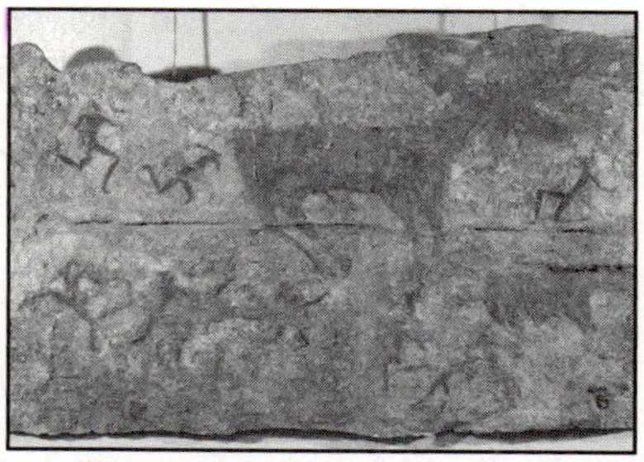

FIG. 01-17 Deer hunt, detail of a wall painting from Level III, Çatal Höyük, Turkey, ca. 5750 BCE. Museum of Anatolian Civilization, Ankara. (page 13)

FIG. 01-18 Landscape with volcanic eruption(?), detail of a watercolor copy of a wall painting from Level VII, Çatal Höyük, Turkey, ca. 6150 BCE. (page 13)

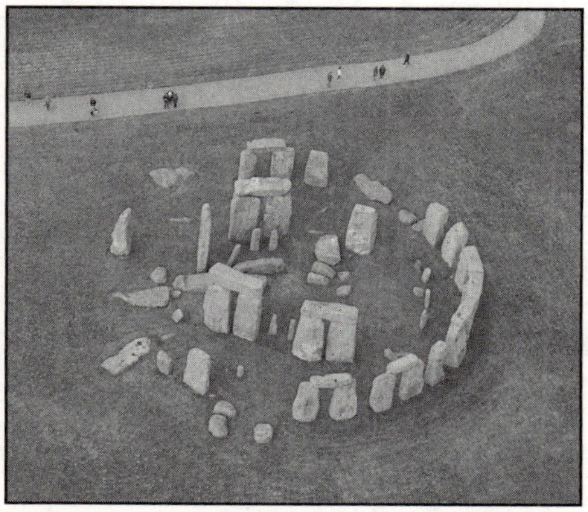

FIG. 01-19 Aerial view of Stonehenge, Salisbury Plain, Wiltshire, England, ca. 2550–1600 BCE. Circle is 97′ in diameter; trilithons approx. 24′ high. (page 14)

Chapter 2

The Rise of Civilization:
The Art of the Ancient Near East

Goals

- Understand the cultural changes in the Neolithic Revolution as they relate to art and architecture.
- Understand the concept of civilization and the importance of Sumer in the ancient Near East.
- Examine the artistic materials, techniques, subject matter, styles, and conventions developed in the ancient Near East.

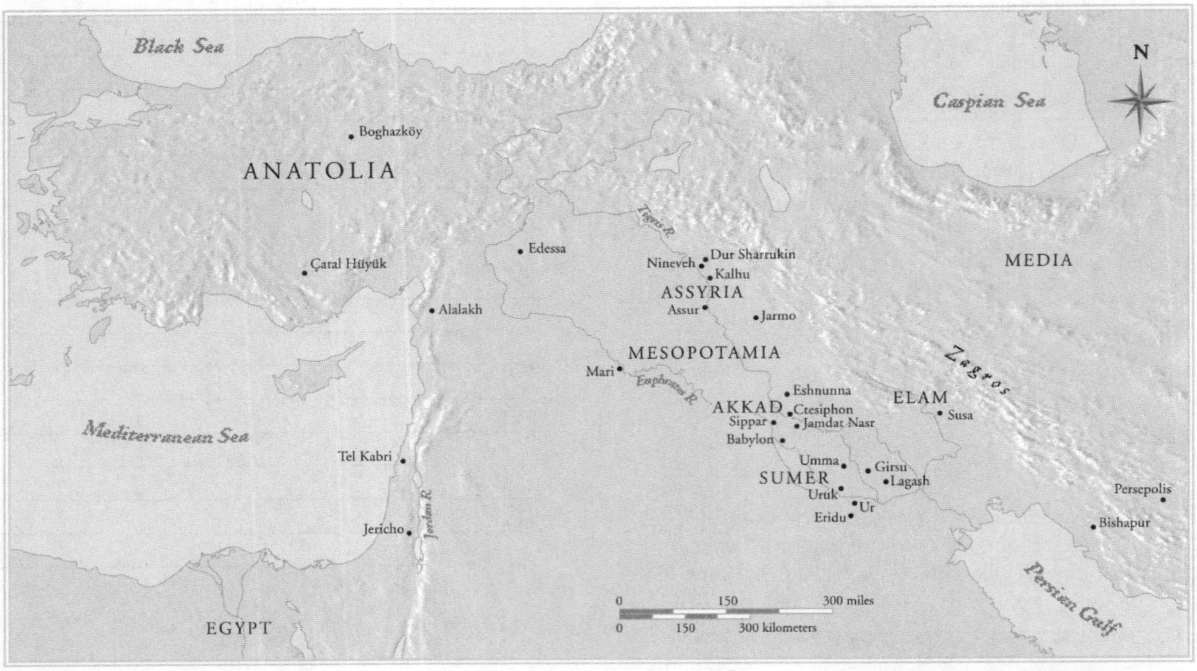

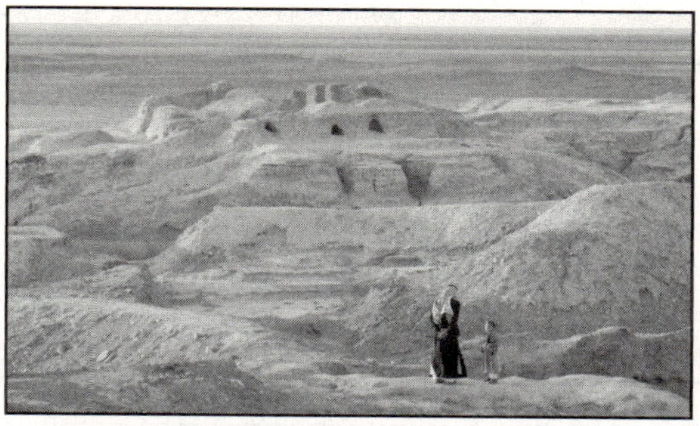

FIG. 02-01 White Temple and ziggurat, Uruk (modern Warka), Iraq, ca. 3200–3000 BCE. (page 18)

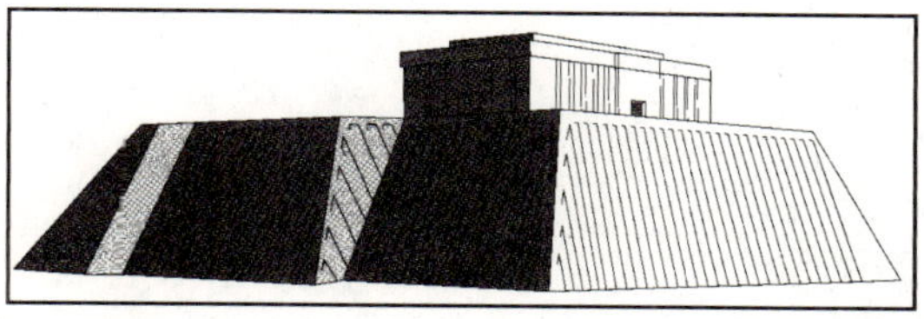

FIG. 02-02 Reconstruction drawing of the White Temple and ziggurat, Uruk (modern Warka), Iraq, ca. 3200–3000 BCE (after S. E. Piggott). (page 19)

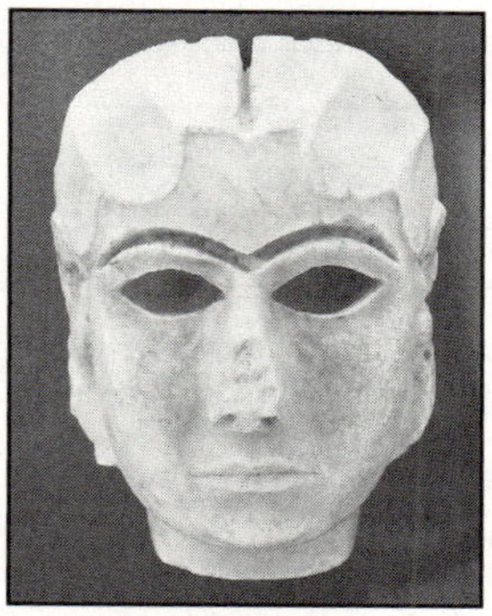

FIG. 02-03 Female head (Inanna?), from Uruk (modern Warka), Iraq, ca. 3200–3000 BCE. Marble, approx. 8″ high. Iraq Museum, Baghdad. (page 20)

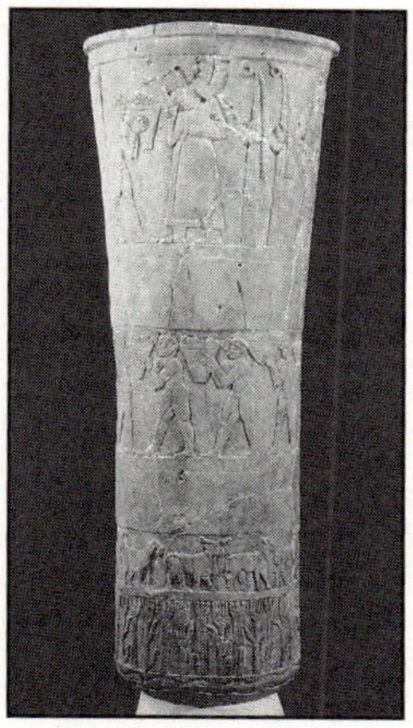

FIG. 02-04 Presentation of offerings to Inanna *(Warka Vase),* from Uruk (modern Warka), Iraq, ca. 3200–3000 BCE. Alabaster, 39 1/4″ high. Iraq Museum, Baghdad. (page 20)

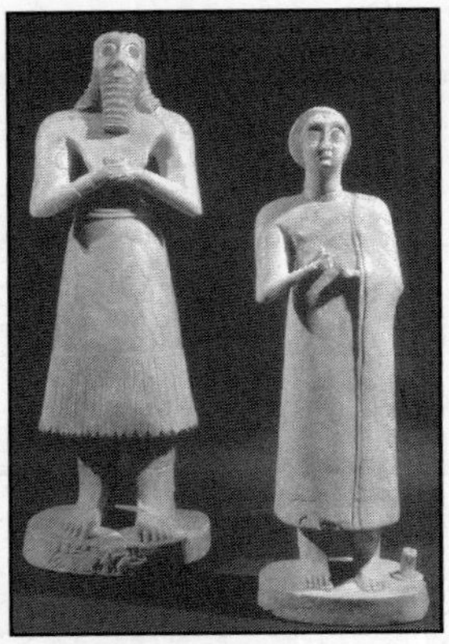

FIG. 02-05 Statuettes of two worshipers, from the Square Temple at Eshnunna (modern Tell Asmar), Iraq, ca. 2700 BCE. Gypsum inlaid with shell and black limestone, male figure approx. 2′ 6″ high. Iraq Museum, Baghdad. (page 22)

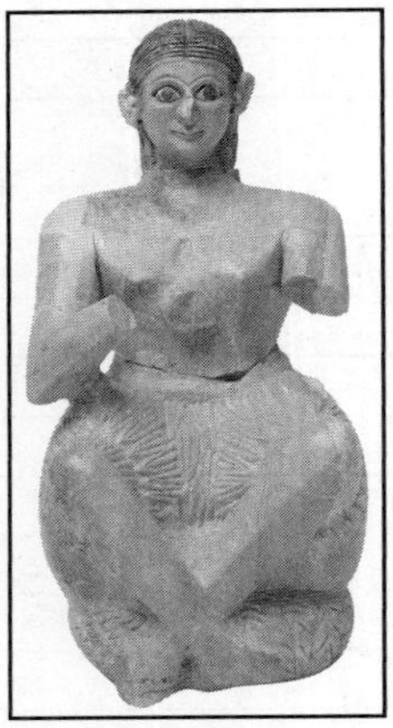

FIG. 02-06 Seated statuette of Urnanshe, from the Temple of Ishtar at Mari (modern Tell Hariri), Syria, ca. 2600–2500 BCE. Gypsum inlaid with shell and lapis lazuli, 10 1/4″ high. National Museum, Damascus. (page 22)

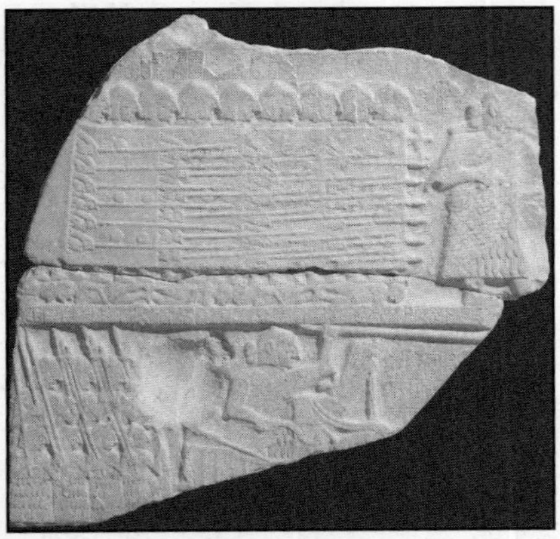

FIG. 02-07 Fragment of the victory stele of Eannatum *(Stele of the Vultures),* from Girsu (modern Telloh), Syria, ca. 2600–2500 BCE. Limestone, full stele approx. 5′ 11″ high. Louvre, Paris. (page 23)

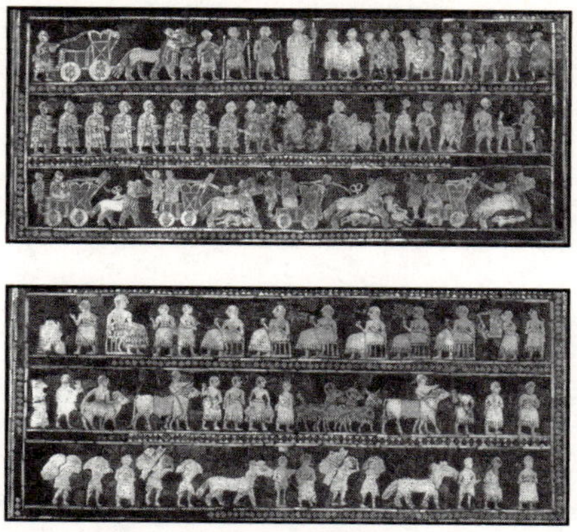

FIG. 02-08 War side *(top)* and peace side *(bottom)* of the *Standard of Ur,* from Tomb 779, Royal Cemetery, Ur (modern Tell Muqayyar), Iraq, ca. 2600 BCE. Wood inlaid with shell, lapis lazuli, and red limestone, approx. 8″ × 1′ 7″. British Museum, London. (page 24)

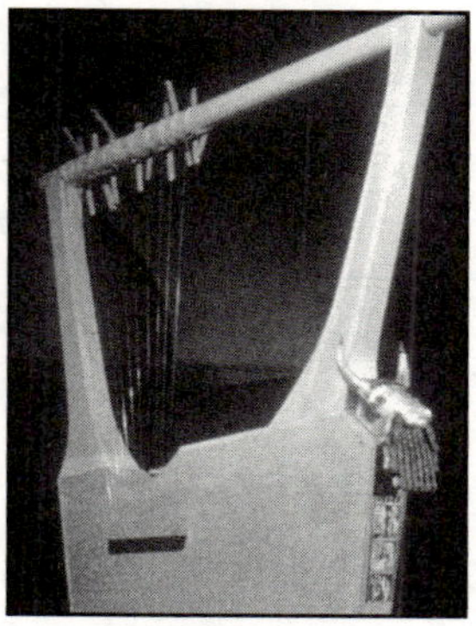

FIG. 02-09 Bull-headed lyre (restored) from Tomb 789 ("King's Grave"), Royal Cemetery, Ur (modern Tell Muqayyar), Iraq, ca. 2600 BCE. Gold leaf and lapis lazuli over a wooden core, approx. 5′ 5″ high. University Museum, University of Pennsylvania, Philadelphia. (page 25)

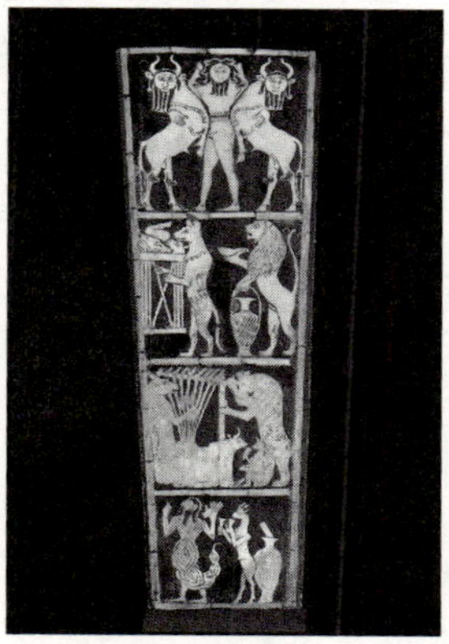

FIG. 02-10 Soundbox of the lyre from Tomb 789 ("King's Grave"), Royal Cemetery, Ur (modern Tell Muqayyar), Iraq, ca. 2600 BCE. Wood with inlaid gold, lapis lazuli, and shell, approx. 1′ 7″ high. University Museum, University of Pennsylvania, Philadelphia. (page 25)

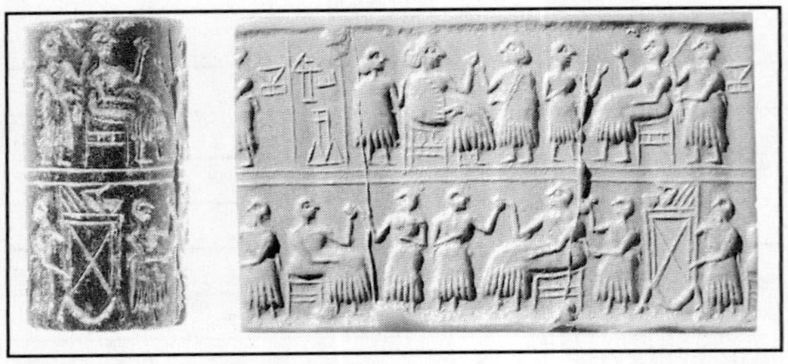

FIG. 02-11 Banquet scene, cylinder seal *(left)* and its modern impression *(right),* from the Tomb of Pu-abi (Tomb 800), Royal Cemetery, Ur (modern Tell Muqayyar), Iraq, ca. 2600 BCE. Lapis lazuli, approx. 20 high. British Museum, London. (page 25)

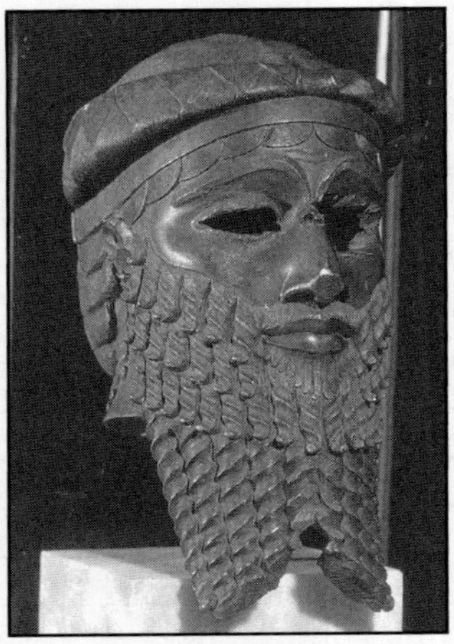

FIG. 02-12 Head of an Akkadian ruler, from Nineveh (modern Kuyunjik), Iraq, ca. 2250–2200 BCE. Copper, 1′ 2 3/8″ high. Iraq Museum, Baghdad. (page 26)

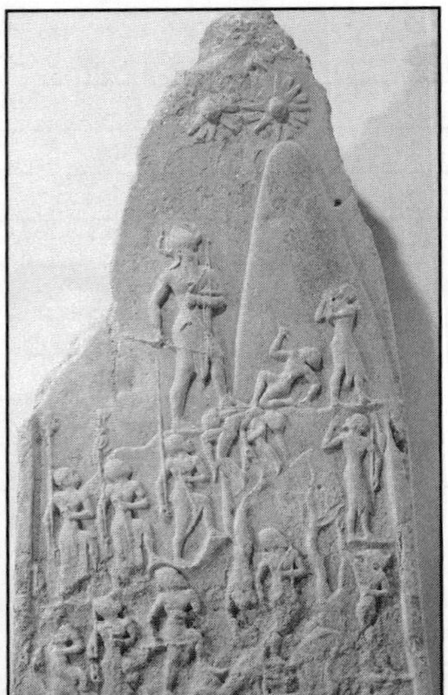

FIG. 02-13 Victory stele of Naram-Sin, from Susa, Iran, 2254–2218 BCE. Pink sandstone, approx. 6′ 7″ high. Louvre, Paris. (page 27)

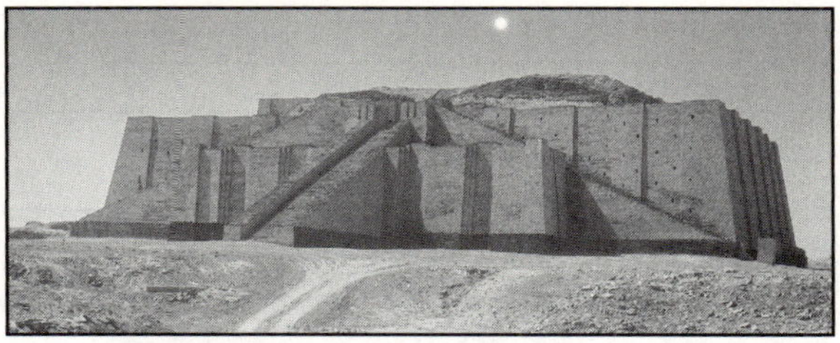

FIG. 02-14 Ziggurat (northeastern facade with restored stairs), Ur (modern Tell Muqayyar), Iraq, ca. 2100 BCE. (page 27)

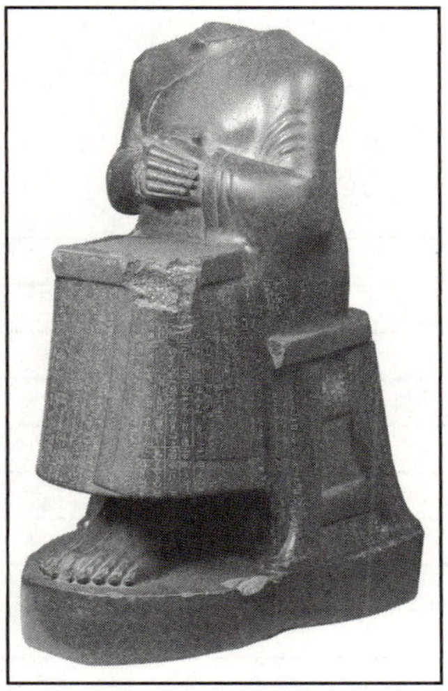

FIG. 02-15 Seated statue of Gudea holding temple plan, from Girsu (modern Telloh), Iraq, ca. 2100 BCE. Diorite, approx. 2′ 5″ high. Louvre, Paris. (page 28)

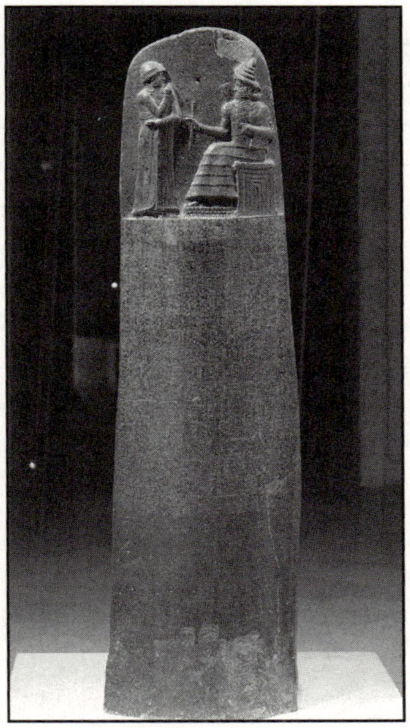

FIG. 02-16 Stele with law code of Hammurabi, from Susa, Iran, ca. 1780 BCE. Basalt, approx. 7′ 4″ high. Louvre, Paris. (page 29)

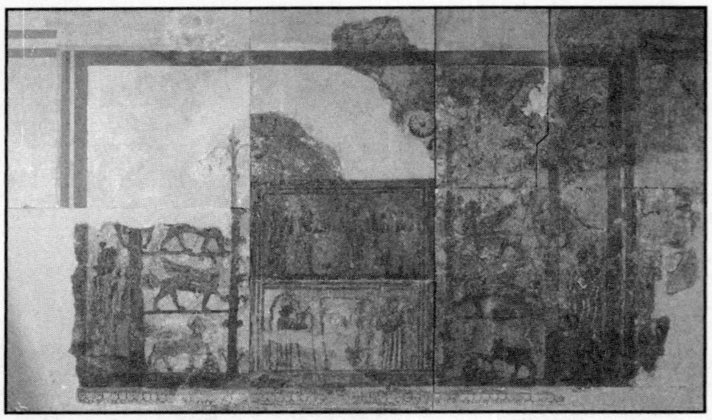

FIG. 02-17 Investiture of Zimri-Lim, mural painting from Court 106 of the palace at Mari (modern Tell Hariri), Syria, ca. 1775–1760 BCE. Louvre, Paris. (page 30)

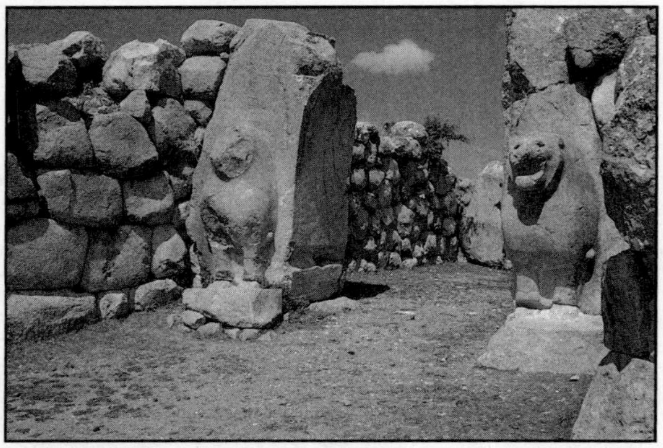

FIG. 02-18 Lion Gate, Boghazköy, Turkey, ca. 1400 BCE. Limestone, lions approx. 7′ high. (page 30)

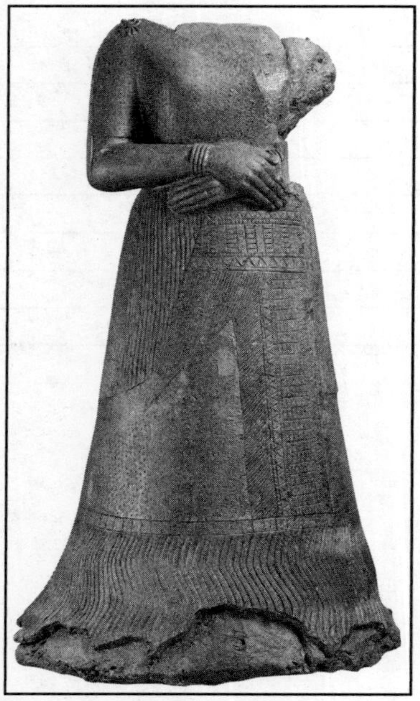

FIG. 02-19 Statue of Queen Napir-Asu, from Susa, Iran, ca. 1350–1300 BCE. Bronze and copper, 4′ 2 3/4″ high. Louvre, Paris. (page 31)

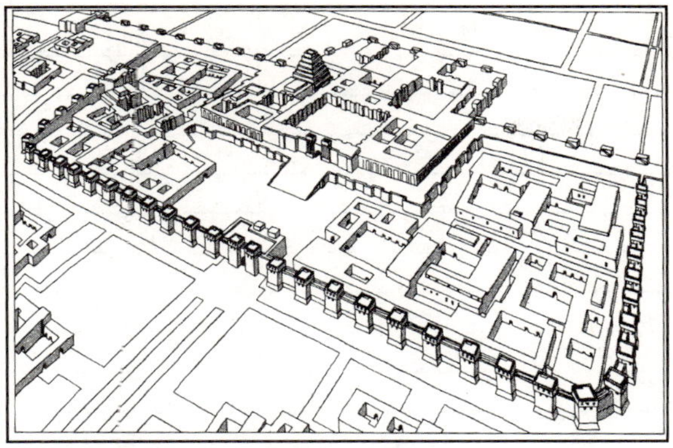

FIG. 02-20 Reconstruction drawing of the citadel of Sargon II, Dur Sharrukin (modern Khorsabad), Iraq, ca. 720–705 BCE (after Charles Altman). (page 32)

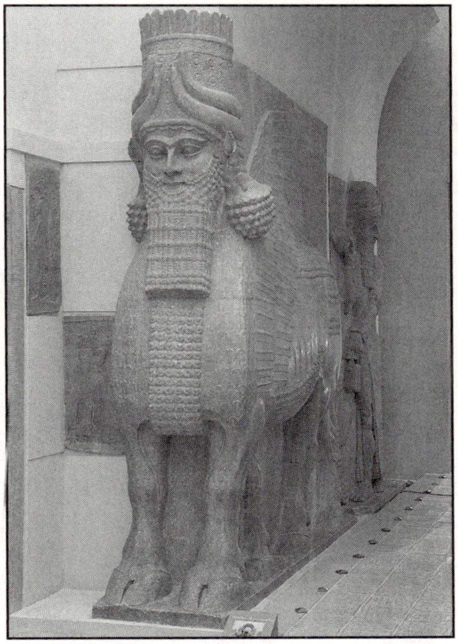

FIG. 02-21 Lamassu (winged, human-headed bull), from the citadel of Sargon II, Dur Sharrukin (modern Khorsabad), Iraq, ca. 720–705 BCE. Limestone, approx. 13′ 10″ high. Louvre, Paris. (page 32)

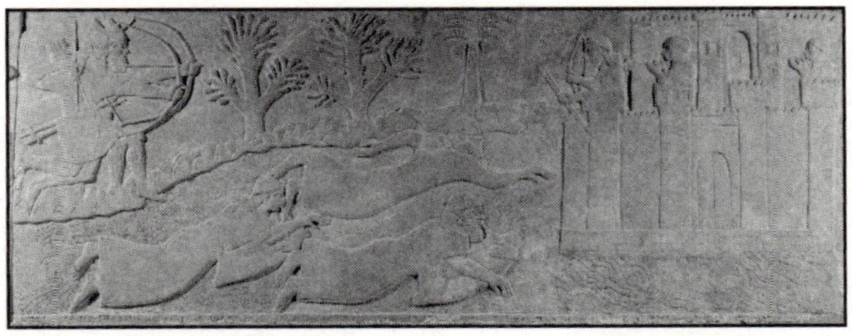

FIG. 02-22 Assyrian archers pursuing enemies, relief from the Northwest Palace of Ashurnasirpal II, Kalhu (modern Nimrud), Iraq, ca. 875–860 BCE. Gypsum, 2′ 10 5/8″ high. British Museum, London. (page 33)

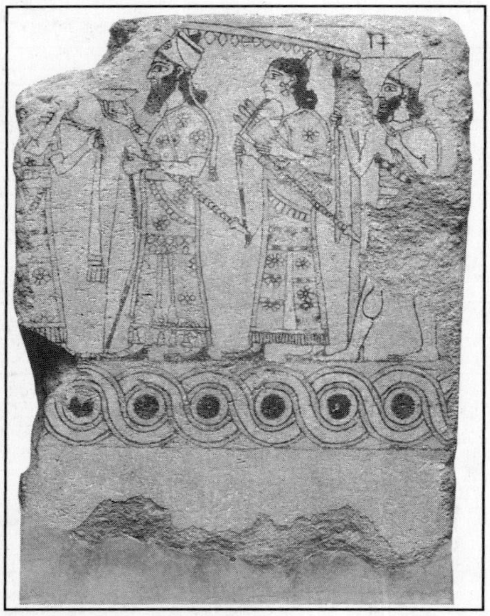

FIG. 02-23 Ashurnasirpal II with attendants and soldier, from his palace at Kalhu, Iraq, ca. 875–860 BCE. Glazed brick, 11 3/4″ high. British Museum, London. (page 34)

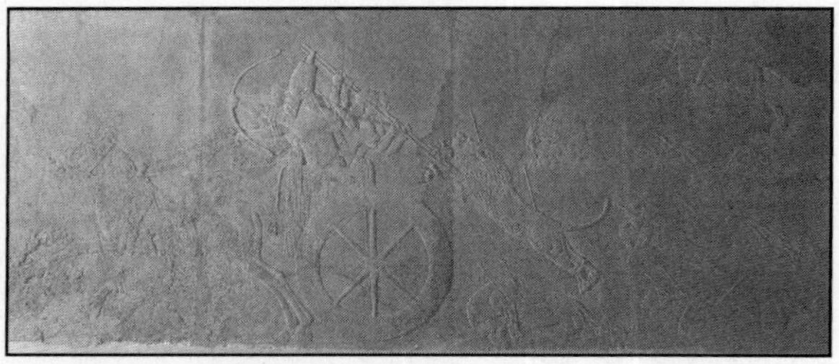

FIG. 02-24 Ashurbanipal hunting lions, relief from the North Palace of Ashurbanipal, Nineveh (modern Kuyunjik), Iraq, ca. 645–640 BCE. Gypsum, 5′ 4″ high. British Museum, London. (page 34)

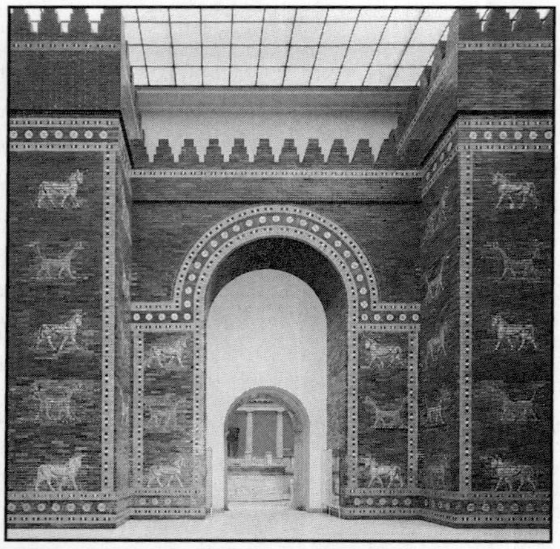

FIG. 02-25 Ishtar Gate (restored), Babylon, Iraq, ca. 575 BCE. Glazed brick. Staatliche Museen, Berlin. (page 35)

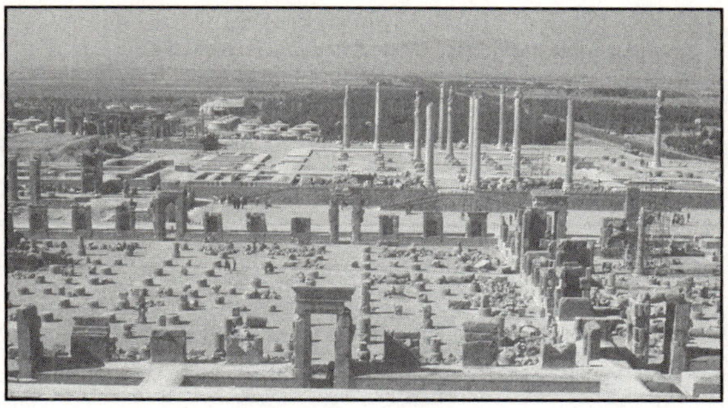

FIG. 02-26 Persepolis (royal audience hall in the background), Iran, ca. 521–465 BCE. (page 36)

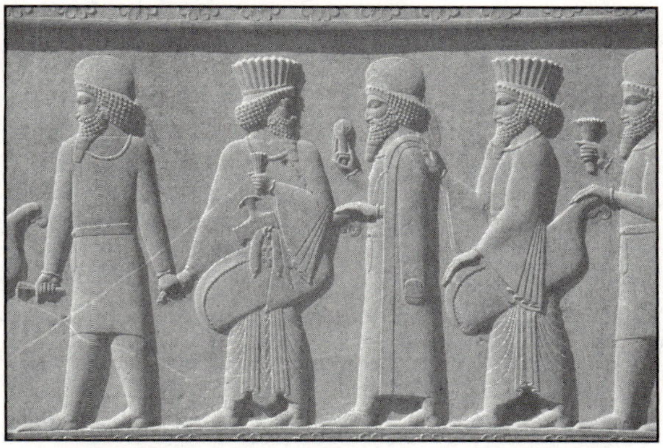

FIG. 02-27 Processional frieze (detail) on the terrace of the royal audience hall *(apadana)*, Persepolis, Iran, ca. 521–465 BCE. (page 37)

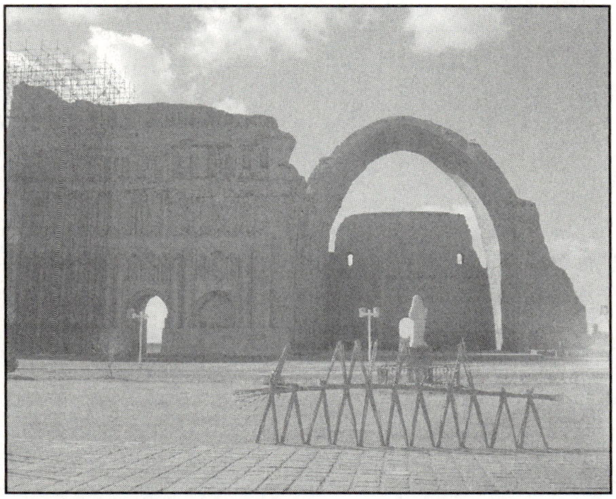

FIG. 02-28 Palace of Shapur I, Ctesiphon, Iraq, ca. 250 CE. (page 37)

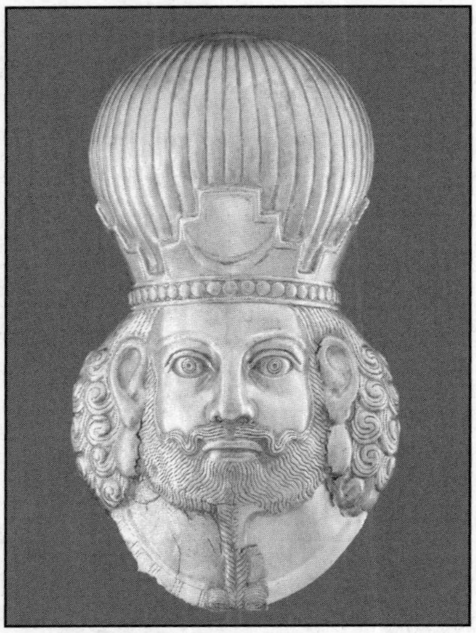

FIG. 02-29 Head of a Sasanian king (Shapur II?), ca. 350 CE. Silver with mercury gilding, 1′ 3 3/4″ high. Metropolitan Museum of Art, New York. (page 38)

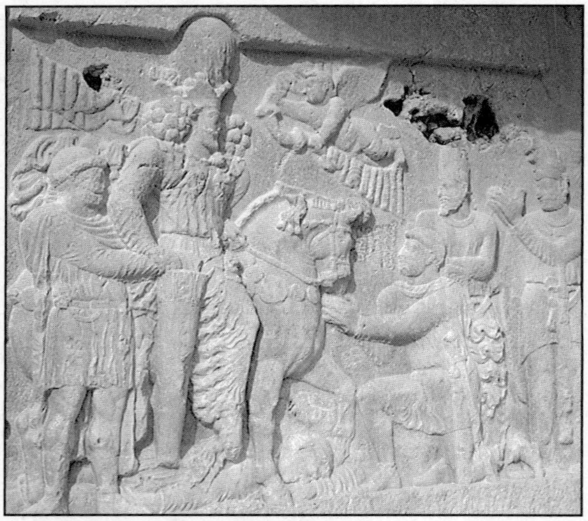

FIG. 02-30 Triumph of Shapur I over Valerian, rock-cut relief, Bishapur, Iran, ca. 260 CE. (page 38)

Chapter 3

Pharaohs and the Afterlife:
The Art of Ancient Egypt

Goals

- Understand the evolution of Egyptian culture and its relationship to the Nile.
- Recognize stylistic conventions of Egyptian art.
- Describe Egyptian funerary art forms from these periods and state reason for the development of these monuments.
- Understand architectural evolution from pyramid to the tomb temple and burial monuments of the Old and Middle Kingdoms.
- Discuss how Egyptian art changed as a result of the Hyksos' invasions.
- Understand aspects of the New Kingdom as reflected in its art.

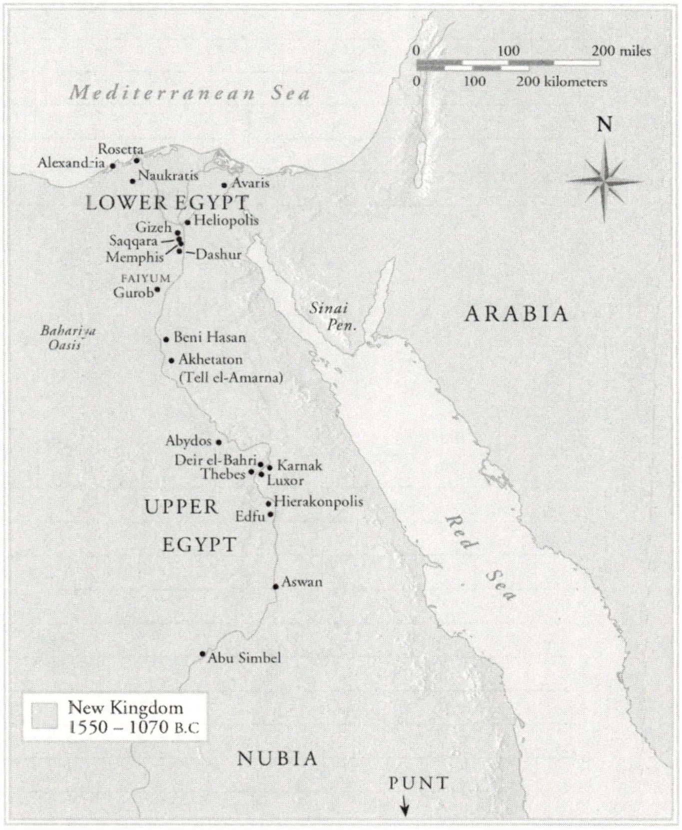

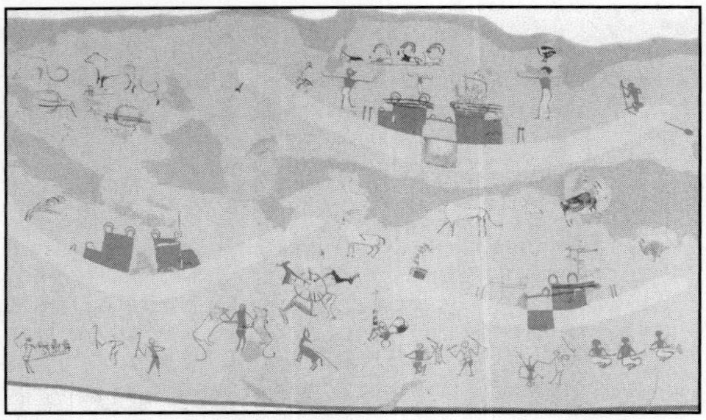

FIG. 03-01 People, boats, and animals, detail of a watercolor copy of a wall painting from Tomb 100 at Hierakonpolis, Egypt, Predynastic, ca. 3500–3200 BCE. Paint on plaster, entire painting approx. 16′ 3″ long. Egyptian Museum, Cairo. (page 42)

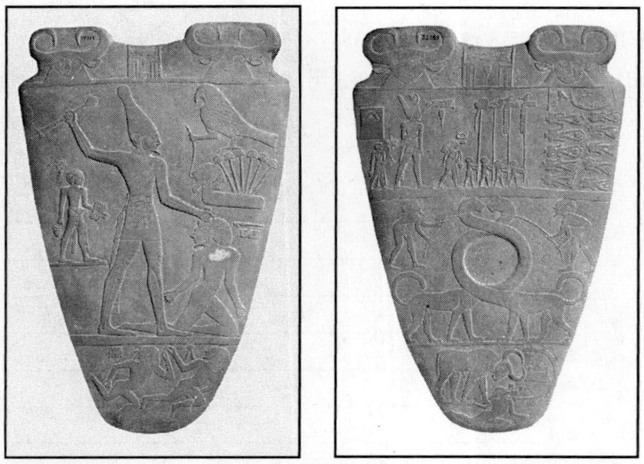

FIG. 03-02 *Palette of King Narmer* (*left,* back; *right,* front), from Hierakonpolis, Egypt, Predynastic, ca. 3000–2920 BCE. Slate, approx. 2′ 1″ high. Egyptian Museum, Cairo. (page 44)

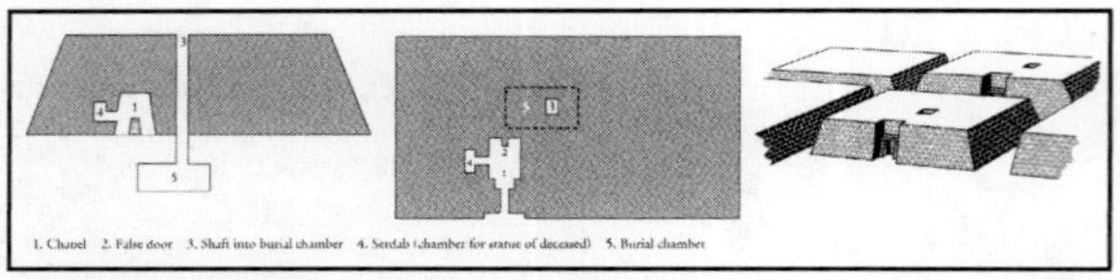

FIG. 03-03 Section *(left),* plan *(center),* and restored view *(right)* of typical Egyptian mastaba tombs. (page 45)

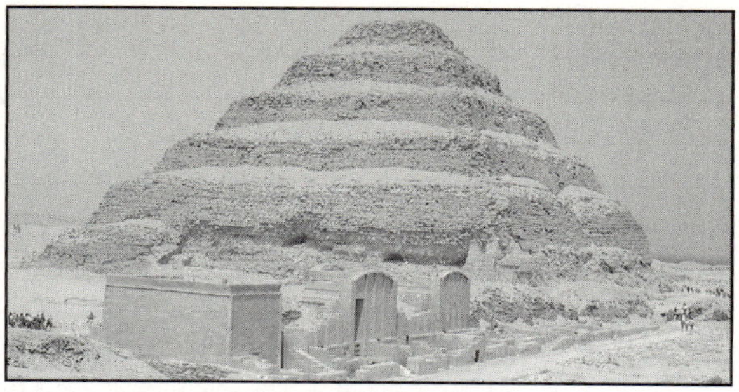

FIG. 03-04 IMHOTEP, Stepped Pyramid and mortuary precinct of Djoser, Saqqara, Egypt, Dynasty III, ca. 2630–2611 BCE. (page 46)

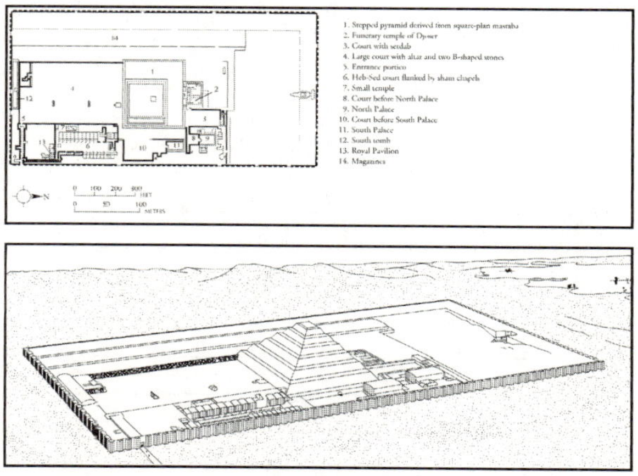

FIG. 03-05 Plan *(top)* and restored view *(bottom)* of the mortuary precinct of Djoser, Saqqara, Egypt, Dynasty III, ca. 2630–2611 BCE. (page 47)

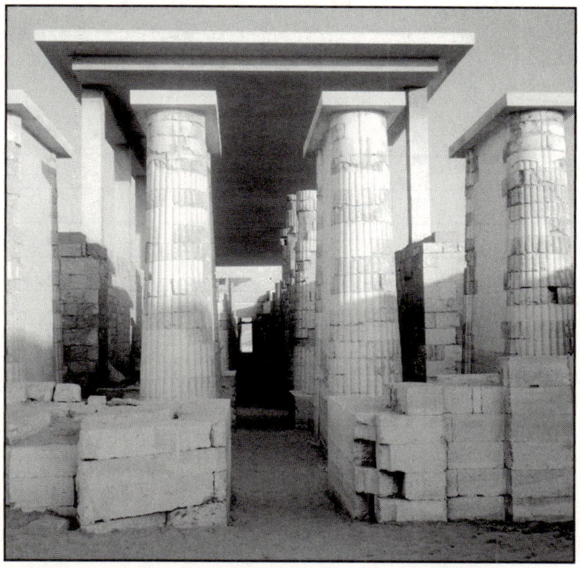

FIG. 03-06 Columnar entrance corridor to the mortuary precinct of Djoser, Saqqara, Egypt, Dynasty III, ca. 2630–2611 BCE. (page 47)

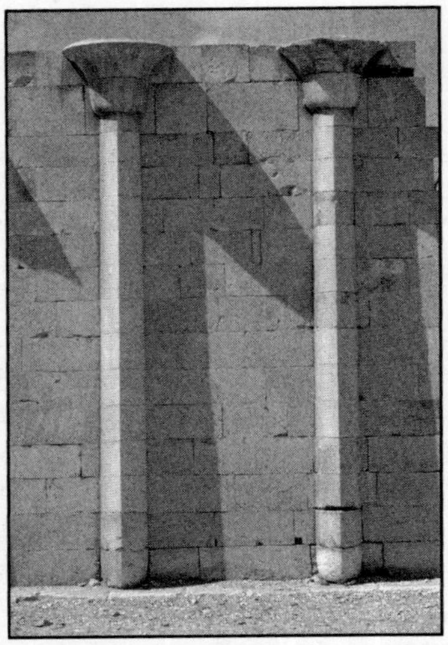

FIG. 03-07 Facade of the North Palace of the mortuary precinct of Djoser, Saqqara, Egypt, Dynasty III, ca. 2630–2611 BCE. (page 48)

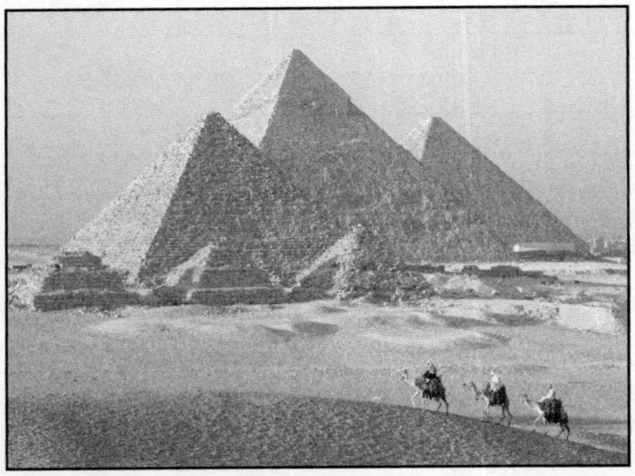

FIG. 03-08 Great Pyramids, Gizeh, Egypt, Dynasty IV. *From left:* Pyramids of Menkaure, ca. 2490–2472 BCE; Khafre, ca. 2520–2494 BCE; and Khufu, ca. 2551–2528 BCE. (page 48)

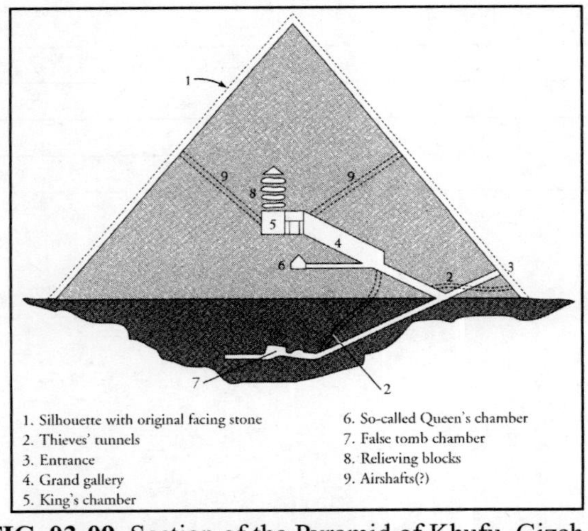

FIG. 03-09 Section of the Pyramid of Khufu, Gizeh, Egypt. (page 49)

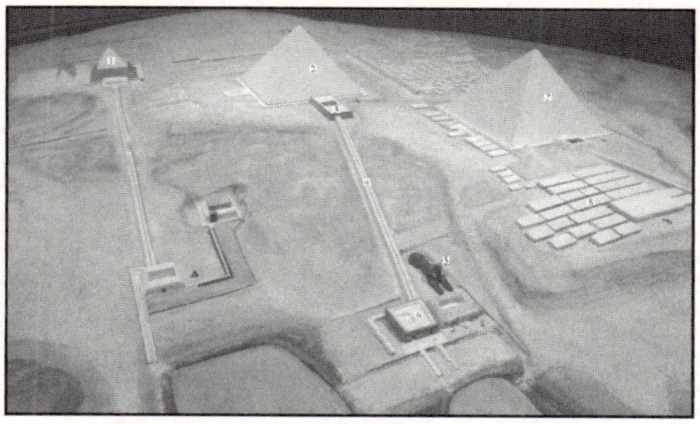

FIG. 03-10 Model of the pyramid complex, Gizeh, Egypt. Cambridge, Massachusetts, Harvard University Semitic Museum. 1) Pyramid of Menkaure, 2) Pyramid of Khafre, 3) Mortuary temple of Khafre, 4) Causeway, 5) Great Sphinx, 6) Valley temple of Khafre, 7) Pyramid of Khufu, 8) Pyramids of the royal family and mastabas of nobles (page 50)

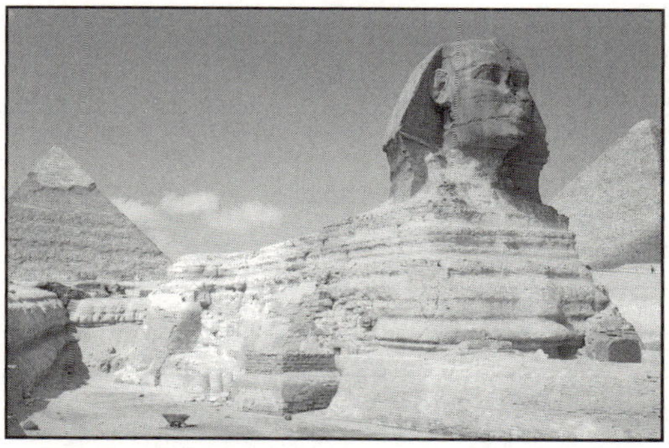

FIG. 03-11 Great Sphinx (with Pyramid of Khafre in the background at left), Gizeh, Egypt, Dynasty IV, ca. 2520–2494 BCE. Sandstone, approx. 65′ high, 240′ long. (page 50)

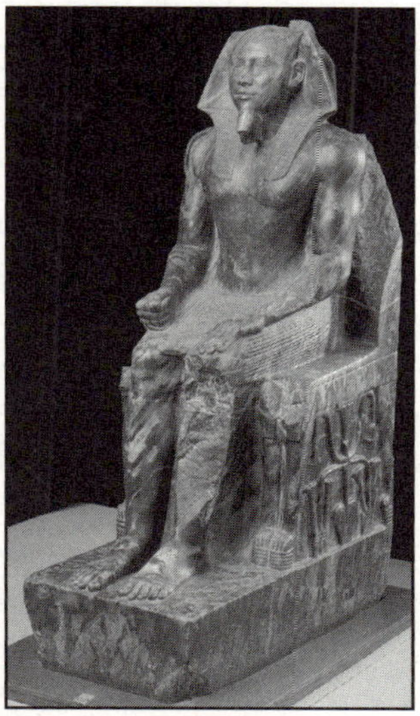

FIG. 03-12 Khafre, from Gizeh, Egypt, Dynasty IV, ca. 2520–2494 BCE. Diorite, approx. 5′ 6″ high. Egyptian Museum, Cairo. (page 51)

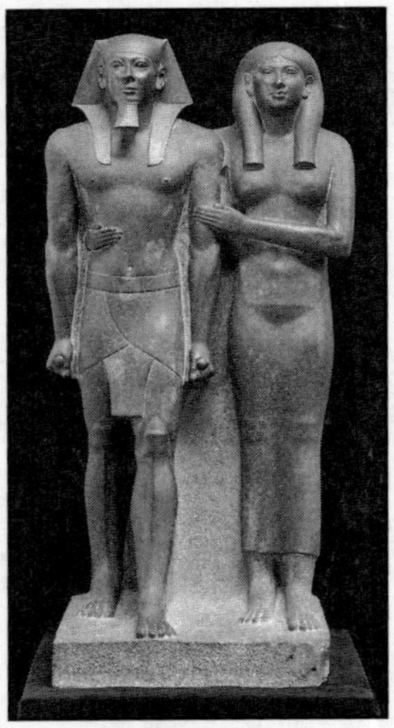

FIG. 03-13 Menkaure and Khamerernebty(?), from Gizeh, Egypt, Dynasty IV, ca. 2490–2472 BCE. Graywacke, approx. 4′ 6 1/2″ high. Museum of Fine Arts, Boston. (page 52)

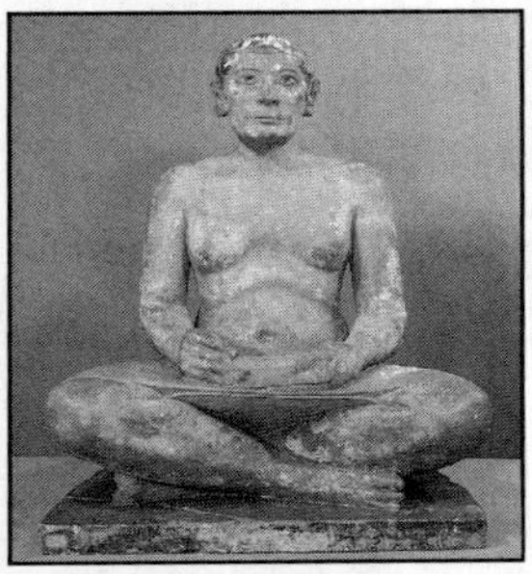

FIG. 03-14 Seated scribe (Kay?), from his mastaba at Saqqara, Egypt, Dynasty V, ca. 2450–2350 BCE. Painted limestone, approx. 1′ 9″ high. Louvre, Paris. (page 52)

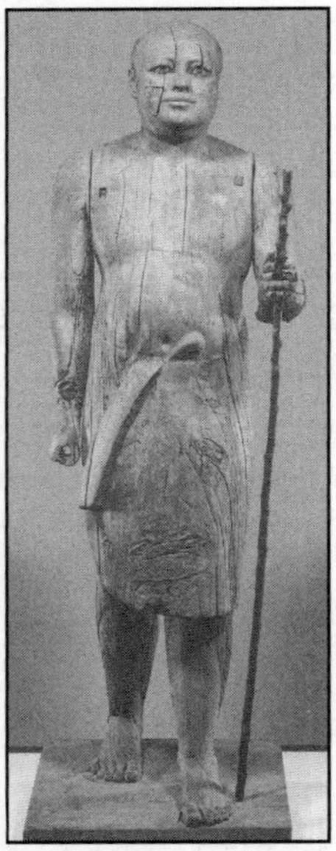

FIG. 03-15 Ka-Aper, from his mastaba at Saqqara, Egypt, Dynasty V, ca. 2450–2350 BCE. Wood, approx. 3′ 7″ high. Egyptian Museum, Cairo. (page 53)

FIG. 03-16 Ti watching a hippopotamus hunt, relief in the mastaba of Ti, Saqqara, Egypt, Dynasty V, ca. 2450–2350 BCE. Painted limestone, hunting scene approx. 4′ high. (page 53)

FIG. 03-17 Goats treading seed and cattle fording a canal, reliefs in the mastaba of Ti, Saqqara, Egypt, Dynasty V, ca. 2450–2350 BCE. Painted limestone. (page 54)

FIG. 03-18 Fragmentary head of Senusret III, Dynasty XII, ca. 1860 BCE. Red quartzite, approx. 6 1/2″ high. Metropolitan Museum of Art, New York. (page 55)

FIG. 03-19 Rock-cut tombs BH 3–5, Beni Hasan, Egypt, Dynasty XII, ca. 1950–1900 BCE. (page 55)

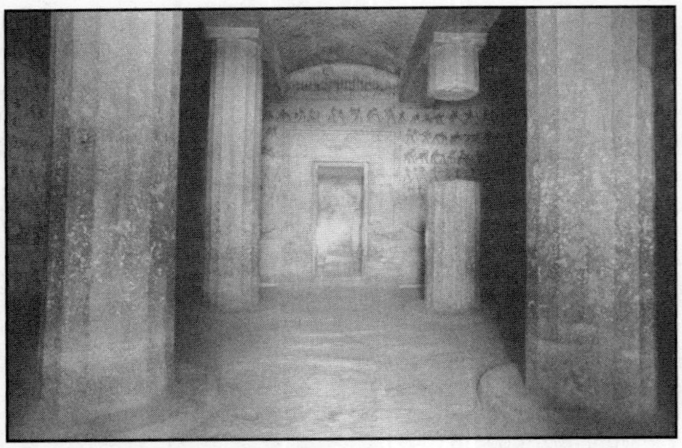

FIG. 03-20 Interior hall of the rock-cut tomb of Amenemhet (BH 2), Beni Hasan, Egypt, Dynasty XII, ca. 1950–1900 BCE. (page 56)

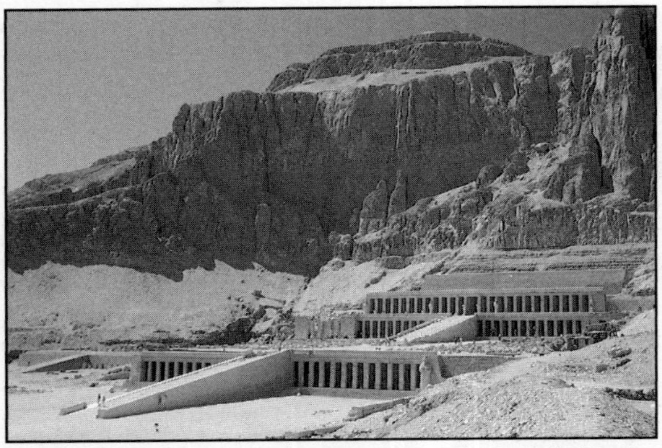

FIG. 03-21 Mortuary temple of Hatshepsut (with the Middle Kingdom mortuary temple of Mentuhotep II at left), Deir el-Bahri, Egypt, Dynasty XVIII, ca. 1473–1458 BCE. (page 57)

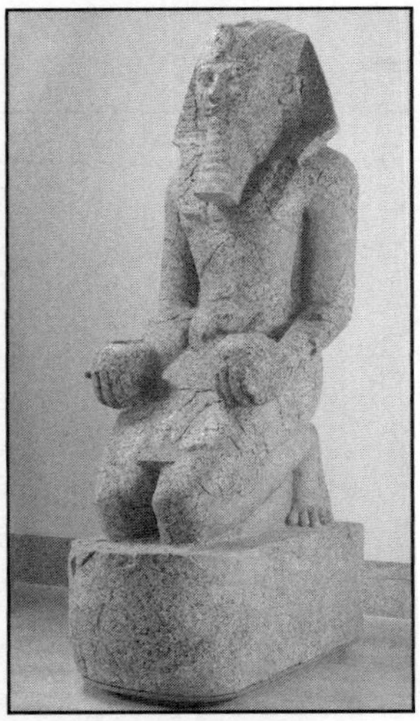

FIG. 03-22 Hatshepsut with offering jars, from the upper court of her mortuary temple, Deir el-Bahri, Egypt, Dynasty XVIII, ca. 1473–1458 BCE. Red granite, approx. 8′ 6″ high. Metropolitan Museum of Art, New York. (page 58)

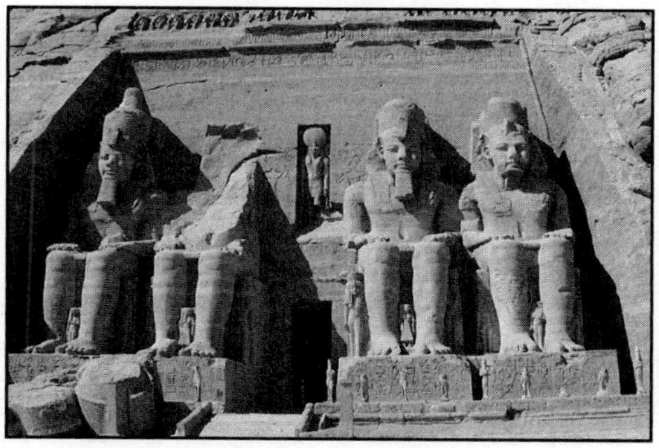

FIG. 03-23 Temple of Ramses II, Abu Simbel, Egypt, Dynasty XIX, ca. 1290–1224 BCE. Sandstone, colossi approx. 65′ high. (page 58)

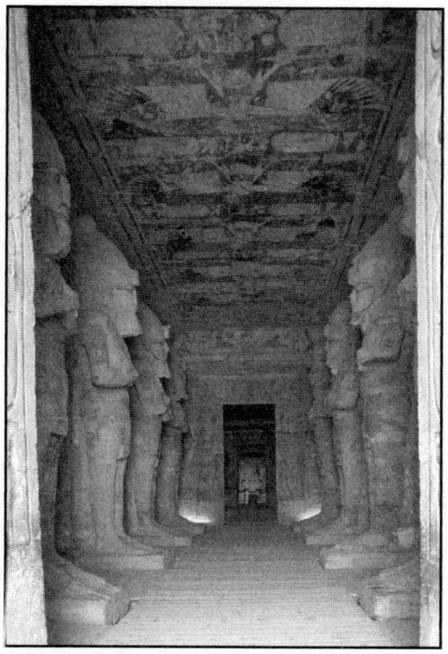

FIG. 03-24 Interior of the temple of Ramses II, Abu Simbel, Egypt, Dynasty XIX, ca. 1290–1224 BCE. Sandstone, pillar statues approx. 32′ high. (page 59)

FIG. 03-25 Restored view of the temple of Amen-Re, Karnak, Egypt, begun 15th century BCE (Jean-Claude Golvin). (page 60)

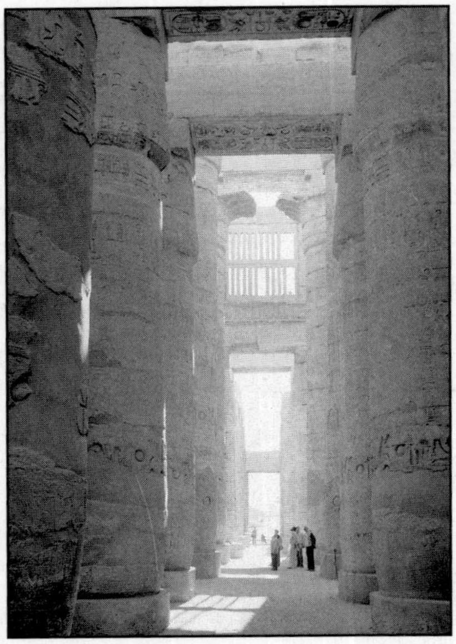

FIG. 03-26 Hypostyle hall, temple of Amen-Re, Karnak, Egypt, Dynasty XIX, ca. 1290 – 1224 BCE. (page 61)

FIG. 03-27 Model of hypostyle hall, temple of Amen-Re, Karnak, Egypt, Dynasty XIX, ca. 1290 – 1224 BCE. Metropolitan Museum of Art, New York. (page 61)

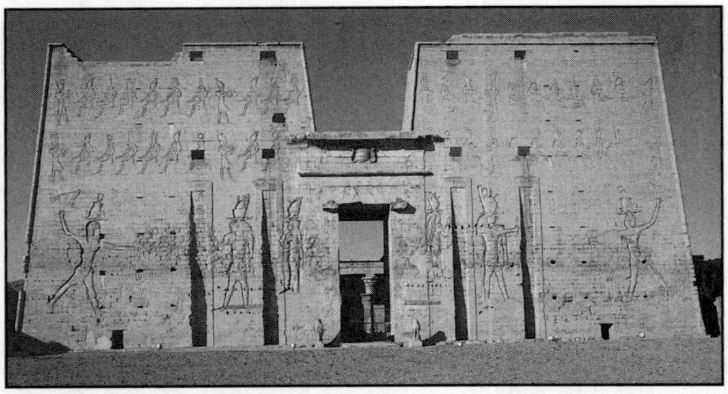

FIG. 03-28 Temple of Horus, Edfu, Egypt, ca. 237 – 47 BCE. (page 61)

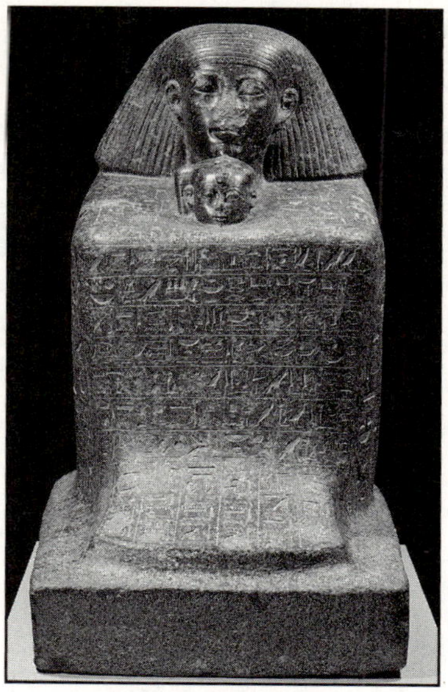

FIG. 03-29 Senmut with Princess Nefrua, from Thebes, Egypt, Dynasty XVIII, ca. 1470–1460 BCE. Granite, approx. 3′ 1/2″ high. Ägyptisches Museum, Berlin. (page 62)

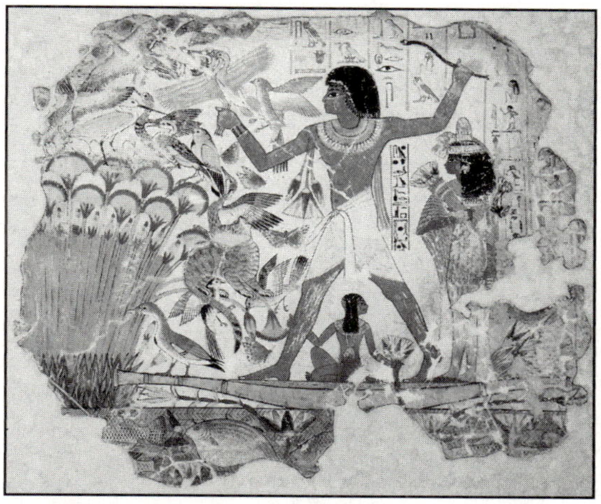

FIG. 03-30 Fowling scene, from the tomb of Nebamun, Thebes, Egypt, Dynasty XVIII, ca. 1400–1350 BCE. Fresco on dry plaster, approx. 2′ 8″ high. British Museum, London. (page 62)

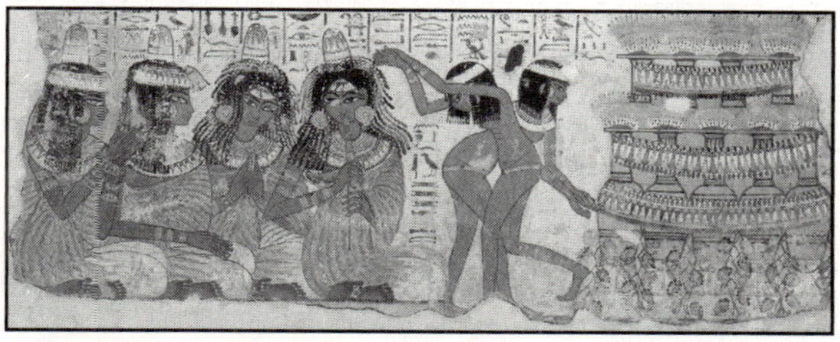

FIG. 03-31 Musicians and dancers, detail of a fresco from the tomb of Nebamun, Thebes, Egypt, Dynasty XVIII, ca. 1400–1350 BCE. Fragment approx. 1′ × 2′ 3″. British Museum, London. (page 63)

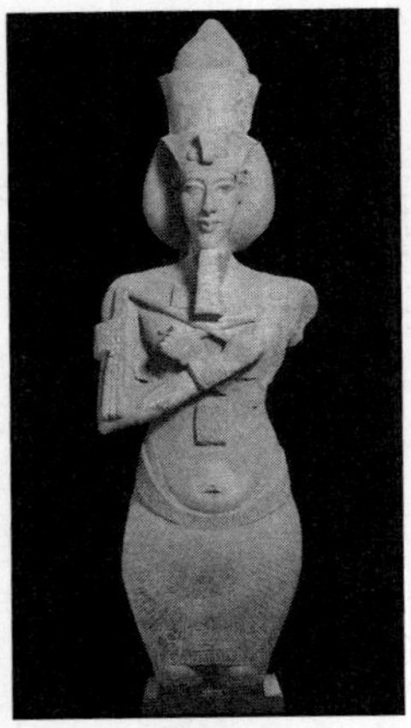

FIG. 03-32 Akhenaton, from the temple of Aton, Karnak, Egypt, Dynasty XVIII, ca. 1353–1335 BCE. Sandstone, approx. 13′ high. Egyptian Museum, Cairo. (page 64)

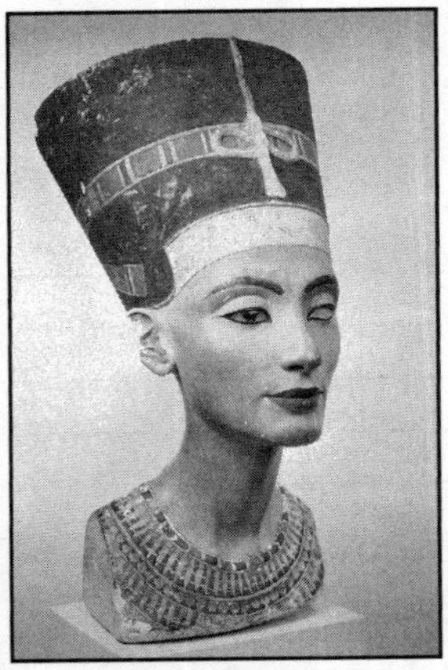

FIG. 03-33 THUTMOSE, Nefertiti, from Tell el-Amarna, Egypt, Dynasty XVIII, ca. 1353–1335 BCE. Painted limestone, approx. 1′ 8″ high. Ägyptisches Museum, Berlin. (page 64)

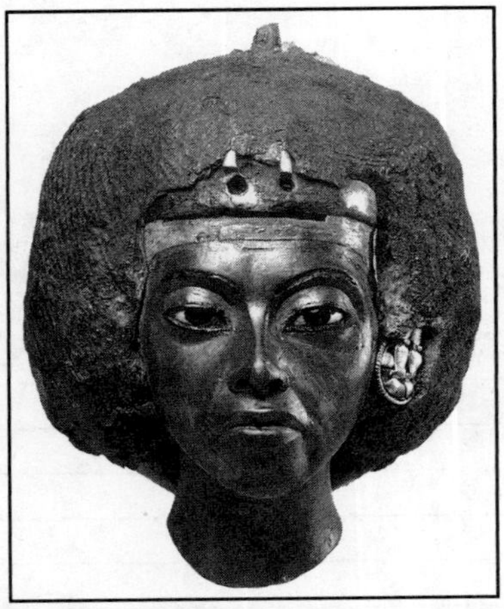

FIG. 03-34 Tiye, from Gurob, Egypt, Dynasty XVIII, ca. 1353–1335 BCE. Wood, with gold, silver, alabaster, and lapis lazuli, approx. 3 3/4″ high. Ägyptisches Museum, Berlin. (page 65)

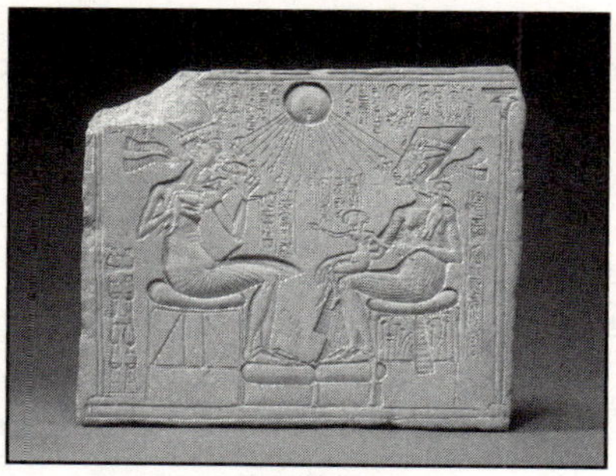

FIG. 03-35 Akhenaton, Nefertiti, and three daughters, from Tell el-Amarna, Egypt, Dynasty XVIII, ca. 1353–1335 BCE. Limestone, approx. 12 1/4″ high. Ägyptisches Museum, Berlin. (page 65)

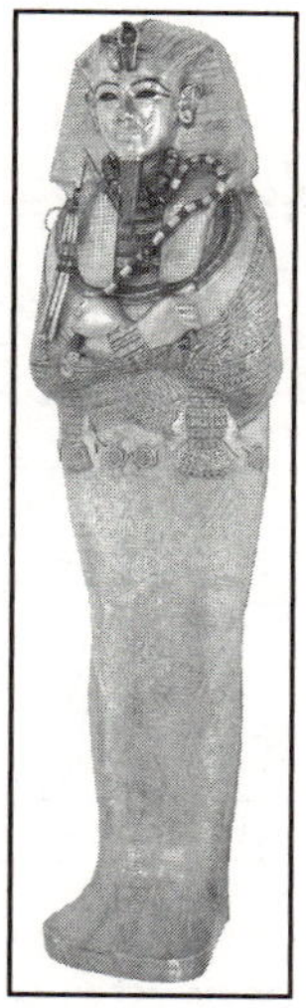

FIG. 03-36 Innermost coffin of Tutankhamen, from his tomb at Thebes, Egypt, Dynasty XVIII, ca. 1323 BCE. Gold with inlay of enamel and semiprecious stones, approx. 6′ 1″ long. Egyptian Museum, Cairo. (page 66)

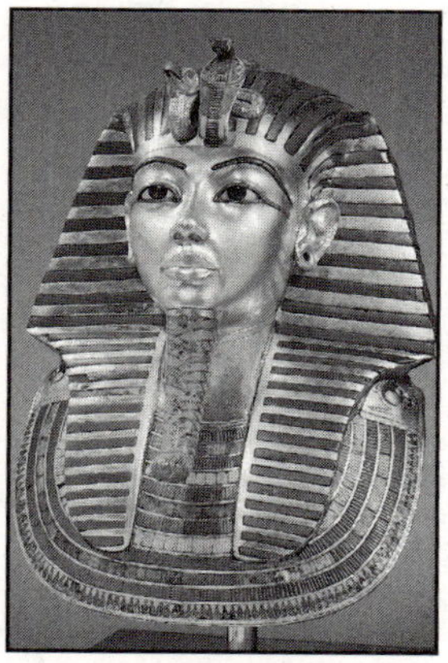

FIG. 03-37 Death mask of Tutankhamen, from the innermost coffin in his tomb at Thebes, Egypt, Dynasty XVIII, ca. 1323 BCE. Gold with inlay of semiprecious stones, 1′ 9 1/4″ high. Egyptian Museum, Cairo. (page 66)

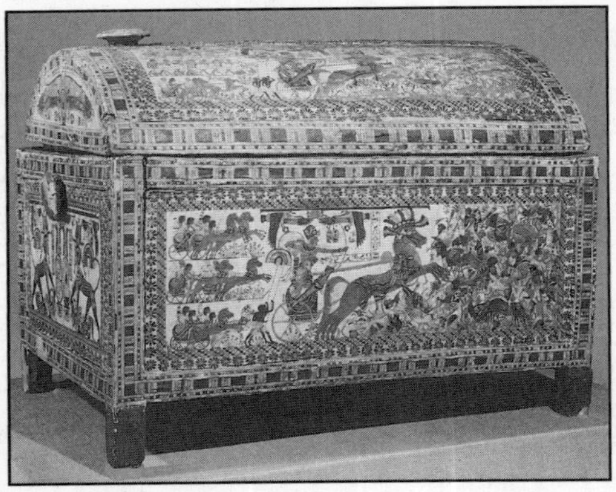

FIG. 03-38 Painted chest, from the Tomb of Tutankhamen, Thebes, Egypt, Dynasty XVIII, ca. 1333–1323 BCE. Wood, approx. 1′ 8″ long. Egyptian Museum, Cairo. (page 67)

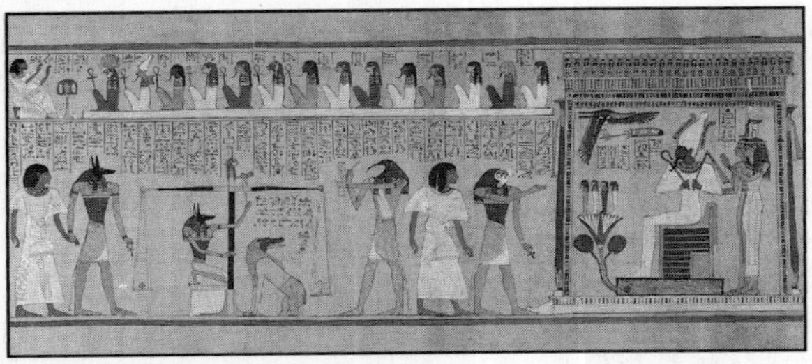

FIG. 03-39 Last judgment of Hu-Nefer, from his tomb at Thebes, Egypt, Dynasty XIX, ca. 1290–1280 BCE. Painted papyrus scroll, approx. 1′ 6″ high. British Museum, London. (page 67)

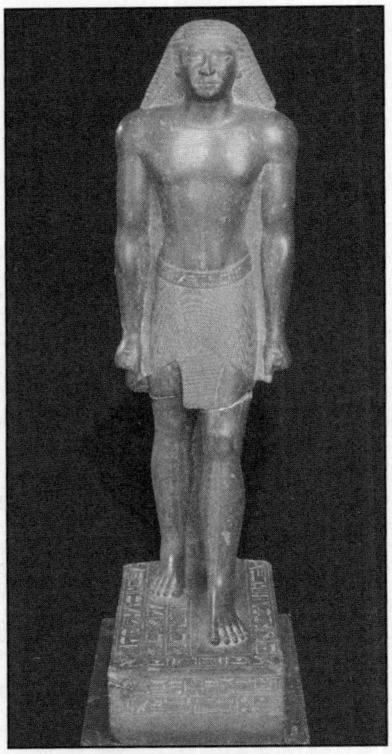

FIG. 03-40 Mentuemhet, from Karnak, Egypt, Dynasty XXVI, ca. 650 BCE. Granite, approx. 4′ 5″ high. Egyptian Museum, Cairo. (page 68)

Chapter 4

Minos and the Heroes of Homer:
The Art of the Prehistoric Aegean

Goals

- Identify the geographic area known as the Aegean.
- Discuss the visual aspects and possible context of the Cycladic sculptures.
- Discuss the Minoan society and architecture.
- Understand visual aspects of Minoan art.
- Relate significant aspects of archeological excavations at Mycenae.
- Understand the link between culture and architecture of Mycenae.
- Discuss the relationship between Minoan and Mycenaean art and culture.

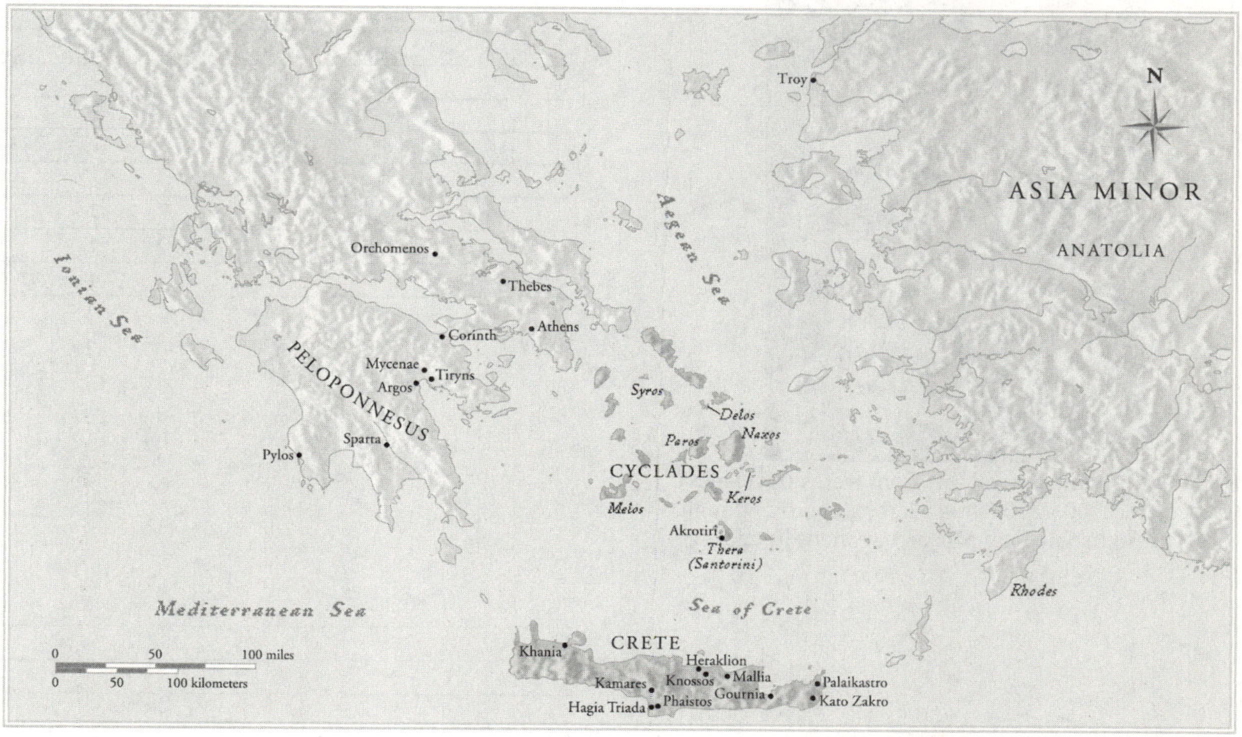

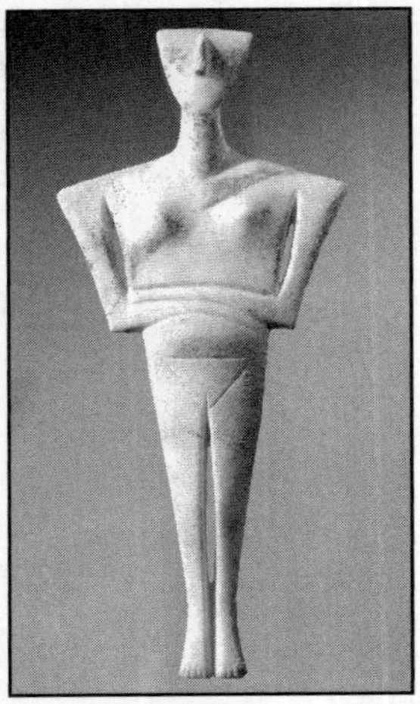

FIG. 04-01 Figurine of a woman, from Syros (Cyclades), Greece, ca. 2500–2300 BCE. Marble, approx. 1′ 6″ high. National Archaeological Museum, Athens. (page 73)

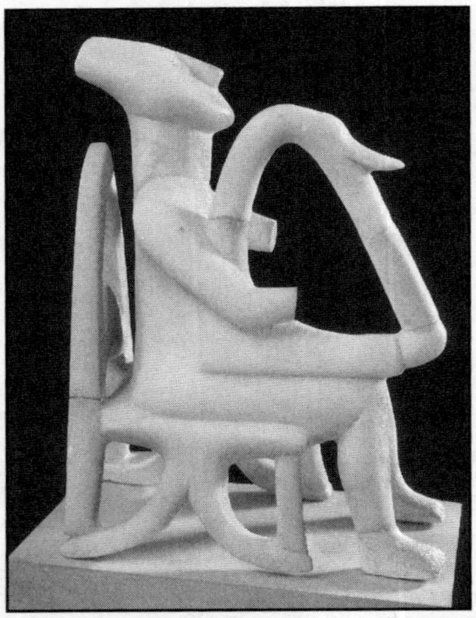

FIG. 04-02 Male lyre player, from Keros (Cyclades), Greece, ca. 2700–2500 BCE. Marble, approx. 9″ high. National Archaeological Museum, Athens. (page 73)

FIG. 04-03 Aerial view (looking northeast) of the palace at Knossos (Crete), Greece, ca. 1700–1400 BCE. (page 75)

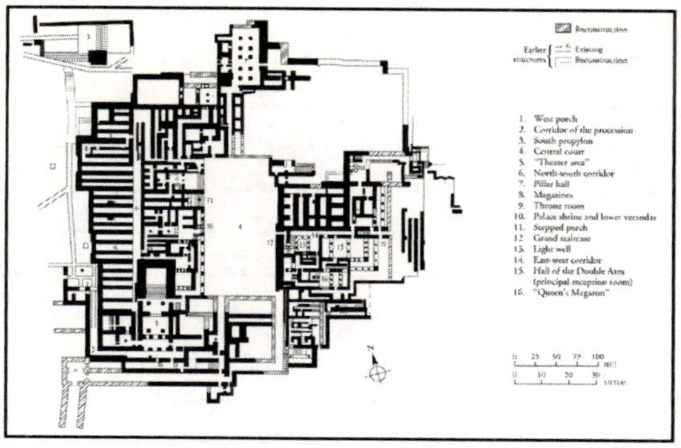

FIG. 04-04 Plan of the palace at Knossos (Crete), Greece, ca. 1700–1400 BCE. (page 75)

FIG. 04-05 Stairwell in the residential quarter of the palace at Knossos (Crete), Greece, ca. 1700–1400 BCE. (page 76)

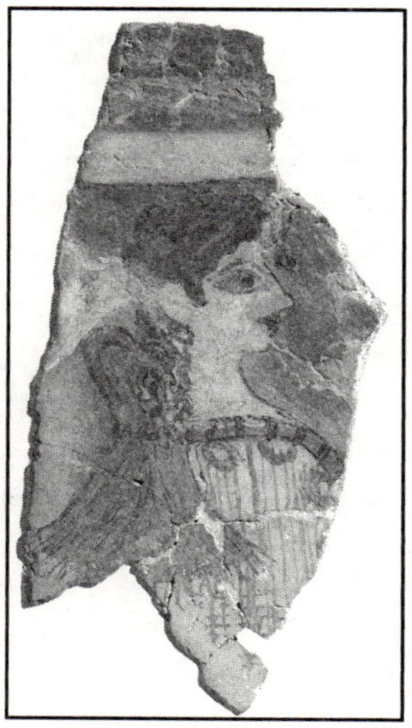

FIG. 04-06 Minoan woman or goddess *(La Parisienne),* from the palace at Knossos (Crete), Greece, ca. 1450–1400 BCE. Fragment of a fresco, approx. 10″ high. Archaeological Museum, Herakleion. (page 76)

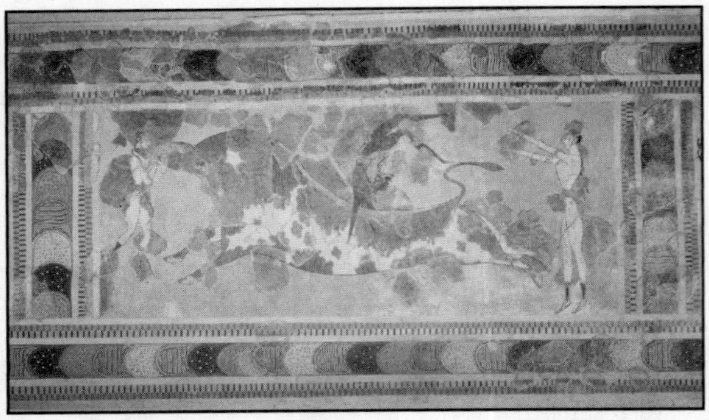

FIG. 04-07 Bull-leaping, from the palace at Knossos (Crete), Greece, ca. 1450–1400 BCE. Fresco, approx. 2′ 8″ high, including border. Archaeological Museum, Herakleion. (page 77)

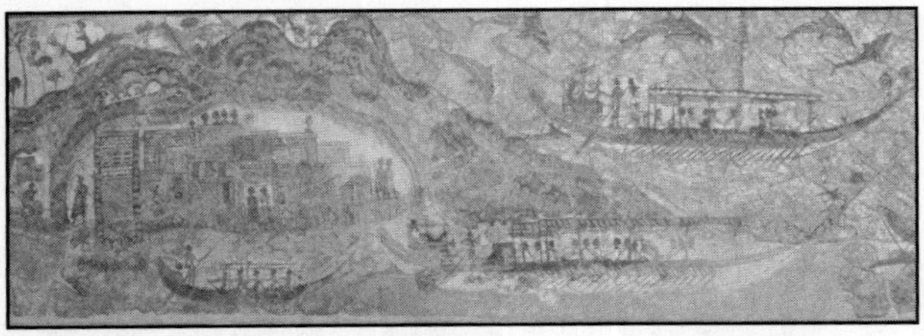

FIG. 04-08 Flotilla, detail of *Miniature Ships Fresco,* from Room 5, West House, Akrotiri, Thera (Cyclades), Greece, ca. 1650 BCE. Fresco, approx. 1′ 5″ high. National Archaeological Museum, Athens. (page 78)

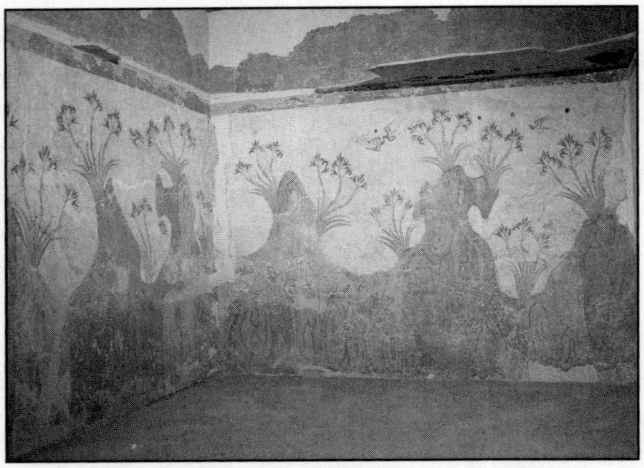

FIG. 04-09 Landscape with swallows *(Spring Fresco),* from Room Delta 2, Akrotiri, Thera (Cyclades), Greece, ca. 1650 BCE. Fresco, approx. 7′ 6″ high. National Archaeological Museum, Athens. (page 79)

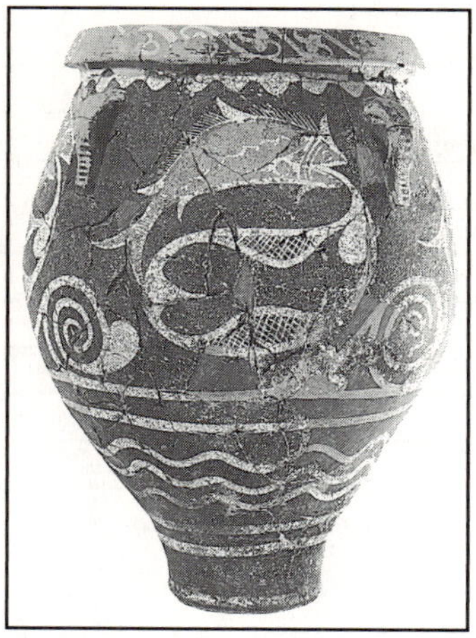

FIG. 04-10 Kamares Ware jar, from Phaistos (Crete), Greece, ca. 1800–1700 BCE. Approx. 1′ 8″ high. Archaeological Museum, Herakleion. (page 79)

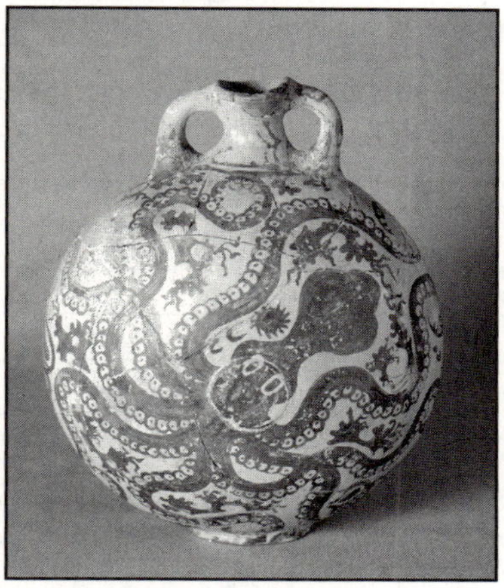

FIG. 04-11 Marine Style octopus jar, from Palaikastro (Crete), Greece, ca. 1500 BCE. Approx. 11″ high. Archaeological Museum, Herakleion. (page 80)

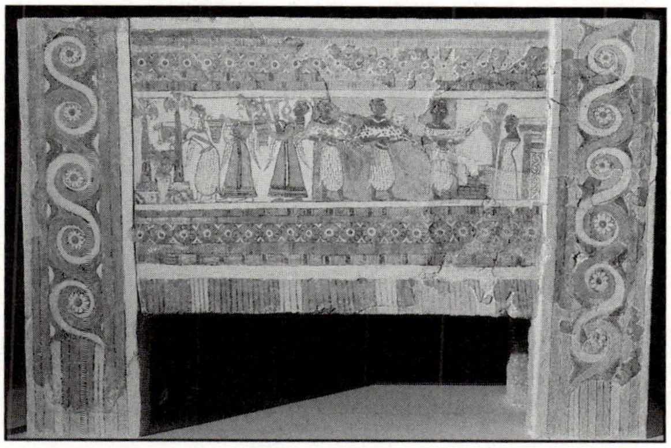

FIG. 04-12 Sarcophagus, from Hagia Triada (Crete), Greece, ca. 1450–1400 BCE. Painted limestone, approx. 4′ 6″ long. Archaeological Museum, Herakleion. (page 80)

FIG. 04-13 *Harvester Vase,* from Hagia Triada (Crete), Greece, ca. 1500 BCE. Steatite, greatest diameter approx. 5″. Archaeological Museum, Herakleion. (page 81)

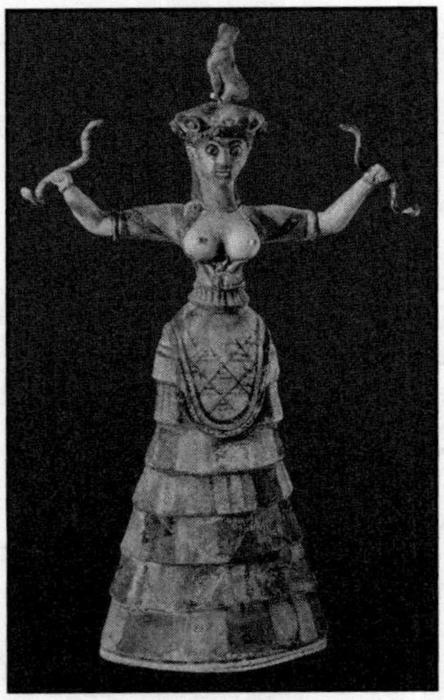

FIG. 04-14 *Snake Goddess,* from the palace at Knossos (Crete), Greece, ca. 1600 BCE. Faience, approx. 1′ 1 1/2″ high. Archaeological Museum, Herakleion. (page 81)

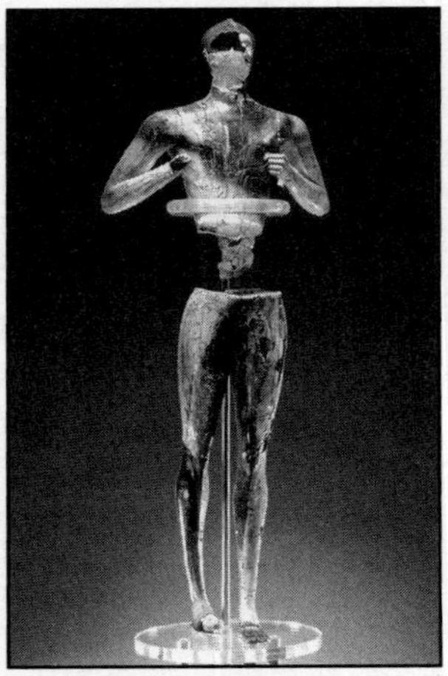

FIG. 04-15 Young god(?), from Palaikastro (Crete), Greece, ca. 1500–1475 BCE. Ivory, gold, serpentine, and rock crystal, original height approx. 1′ 7 1/2″. Archaeological Museum, Siteia. (page 82)

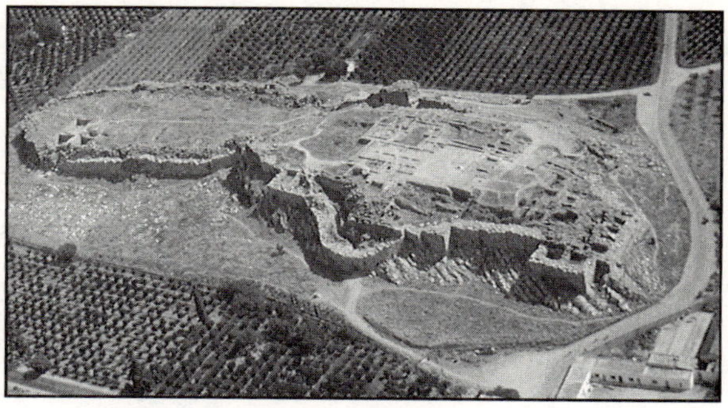

FIG. 04-16 Aerial view of the citadel at Tiryns, Greece, ca. 1400–1200 BCE. (page 83)

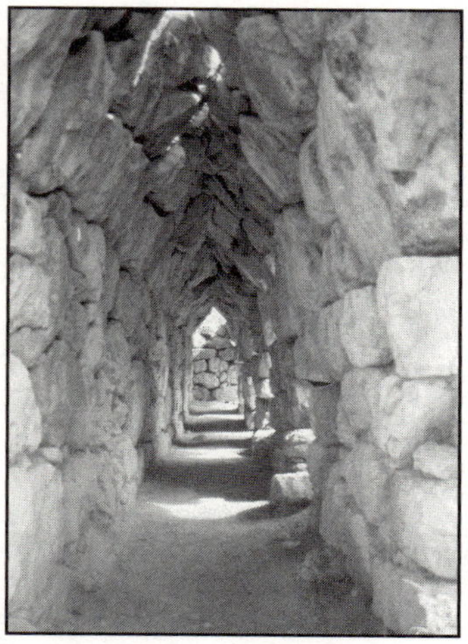

FIG. 04-17 Corbeled gallery in the walls of the citadel, Tiryns, Greece, ca. 1400–1200 BCE. (page 83)

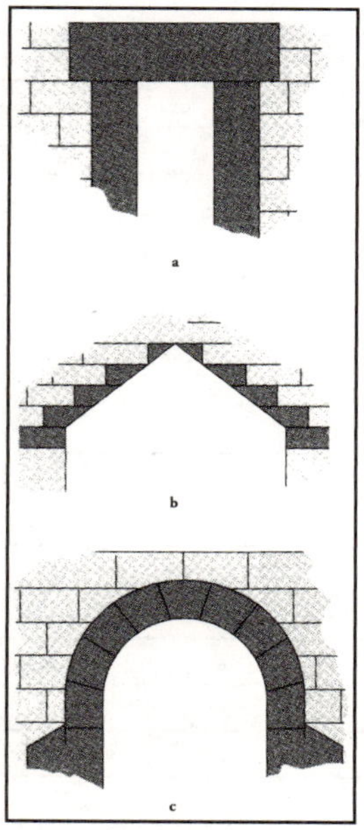

FIG. 04-18 Three methods of spanning a passageway: *(a)* post and lintel, *(b)* corbeled arch, *(c)* arch. (page 83)

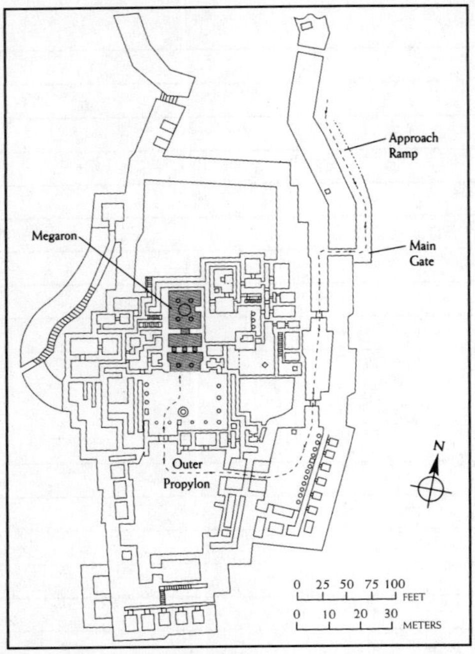

FIG. 04-19 Plan of the palace and southern part of the citadel, Tiryns, Greece, ca. 1400–1200 BCE. (page 84)

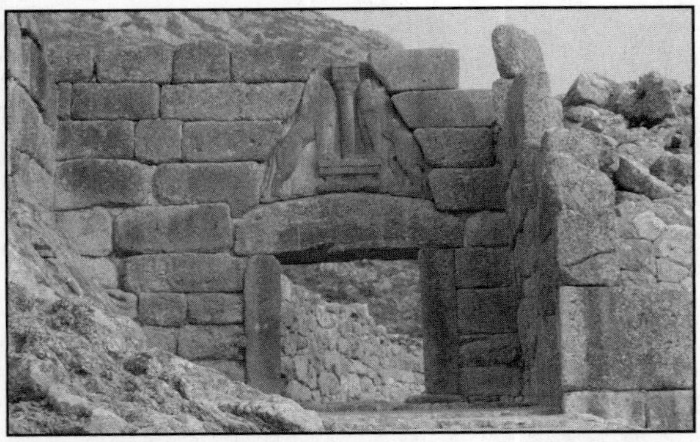

FIG. 04-20 Lion Gate, Mycenae, Greece, ca. 1300–1250 BCE. Limestone, relief panel approx. 9′ 6″ high. (page 84)

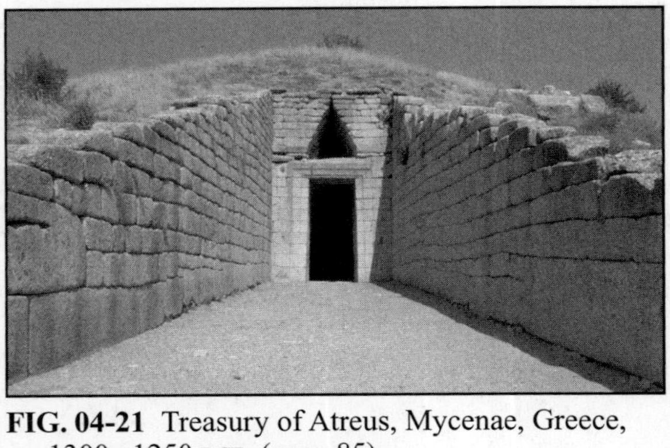

FIG. 04-21 Treasury of Atreus, Mycenae, Greece, ca. 1300–1250 BCE. (page 85)

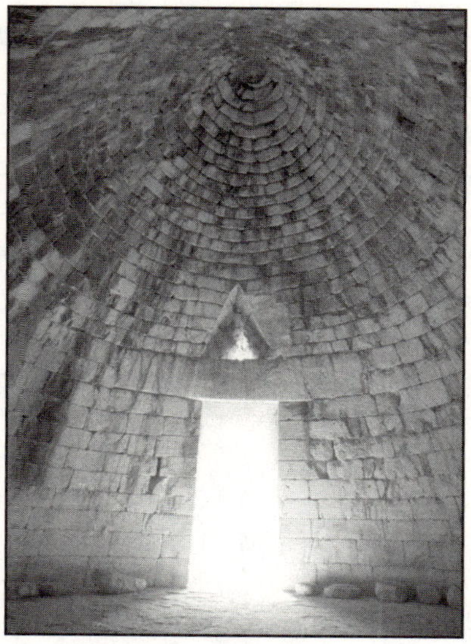

FIG. 04-22 Vault of the tholos of the Treasury of Atreus, Mycenae, Greece, ca. 1300–1250 BCE. Approx. 43′ high. (page 85)

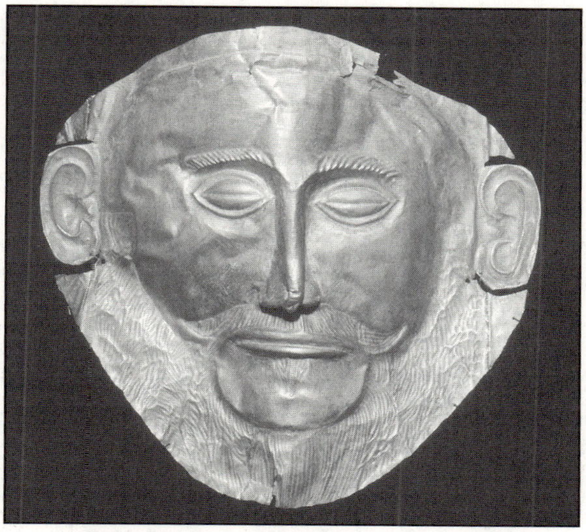

FIG. 04-23 Funerary mask, from Grave Circle A, Mycenae, Greece, ca. 1600–1500 BCE. Beaten gold, approx. 1′ high. National Archaeological Museum, Athens. (page 86)

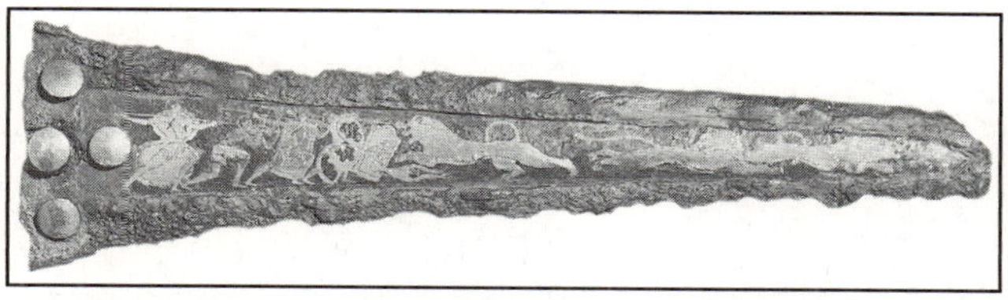

FIG. 04-24 Inlaid dagger blade with lion hunt, from Grave Circle A, Mycenae, Greece, ca. 1600–1500 BCE. Bronze, inlaid with gold, silver, and niello, approx. 9″ long. National Archaeological Museum, Athens. (page 87)

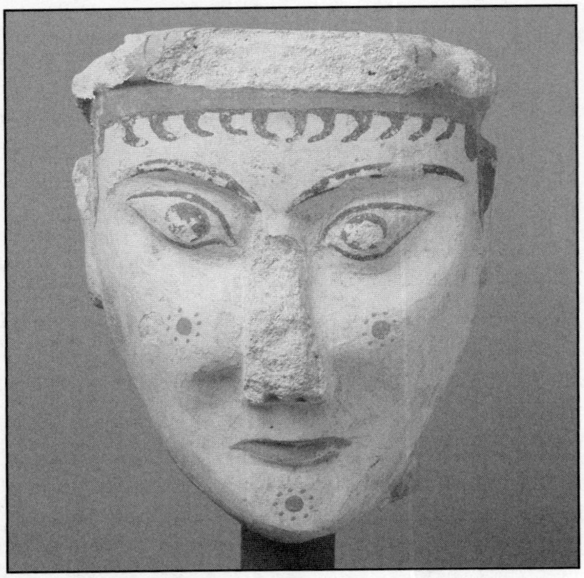

FIG. 04-25 Female head, from Mycenae, Greece, ca. 1300–1250 BCE. Painted plaster, approx. 6 1/2″ high. National Archaeological Museum, Athens. (page 87)

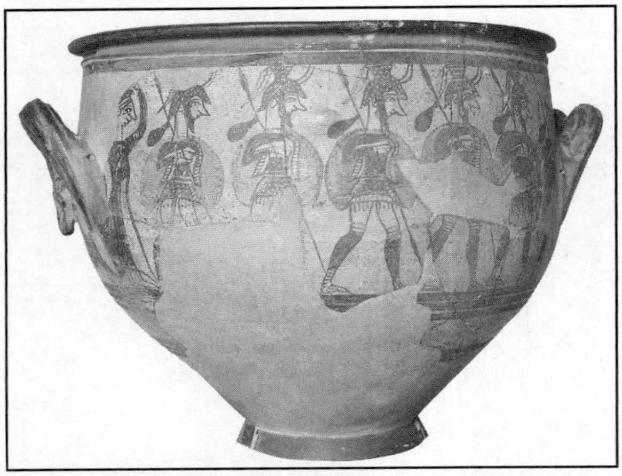

FIG. 04-26 *Warrior Vase,* from Mycenae, Greece, ca. 1200 BCE. Approx. 1′ 4″ high. National Archaeological Museum, Athens. (page 88)

Chapter 5

Gods, Heroes, and Athletes:
The Art of Ancient Greece

Goals

- Understand the diverse cultural influences on Greek artistic development.
- Discuss the evolution of the human figure and how it is represented in Greek art.
- Relate the development of temple architecture.
- Cite architectural components and terminology.
- Understand the impact of the conquest of the Greeks on their respective art forms.
- Discuss individual artists and their respective styles.

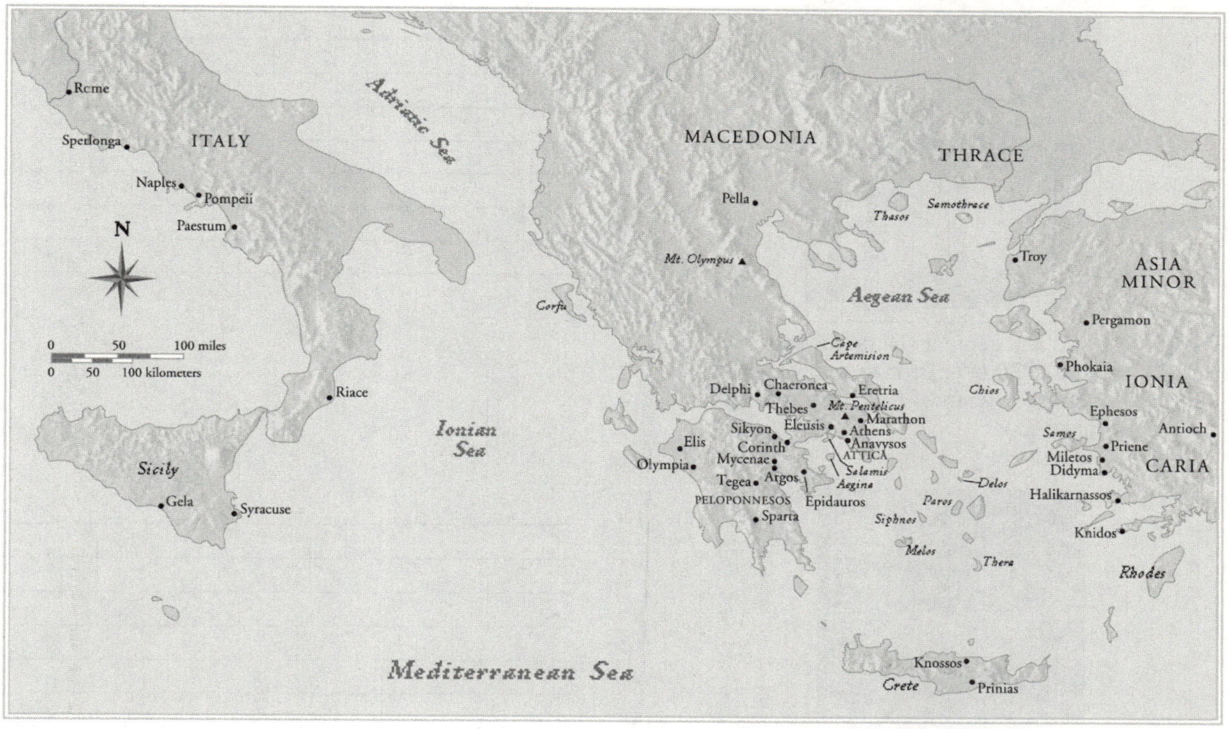

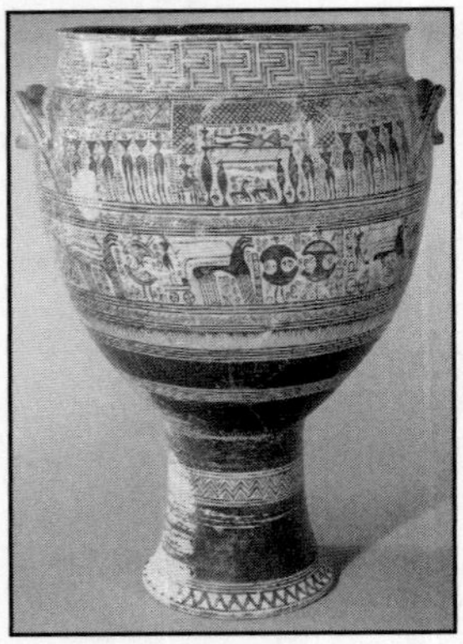

FIG. 05-01 Geometric krater, from the Dipylon cemetery, Athens, Greece, ca. 740 BCE. Approx. 3′ 4 1/2″ high. Metropolitan Museum of Art, New York. (page 94)

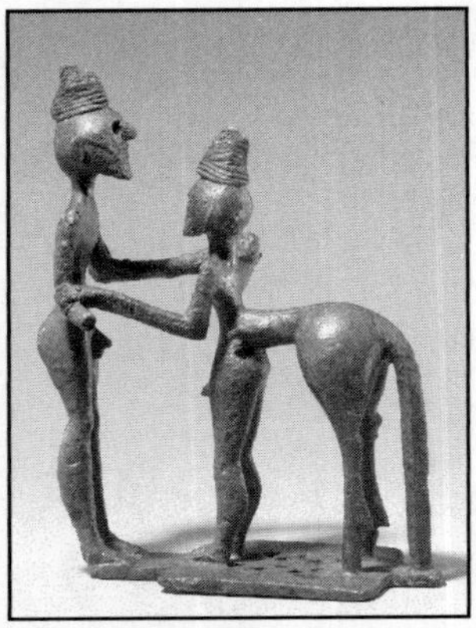

FIG. 05-02 Hero and centaur (Herakles and Nessos?), ca. 750–730 BCE. Bronze, approx. 4 1/2″ high. Metropolitan Museum of Art, New York (gift of J. Pierpont). (page 95)

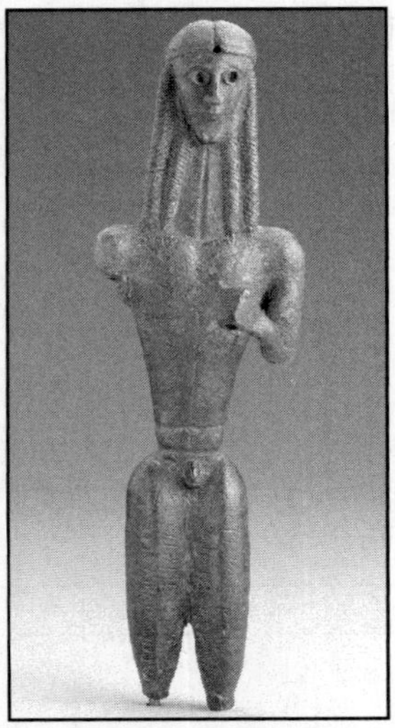

FIG. 05-03 *Mantiklos Apollo,* statuette of a youth dedicated by Mantiklos to Apollo, from Thebes, Greece, ca. 700–680 BCE. Bronze, approx. 8″ high. Museum of Fine Arts, Boston. (page 96)

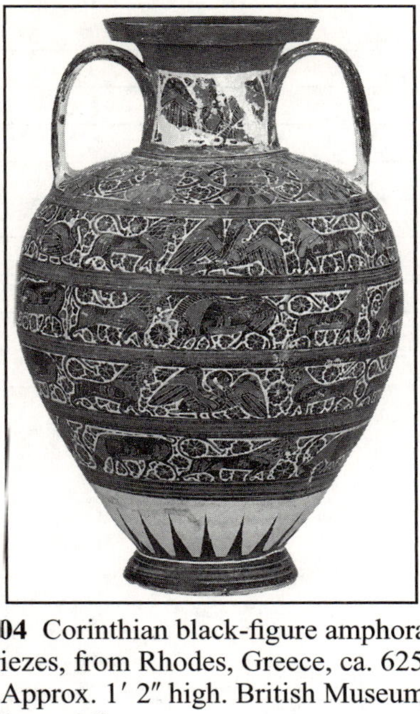

FIG. 05-04 Corinthian black-figure amphora with animal friezes, from Rhodes, Greece, ca. 625–600 BCE. Approx. 1′ 2″ high. British Museum, London. (page 96)

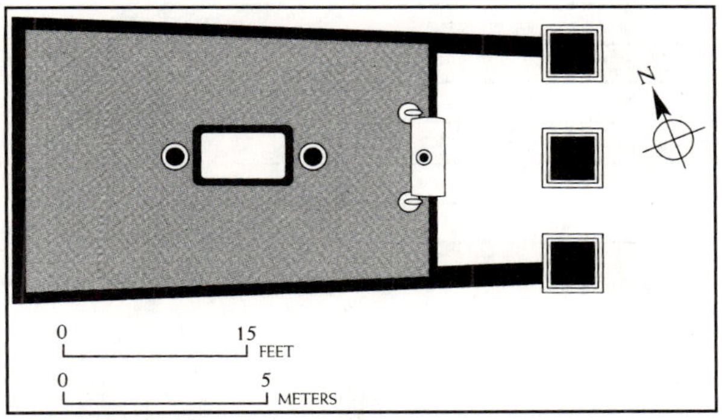

FIG. 05-05 Plan of Temple A, Prinias, Greece, ca. 625 BCE. (page 97)

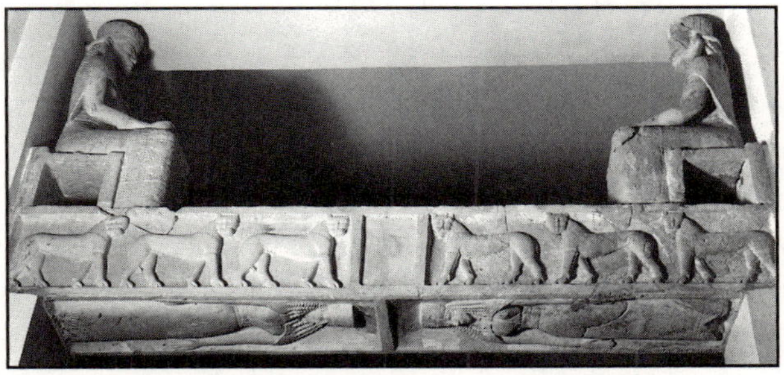

FIG. 05-06 Lintel of Temple A, Prinias, Greece, ca. 625 BCE. Limestone, approx. 2′ 9″ high. Archaeological Museum, Herakleion. (page 97)

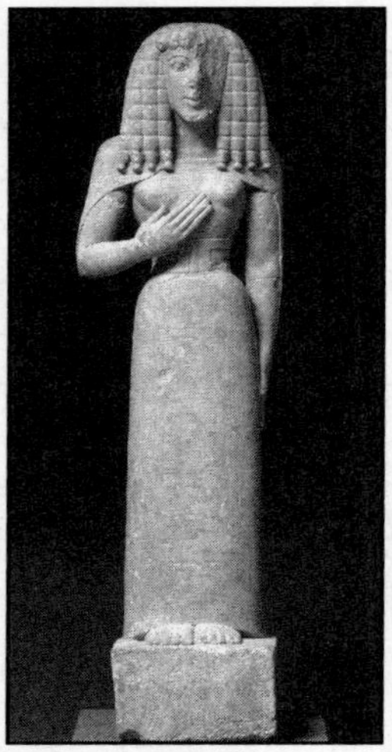

FIG. 05-07 *Lady of Auxerre,* statue of a goddess or kore, ca. 650–625 BCE. Limestone, approx. 2′ 1 1/2″ high. Louvre, Paris. (page 98)

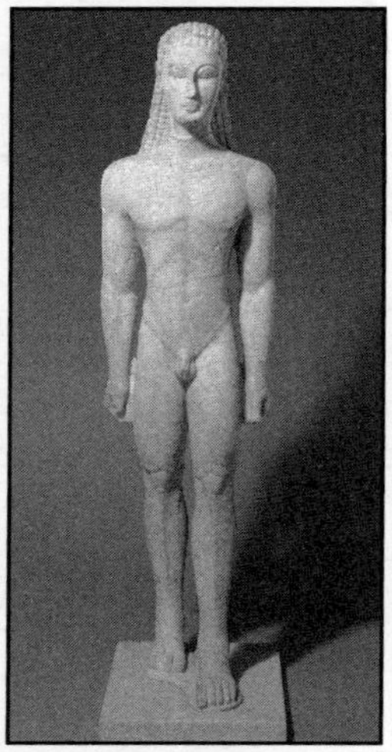

FIG. 05-08 Kouros, ca. 600 BCE. Marble, approx. 6′ 1/2″ high. Metropolitan Museum of Art, New York. (page 98)

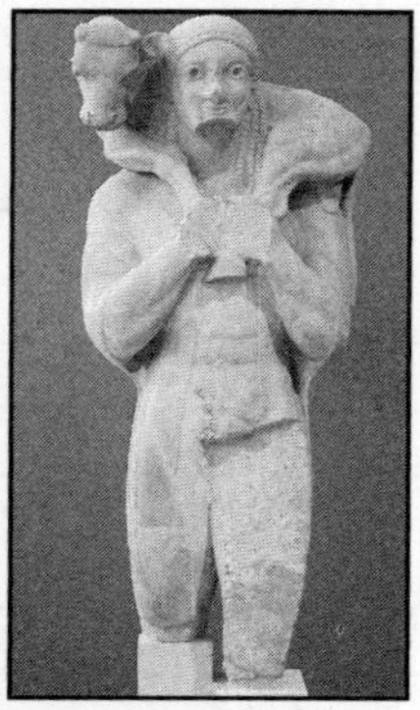

FIG. 05-09 Calf Bearer, dedicated by Rhonbos on the Acropolis, Athens, Greece, ca. 560 BCE. Marble, restored height approx. 5′ 5″. Acropolis Museum, Athens. (page 99)

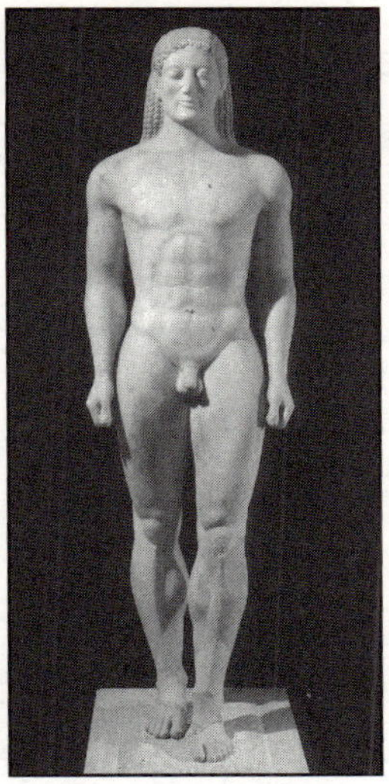

FIG. 05-10 Kroisos, from Anavysos, Greece, ca. 530 BCE. Marble, approx. 6′ 4″ high. National Archaeological Museum, Athens. (page 99)

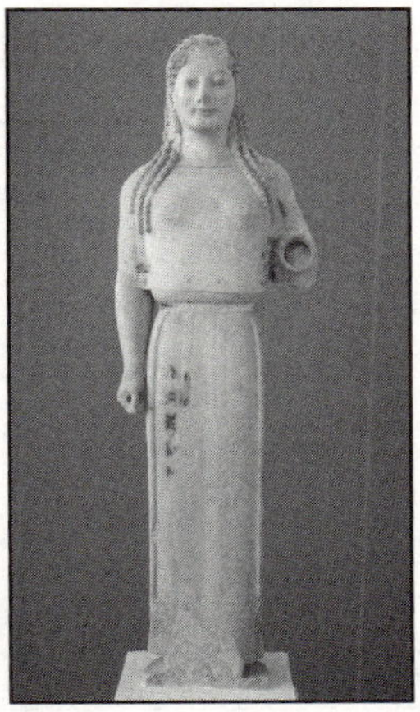

FIG. 05-11 *Peplos Kore,* from the Acropolis, Athens, Greece, ca. 530 BCE. Marble, approx. 4′ high. Acropolis Museum, Athens. (page 100)

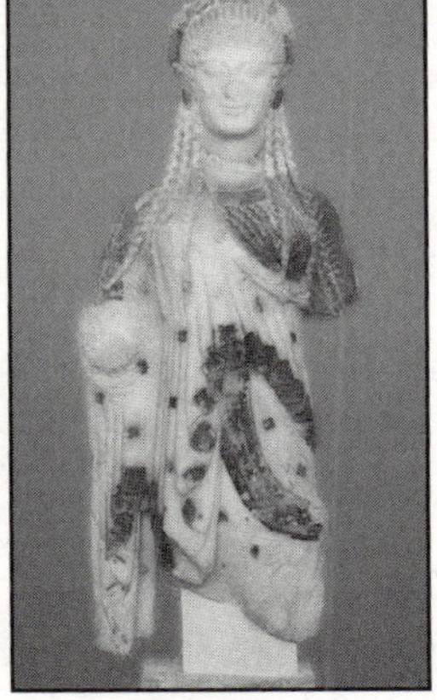

FIG. 05-12 Kore, from the Acropolis, Athens, Greece, ca. 520–510 BCE. Marble, approx. 1′ 9 1/2″ high. Acropolis Museum, Athens. (page 101)

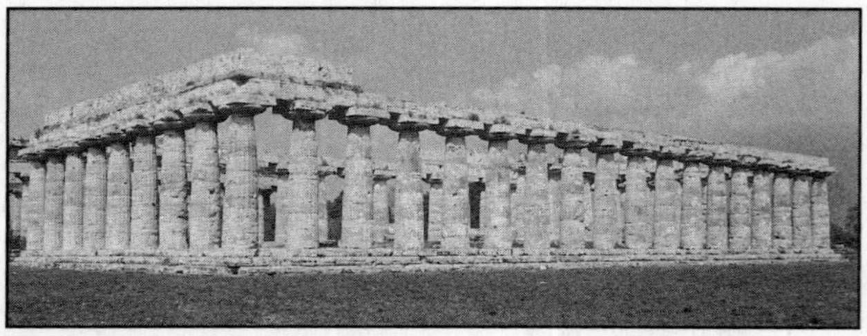

FIG. 05-13 Temple of Hera I ("Basilica"), Paestum, Italy, ca. 550 BCE. (page 103)

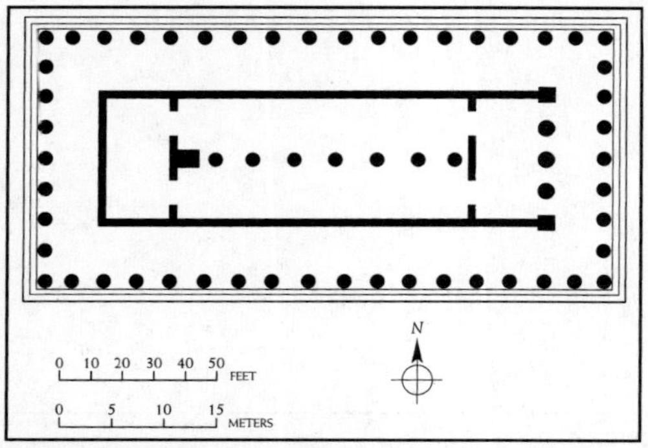

FIG. 05-14 Plan of the Temple of Hera I, Paestum, Italy, ca. 550 BCE. (page 104)

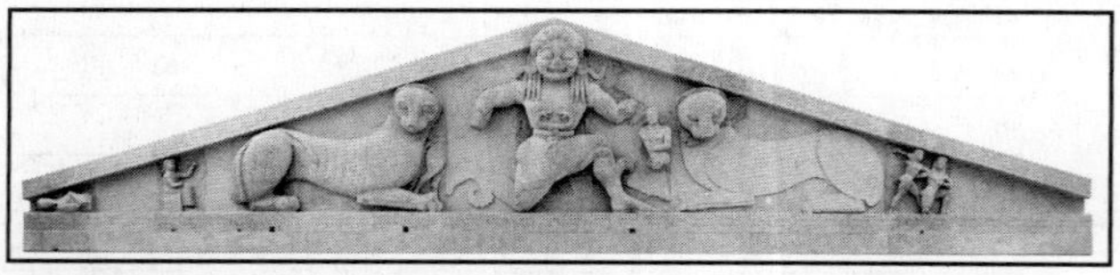

FIG. 05-15 West pediment from the Temple of Artemis, Corfu, Greece, ca. 600–580 BCE. Limestone, greatest height approx. 9′ 4″. Archaeological Museum, Corfu. (page 104)

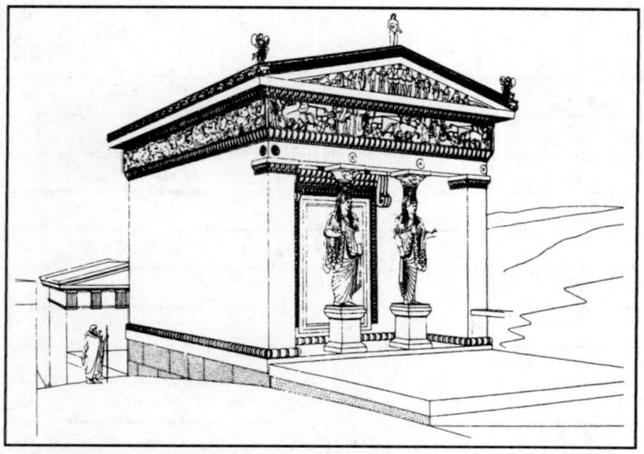

FIG. 05-16 Reconstruction drawing of the Siphnian Treasury, Delphi, Greece, ca. 530 BCE. (page 105)

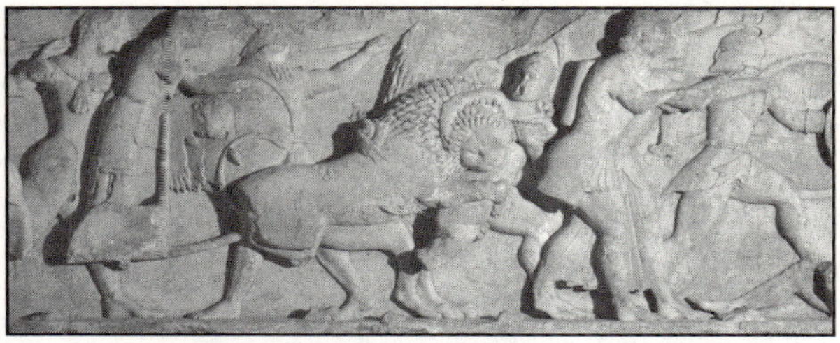

FIG. 05-17 Gigantomachy, detail of the north frieze of the Siphnian Treasury, Delphi, Greece, ca. 530 BCE. Marble, approx. 2′ 1″ high. Archaeological Museum, Delphi. (page 105)

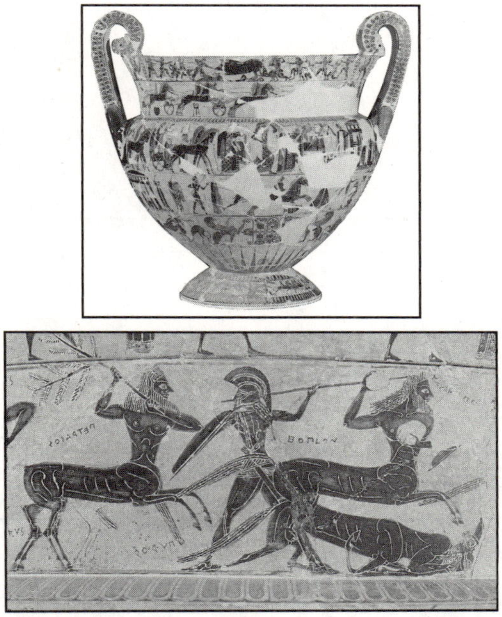

FIG. 05-18 KLEITIAS and ERGOTIMOS, *François Vase* (Attic black-figure volute krater), from Chiusi, Italy, ca. 570 BCE. General view *(top)* and detail of centauromachy on other side of vase *(bottom)*. Approx. 2′ 2″ high. Museo Archeologico, Florence. (page 106)

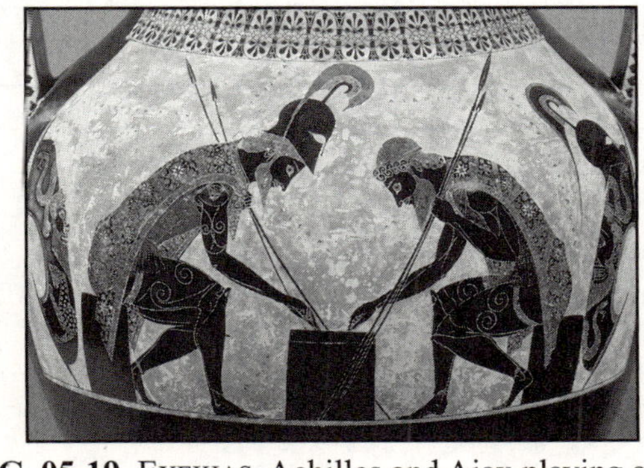

FIG. 05-19 EXEKIAS, Achilles and Ajax playing a dice game (detail from an Attic black-figure amphora), from Vulci, Italy, ca. 540–530 BCE. Whole vessel approx. 2′ high. Vatican Museums, Rome. (page 107)

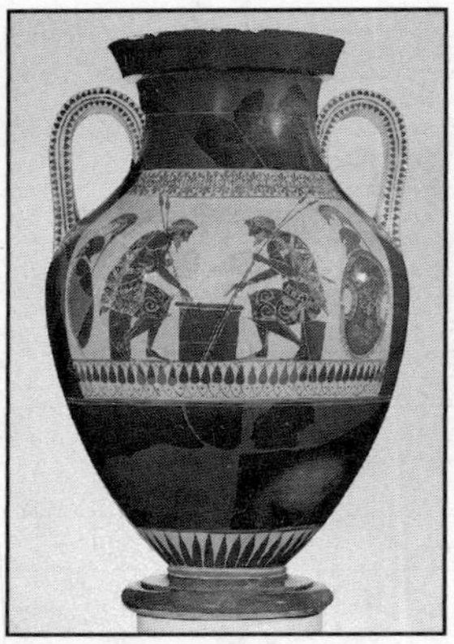
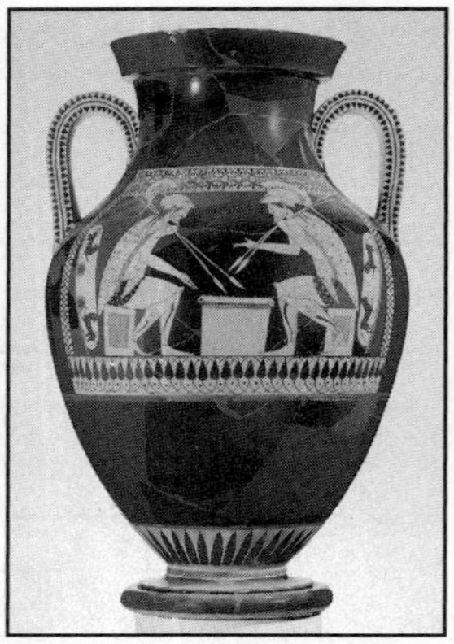

FIG. 05-20 ANDOKIDES PAINTER, Achilles and Ajax playing a dice game (Attic bilingual amphora), from Orvieto, Italy, ca. 525–520 bce. Black-figure side *(left)* and red-figure side *(right)*. Approx. 1′ 9″ high. Museum of Fine Arts, Boston. (page 108)

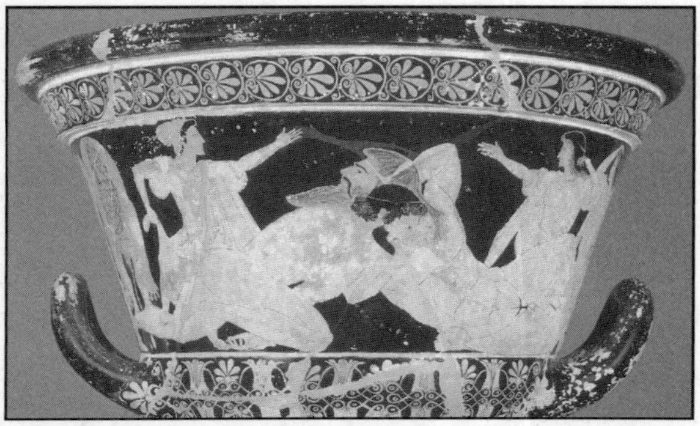

FIG. 05-21 EUPHRONIOS, Herakles wrestling Antaios (detail of an Attic red-figure calyx krater), from Cerveteri, Italy, ca. 510 BCE. Whole vessel approx. 1′ 7″ high. Louvre, Paris. (page 109)

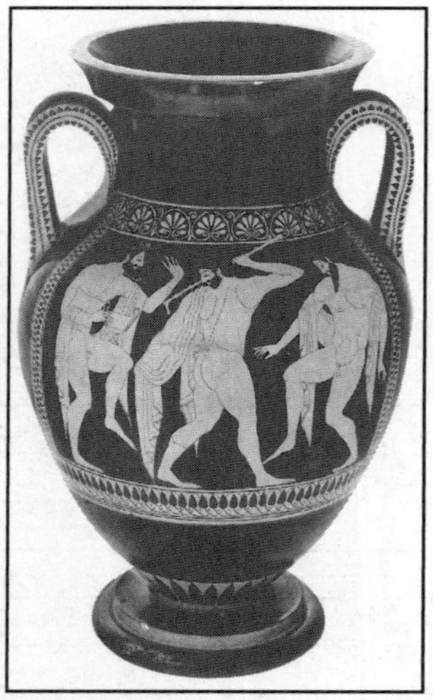

FIG. 05-22 EUTHYMIDES, Three revelers (Attic red-figure amphora), from Vulci, Italy, ca. 510 BCE. Approx. 2′ high. Staatliche Antikensammlungen, Munich. (page 110)

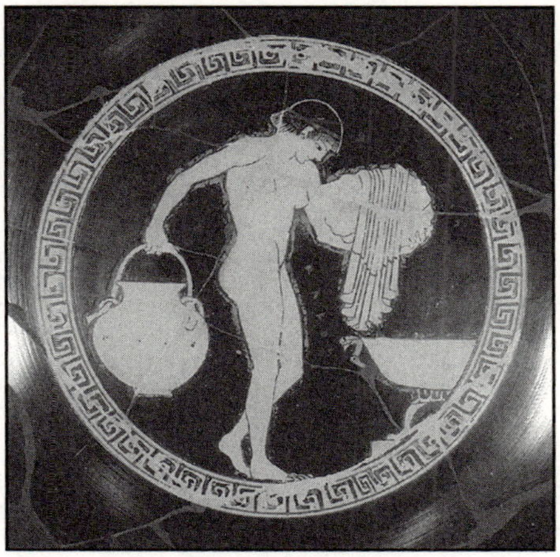

FIG. 05-23 ONESIMOS, Girl preparing to bathe (interior of an Attic red-figure kylix), from Chiusi, Italy, ca. 490 BCE. Tondo approx. 6″ in diameter. Musées Royaux, Brussels. (page 110)

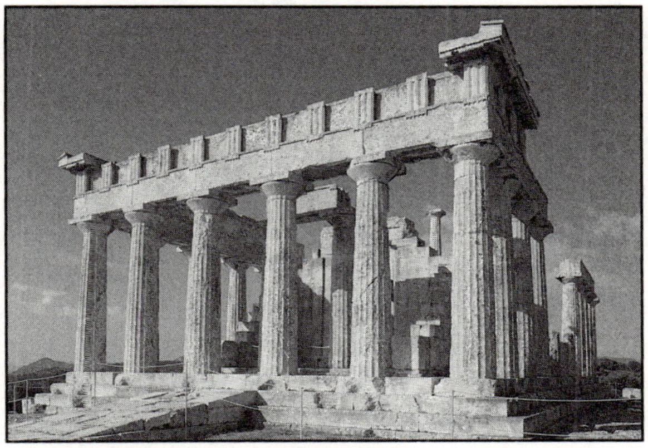

FIG. 05-24 Temple of Aphaia, Aegina, Greece, ca. 500–490 BCE. (page 111)

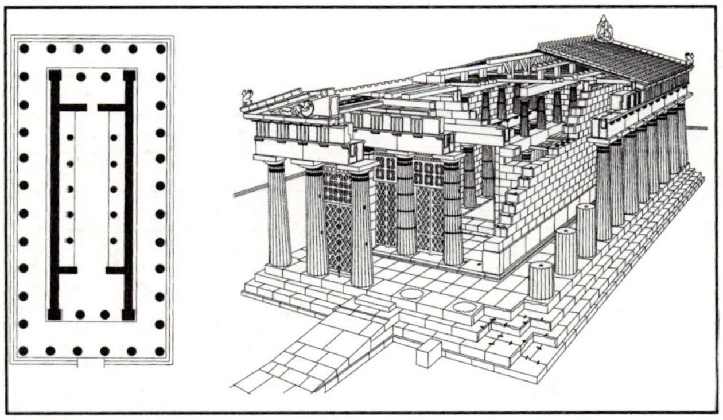

FIG. 05-25 Plan *(left)* and restored cutaway view *(right)* of the Temple of Aphaia, Aegina, Greece, ca. 500–490 BCE. (page 111)

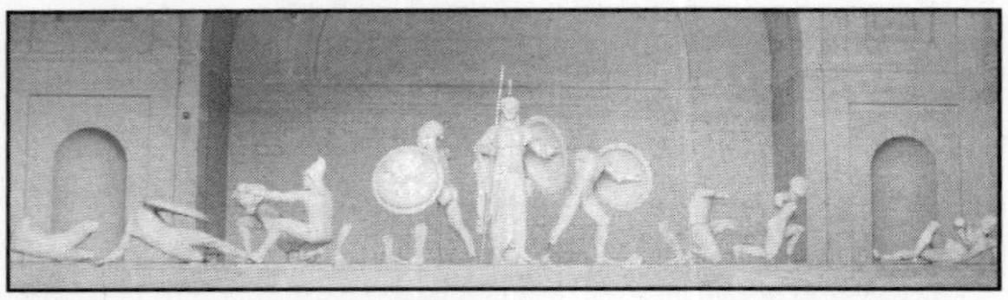

FIG. 05-26 West pediment of the Temple of Aphaia, Aegina, Greece, ca. 500–490 BCE. Marble, approx. 5′ 8″ high at center. Glyptothek, Munich. (page 112)

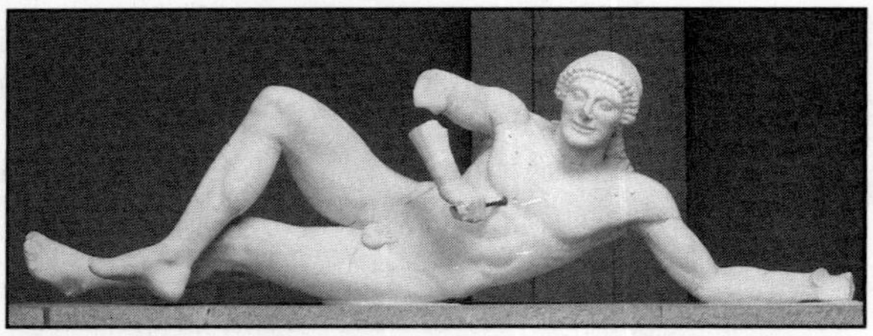

FIG. 05-27 Dying warrior, from the west pediment of the Temple of Aphaia, Aegina, Greece, ca. 500–490 BCE. Marble, approx. 5′ 2 1/2″ long. Glyptothek, Munich. (page 112)

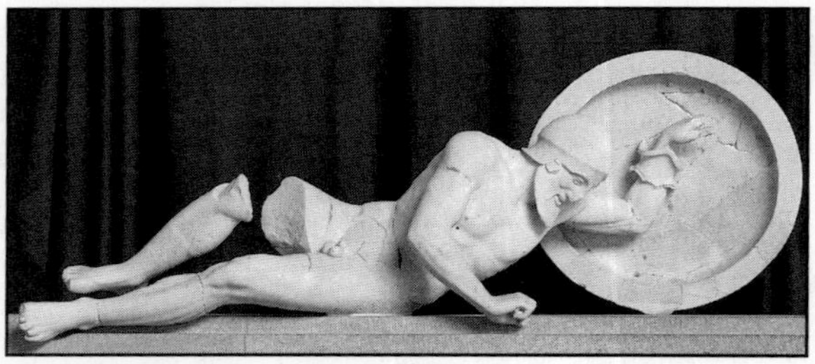

FIG. 05-28 Dying warrior, from the east pediment of the Temple of Aphaia, Aegina, Greece, ca. 490–480 BCE. Marble, approx. 6′ 1″ long. Glyptothek, Munich. (page 112)

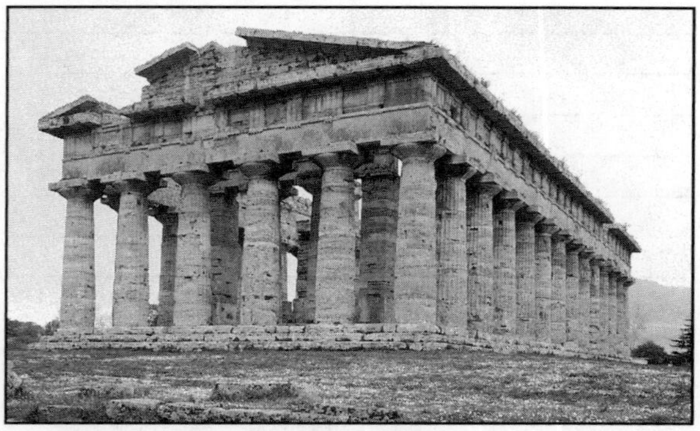

FIG. 05-29 Temple of Hera II, Paestum, Italy, ca. 460 BCE. (page 113)

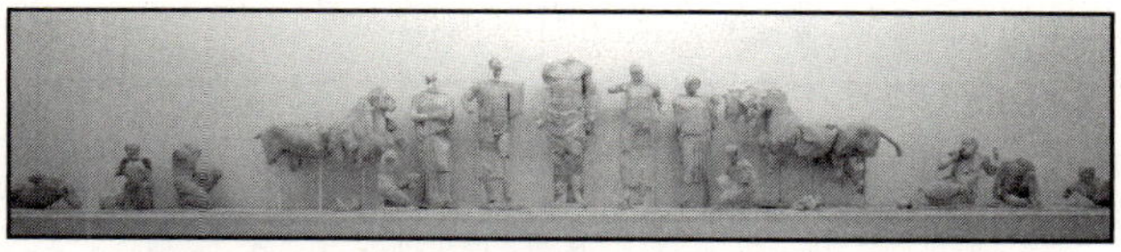

FIG. 05-30 East pediment from the Temple of Zeus, Olympia, Greece, ca. 470–456 BCE. Marble, approx. 87′ wide. Archaeological Museum, Olympia. (page 113)

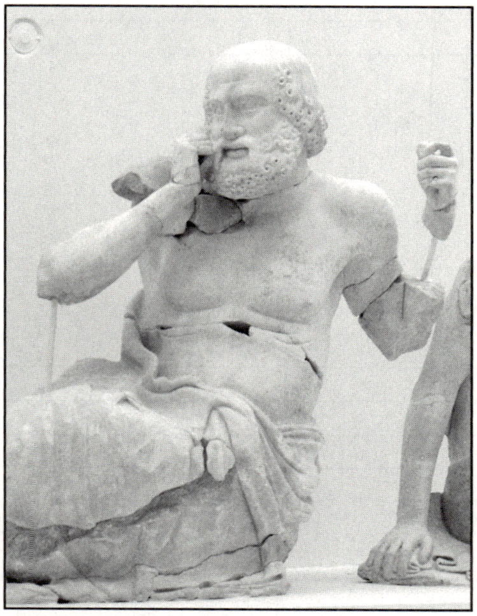

FIG. 05-31 Seer, from the east pediment of the Temple of Zeus, Olympia, Greece, ca. 470–456 BCE. Marble, full figure approx. 4′ 6″ high. Archaeological Museum, Olympia. (page 114)

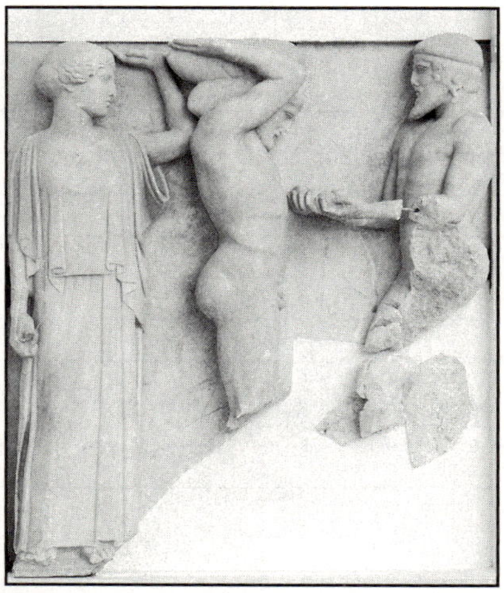

FIG. 05-32 Athena, Herakles, and Atlas with the apples of the Hesperides, metope from the Temple of Zeus, Olympia, Greece, ca. 470–456 BCE. Marble, approx. 5′ 3″ high. Archaeological Museum, Olympia. (page 114)

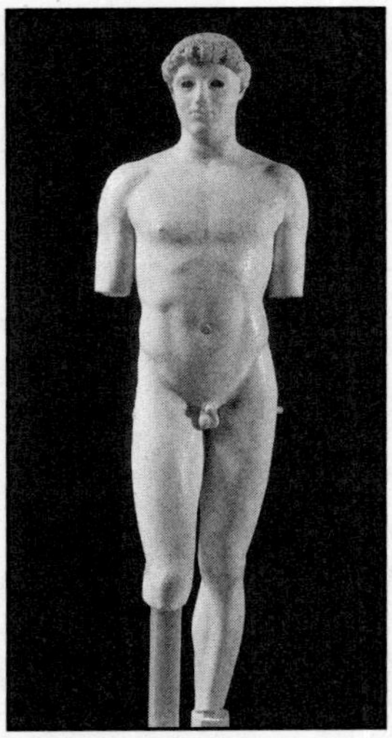

FIG. 05-33 *Kritios Boy,* from the Acropolis, Athens, Greece, ca. 480 BCE. Marble, approx. 2′ 10″ high. Acropolis Museum, Athens. (page 115)

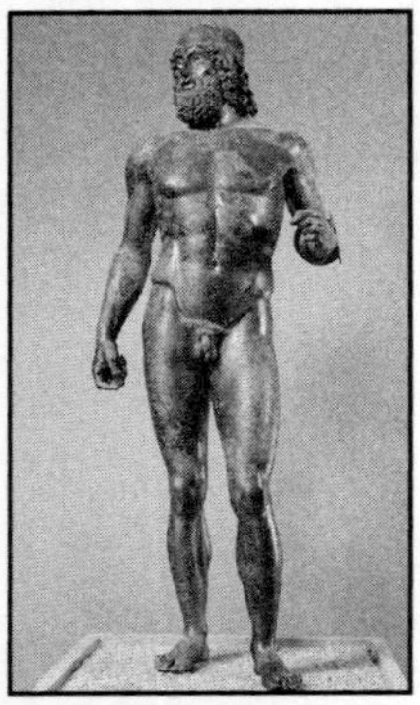

FIG. 05-34 Warrior, from the sea off Riace, Italy, ca. 460–450 BCE. Bronze, approx. 6′ 6″ high. Archaeological Museum, Reggio Calabria. (page 115)

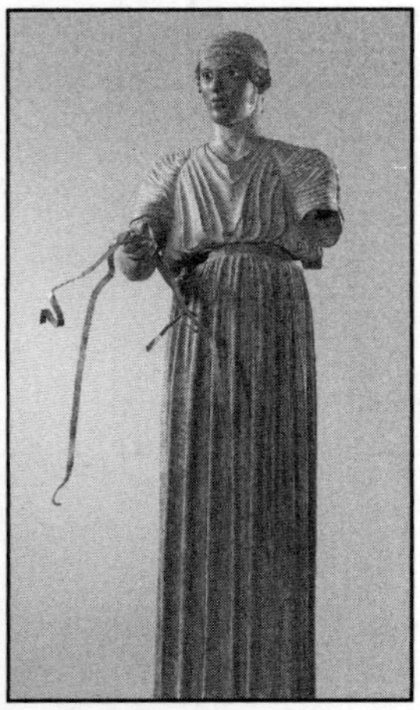

FIG. 05-35 Charioteer, from a group dedicated by Polyzalos of Gela in the Sanctuary of Apollo, Delphi, Greece, ca. 470 BCE. Bronze, approx. 5′ 11″ high. Archaeological Museum, Delphi. (page 116)

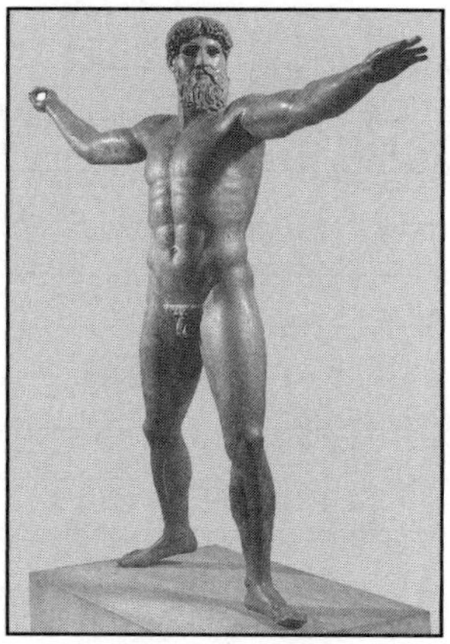

FIG. 05-36 Zeus (or Poseidon?), from the sea off Cape Artemision, Greece, ca. 460–450 BCE. Bronze, approx. 6′ 10″ high. National Archaeological Museum, Athens. (page 116)

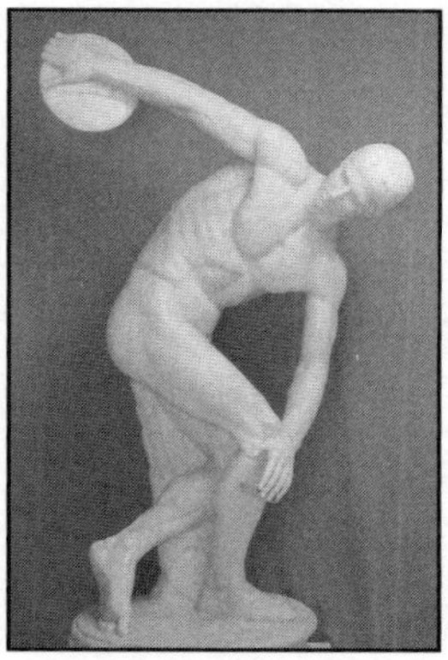

FIG. 05-37 MYRON, *Diskobolos (Discus Thrower)*. Roman copy after a bronze original of ca. 450 BCE, 5′ 1″ high. Museo Nazionale Romano—Palazzo Massimo alle Terme, Rome. (page 117)

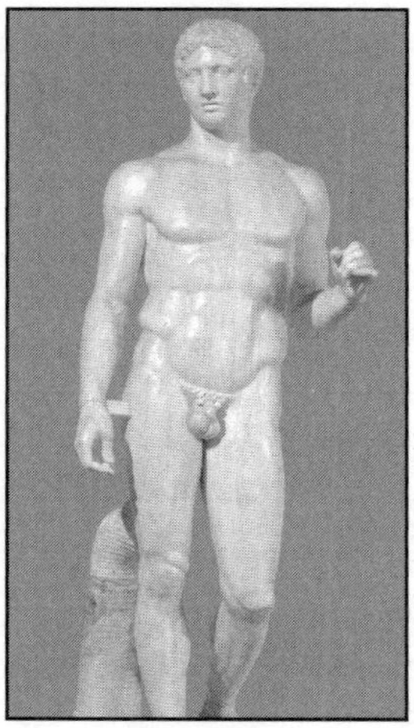

FIG. 05-38 POLYKLEITOS, *Doryphoros (Spear Bearer)*. Roman copy from Pompeii, Italy, after a bronze original of ca. 450–440 BCE, 6′ 11″ high. Museo Nazionale, Naples. (page 118)

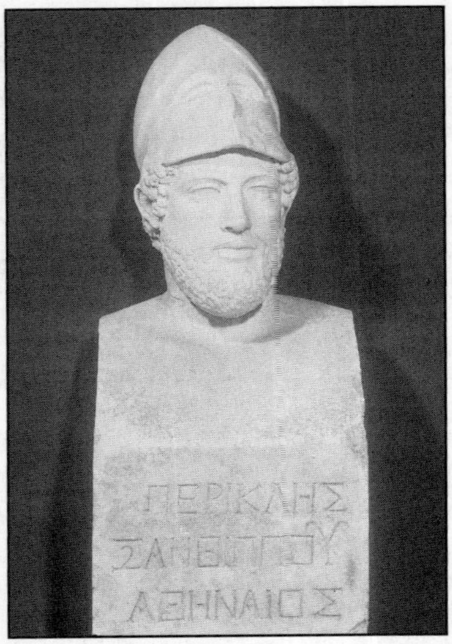

FIG. 05-39 KRESILAS, Pericles. Roman herm copy after a bronze original of ca. 429 BCE, approx. 6′ high. Vatican Museums, Rome. (page 119)

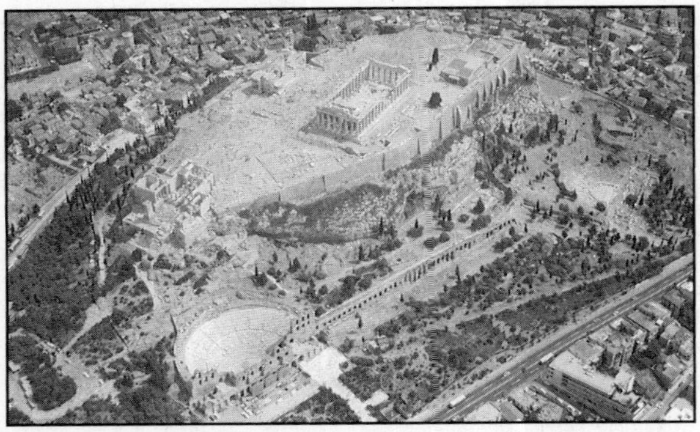

FIG. 05-40 Aerial view of the Acropolis, Athens, Greece. (page 120)

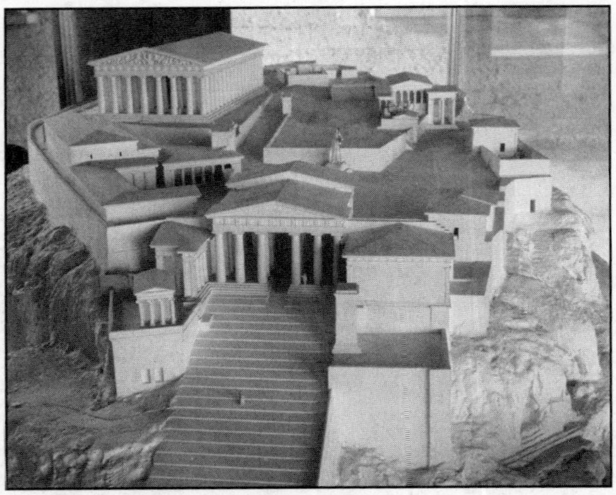

FIG. 05-41 Model of the Acropolis, Athens, Greece. Acropolis Museum, Athens. 1) Parthenon, 2) Propylaia, 3) Erechtheion, 4) Temple of Athena Nike. (page 120)

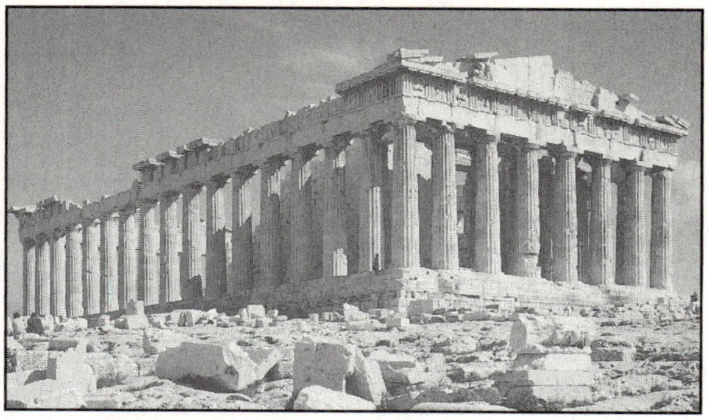

FIG. 05-42 IKTINOS and KALLIKRATES, Parthenon, the Temple of Athena Parthenos (view from the northwest), Acropolis, Athens, Greece, 447–438 BCE. (page 121)

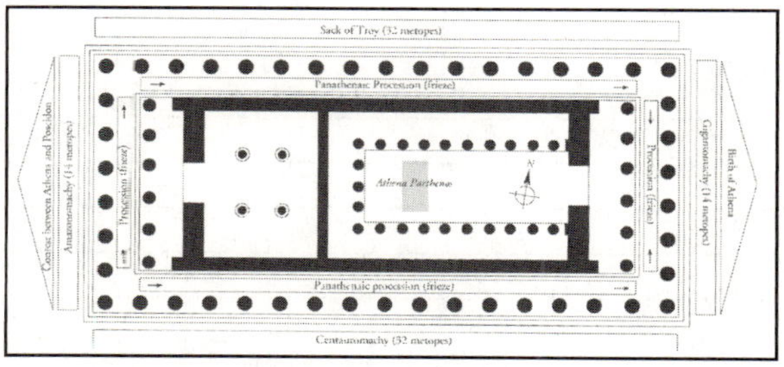

FIG. 05-43 Plan of the Parthenon, Acropolis, Athens, Greece, with diagram of sculptural program (after A. Stewart), 447–432 BCE. (page 122)

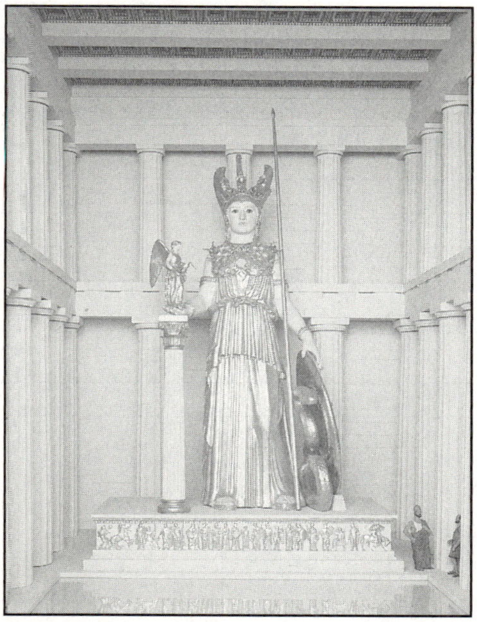

FIG. 05-44 PHIDIAS, *Athena Parthenos,* in the cella of the Parthenon, Acropolis, Athens, Greece, ca. 438 BCE. Model of the lost statue, which was approx. 38′ tall. Royal Ontario Museum, Toronto. (page 122)

FIG. 05-45 Lapith versus centaur, metope from the south side of the Parthenon, Acropolis, Athens, Greece, ca. 447–438 BCE. Marble, approx. 4′ 8″ high. British Museum, London. (page 123)

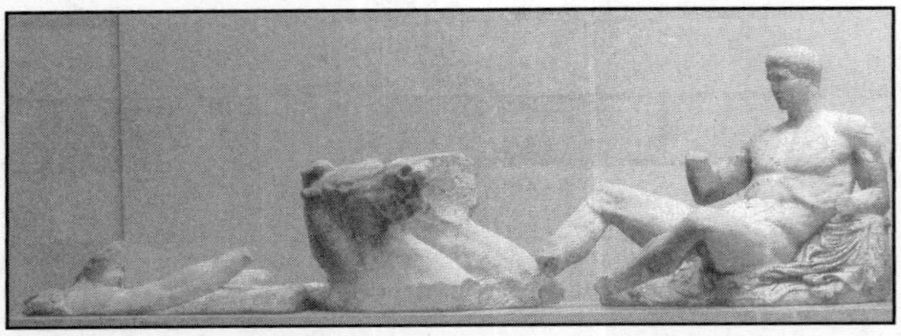

FIG. 05-46 Helios and his horses, and Dionysos (Herakles?), from the east pediment of the Parthenon, Acropolis, Athens, Greece, ca. 438–432 BCE. Marble, greatest height approx. 4′ 3″. British Museum, London. (page 123)

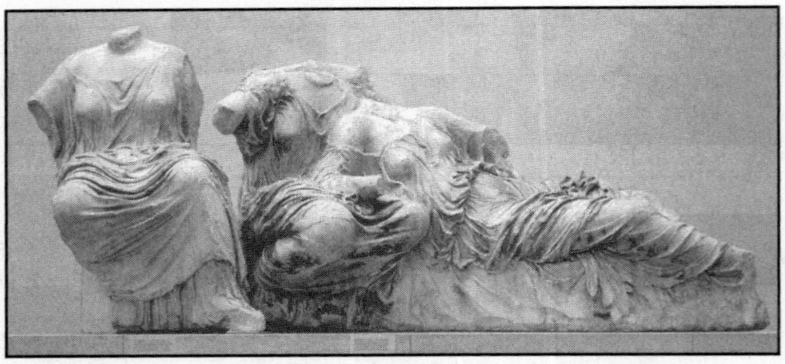

FIG. 05-47 Three goddesses (Hestia, Dione, and Aphrodite?), from the east pediment of the Parthenon, Acropolis, Athens, Greece, ca. 438–432 BCE. Marble, greatest height approx. 4′ 5″. British Museum, London. (page 123)

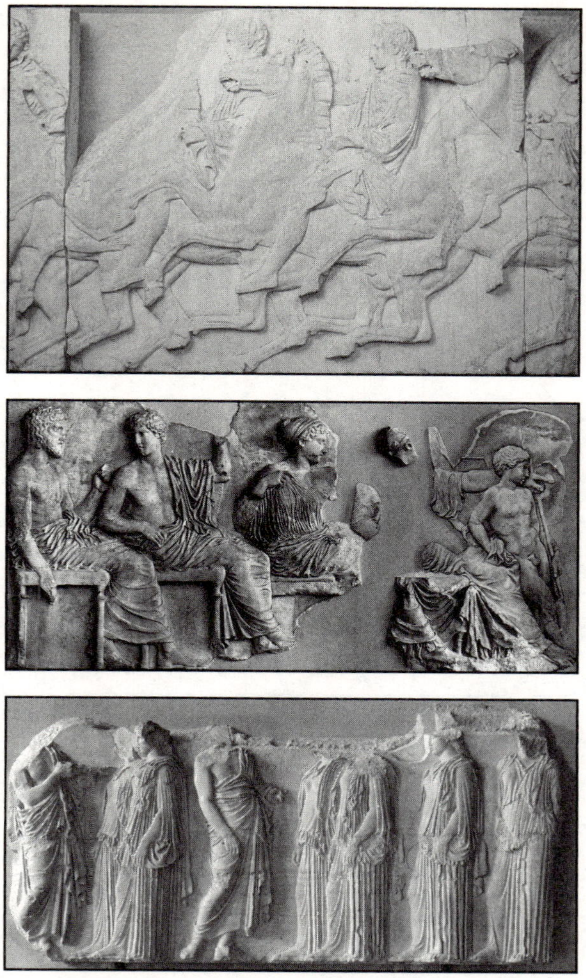

FIG. 05-48 Details of the Panathenaic Festival procession frieze, from the Parthenon, Acropolis, Athens, Greece, ca. 447–438 BCE. Marble, approx. 3′ 6″ high. Horsemen of north frieze *(top)*, British Museum, London; seated gods and goddesses (Poseidon, Apollo, Artemis, Aphrodite, and Eros) of east frieze *(center)*, Acropolis Museum, Athens; and elders and maidens of east frieze *(bottom)*, Louvre, Paris. (page 124)

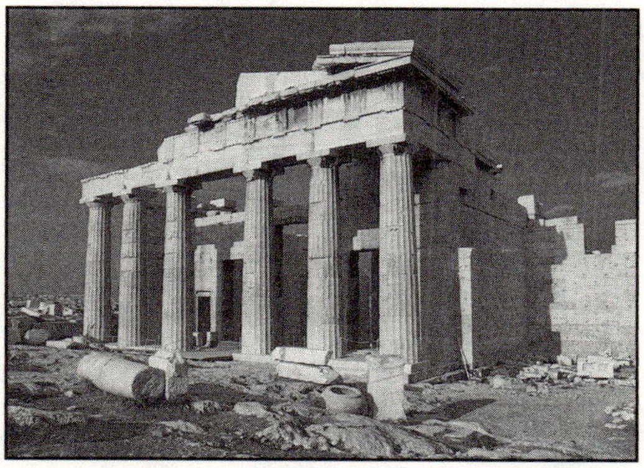

FIG. 05-49 MNESIKLES, Propylaia (view from the northeast), Acropolis, Athens, Greece, 437–432 BCE. (page 125)

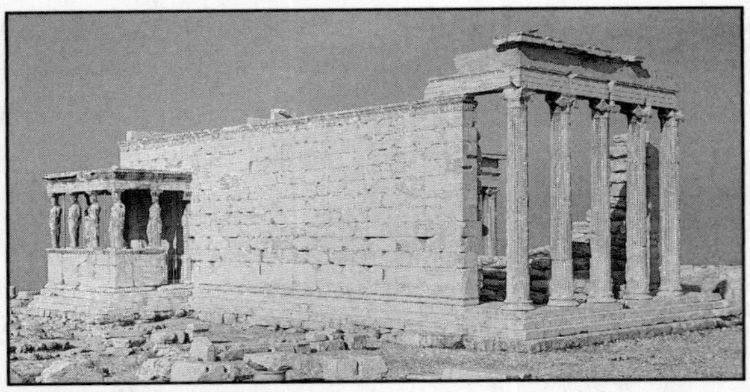

FIG. 05-50 Erechtheion (view from the southeast), Acropolis, Athens, Greece, ca. 421–405 BCE. (page 126)

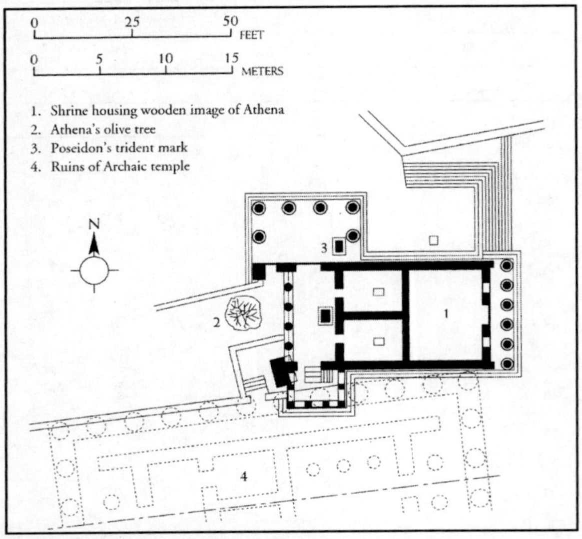

FIG. 05-51 Plan of the Erechtheion, Acropolis, Athens, Greece, ca. 421–405 BCE. (page 126)

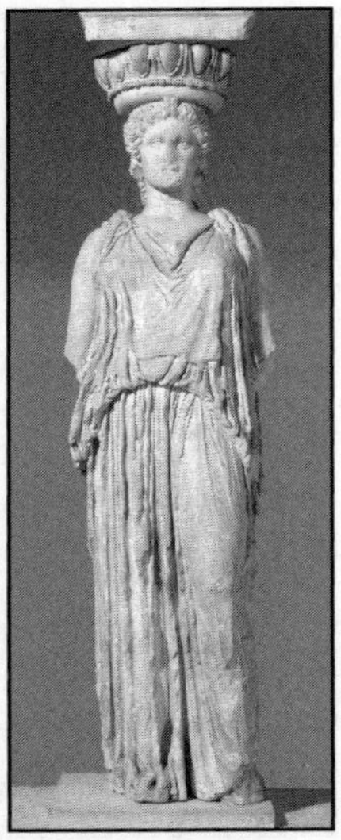

FIG. 05-52 Caryatid from the south porch of the Erechtheion, Acropolis, Athens, Greece, ca. 421–405 BCE. Marble, 7′ 7″ high. British Museum, London. (page 127)

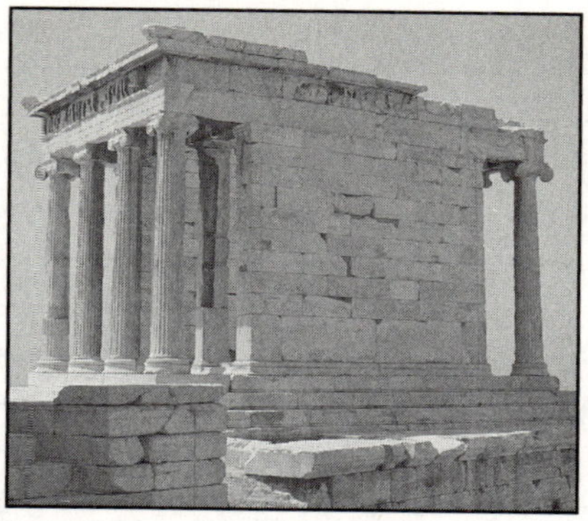

FIG. 05-53 KALLIKRATES, Temple of Athena Nike (view from the northeast), Acropolis, Athens, Greece, ca. 427–424 BCE. (page 127)

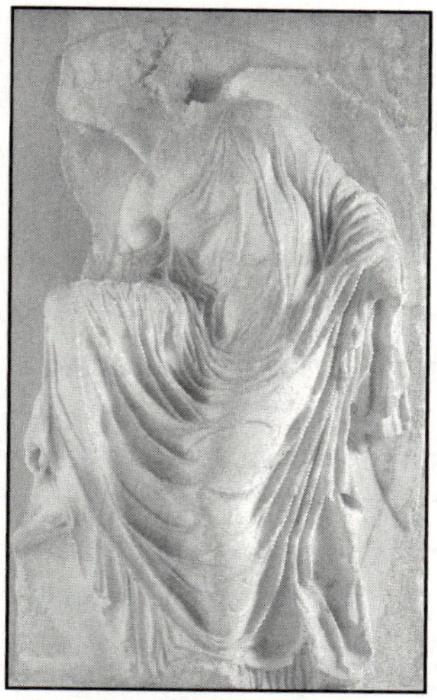

FIG. 05-54 Nike adjusting her sandal, from the south side of the parapet of the Temple of Athena Nike, Acropolis, Athens, Greece, ca. 410 BCE. Marble, approx. 3′ 6″ high. Acropolis Museum, Athens. (page 127)

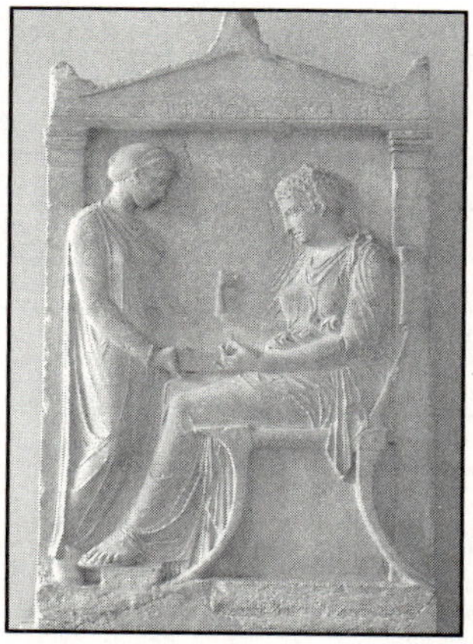

FIG. 05-55 Grave stele of Hegeso, from the Dipylon cemetery, Athens, Greece, ca. 400 BCE. Marble, 5′ 2″ high. National Archaeological Museum, Athens. (page 128)

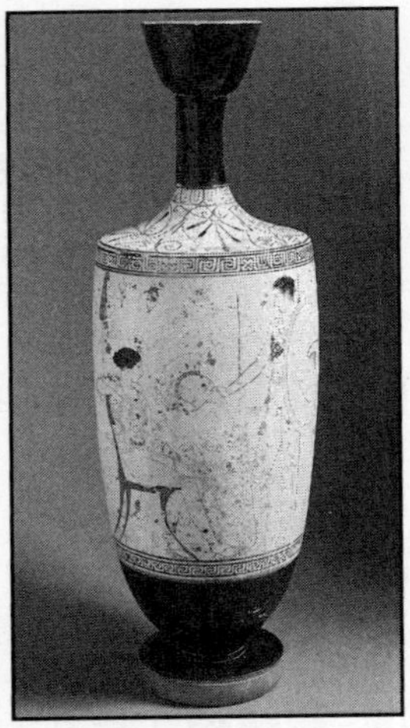

FIG. 05-56 ACHILLES PAINTER, Warrior taking leave of his wife (Attic white-ground lekythos), from Eretria, Greece, ca. 440 BCE. Approx. 1′ 5″ high. National Archaeological Museum, Athens. (page 129)

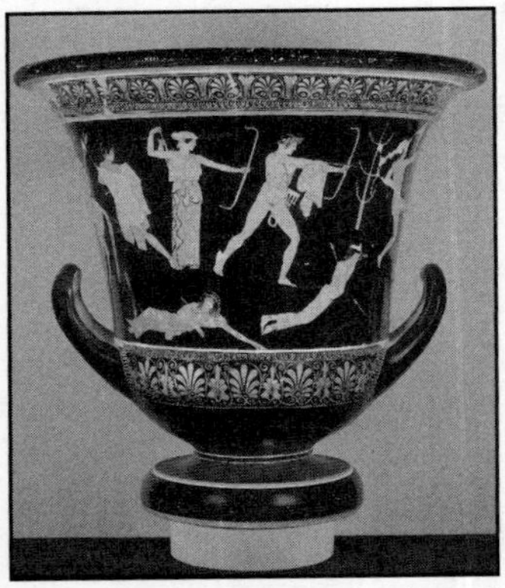

FIG. 05-57 NIOBID PAINTER, Artemis and Apollo slaying the children of Niobe (Attic red-figure calyx krater), from Orvieto, Italy, ca. 450 BCE. Approx. 1′ 9″ high. Louvre, Paris. (page 130)

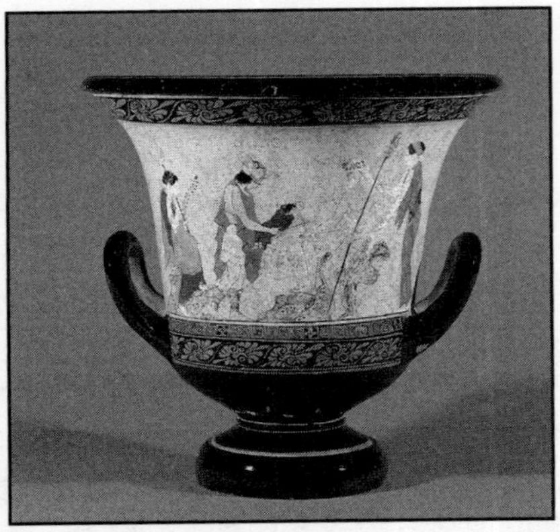

FIG. 05-58 PHIALE PAINTER, Hermes bringing the infant Dionysos to Papposilenos (Attic white-ground calyx krater), from Vulci, Italy, ca. 440–435 BCE. Approx. 1′ 2″ high. Vatican Museums, Rome. (page 130)

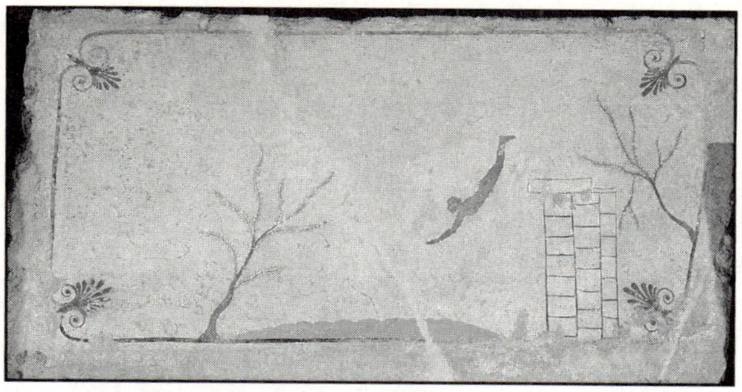

FIG. 05-59 Youth diving, painted ceiling of the Tomb of the Diver, Paestum, Italy, ca. 480 BCE. Approx. 3′ 4″ high. Museo Archeologico Nazionale, Paestum. (page 130)

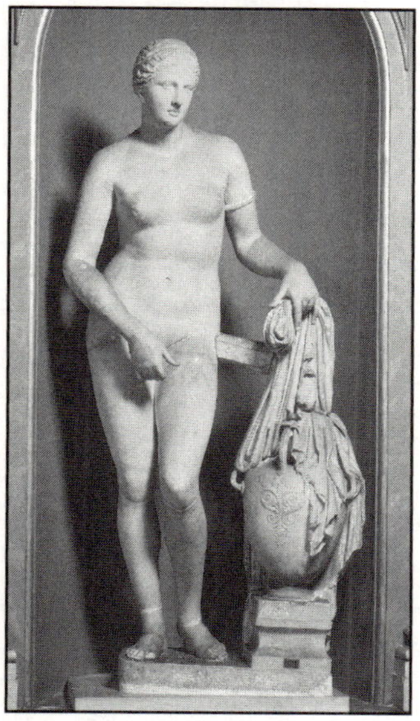

FIG. 05-60 PRAXITELES, *Aphrodite of Knidos*. Roman copy after an original of ca. 350–340 BCE. Approx. 6′ 8″ high. Vatican Museums, Rome. (page 131)

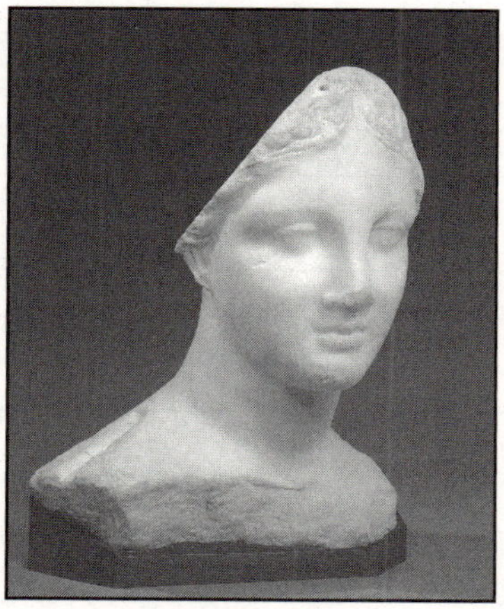

FIG. 05-61 Head of a woman, from Chios, Greece, ca. 320–300 BCE. Marble, approx. 1′ 2″ high. Museum of Fine Arts, Boston. (page 132)

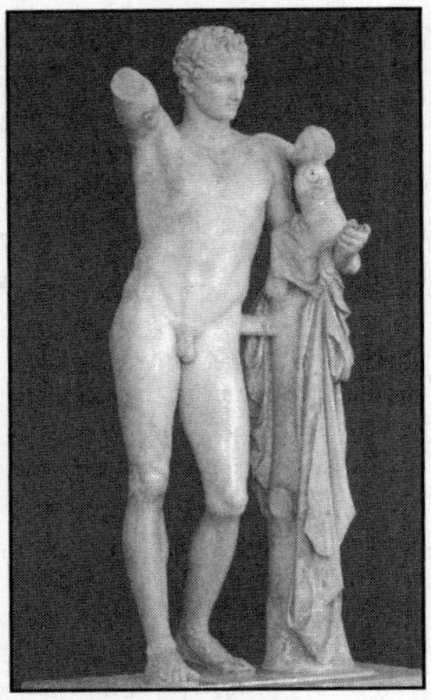

FIG. 05-62 PRAXITELES, Hermes and the infant Dionysos, from the Temple of Hera, Olympia, Greece. Copy after an original of ca. 340 BCE, approx. 7′ 1″ high. Archaeological Museum, Olympia. (page 132)

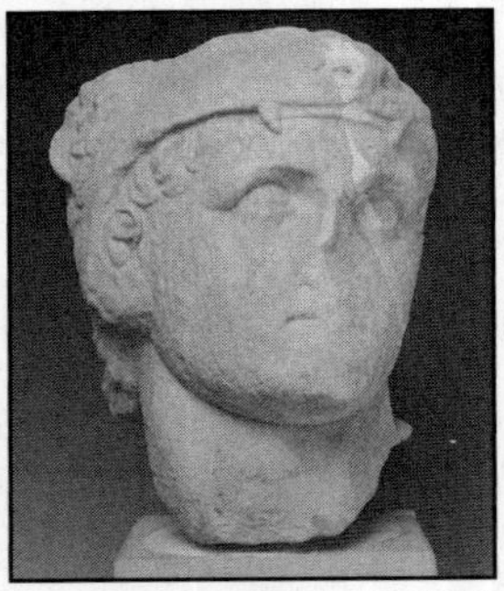

FIG. 05-63 Head of Herakles or Telephos, from the west pediment of the Temple of Athena Alea, Tegea, Greece, ca. 340 BCE. Marble, approx. 19 1/2″ high. (Stolen from) Archaeological Museum, Tegea. (page 133)

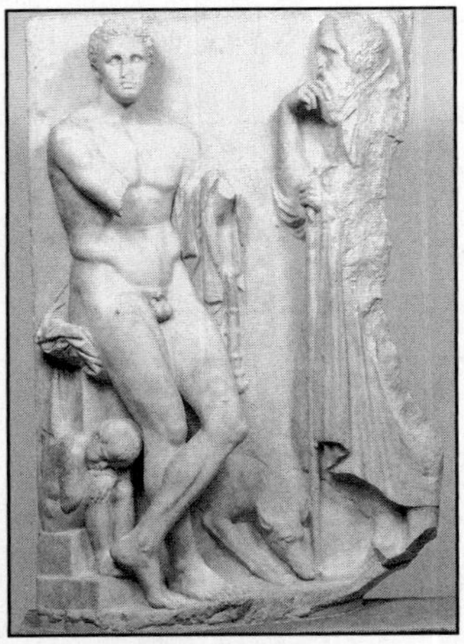

FIG. 05-64 Grave stele of a young hunter, found near the Ilissos River, Athens, Greece, ca. 340–330 BCE. Marble, approx. 5′ 6″ high. National Archaeological Museum, Athens. (page 133)

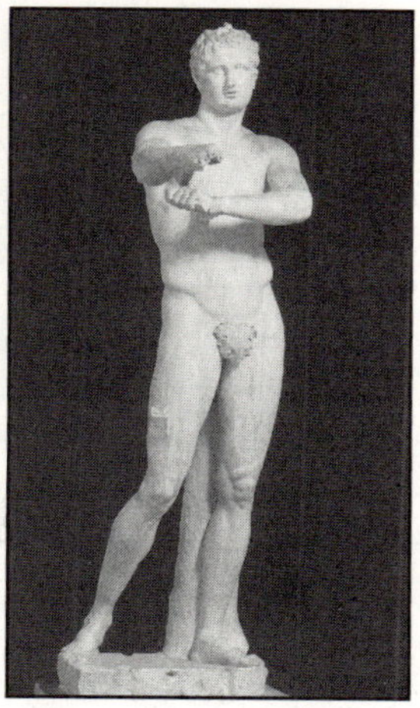

FIG. 05-65 LYSIPPOS, *Apoxyomenos (Scraper)*. Roman copy after a bronze original of ca. 330 BCE, approx. 6′ 9″ high. Vatican Museums, Rome. (page 134)

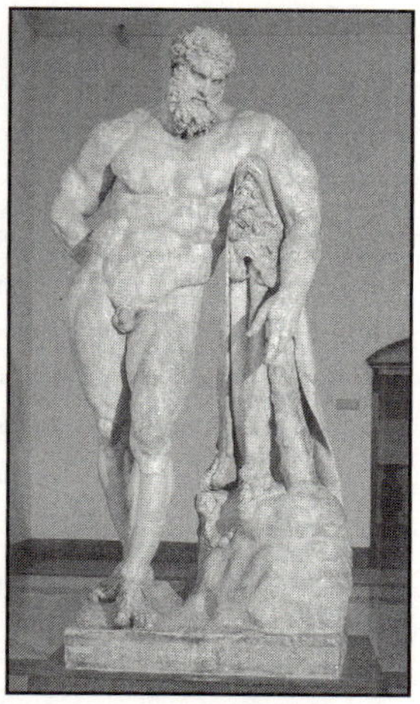

FIG. 05-66 LYSIPPOS, Weary Herakles *(Farnese Herakles)*. Roman copy from Rome, Italy, signed by Glykon of Athens, after a bronze original of ca. 320 BCE. Approx. 10′ 5″ high. Museo Nazionale, Naples. (page 134)

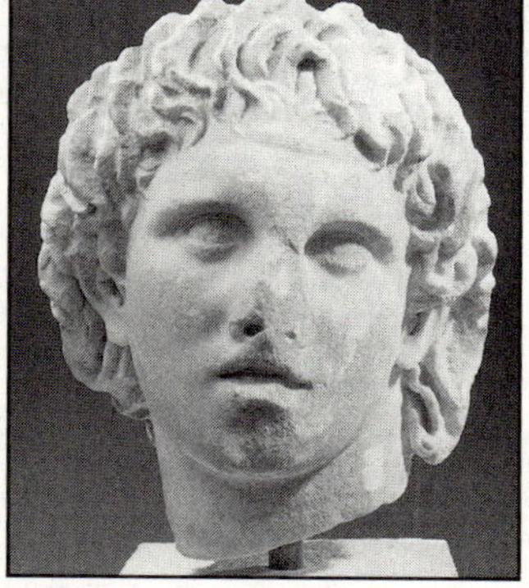

FIG. 05-67 Head of Alexander the Great, from Pella, Greece, ca. 200–150 BCE. Marble, approx. 1′ high. Archaeological Museum, Pella. (page 135)

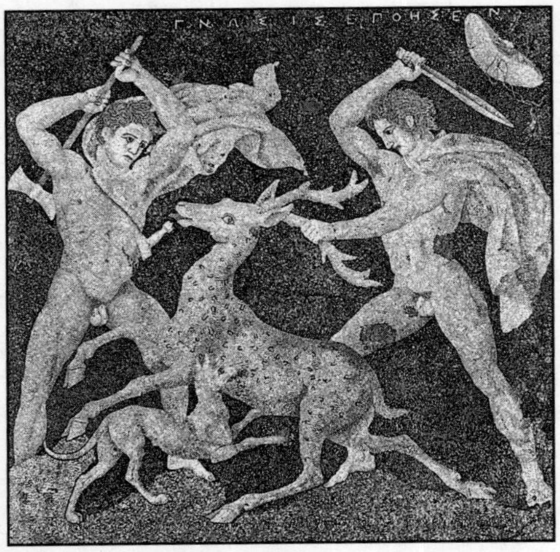

FIG. 05-68 GNOSIS, Stag hunt, from Pella, Greece, ca. 300 BCE. Pebble mosaic, figural panel 10′ 2″ high. Archaeological Museum, Pella. (page 135)

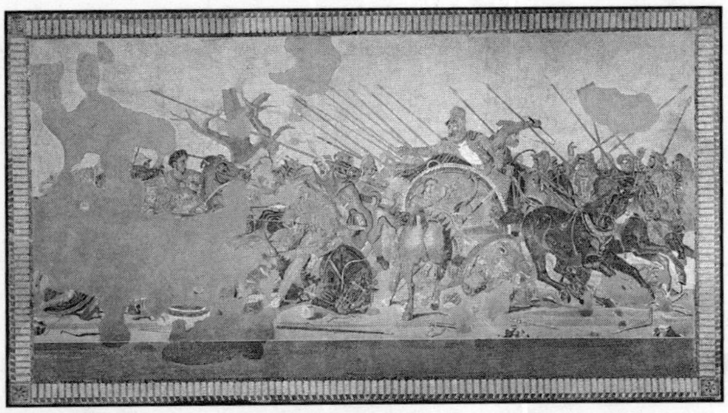

FIG. 05-69 PHILOXENOS OF ERETRIA, *Battle of Issus,* ca. 310 BCE. Roman copy *(Alexander Mosaic)* from the House of the Faun, Pompeii, Italy, late second or early first century BCE. Tessera mosaic, approx. 8′ 10″ × 16′ 9″. Museo Nazionale, Naples. (page 136)

FIG. 05-70 POLYKLEITOS THE YOUNGER, Theater, Epidauros, Greece, ca. 350 BCE. (page 137)

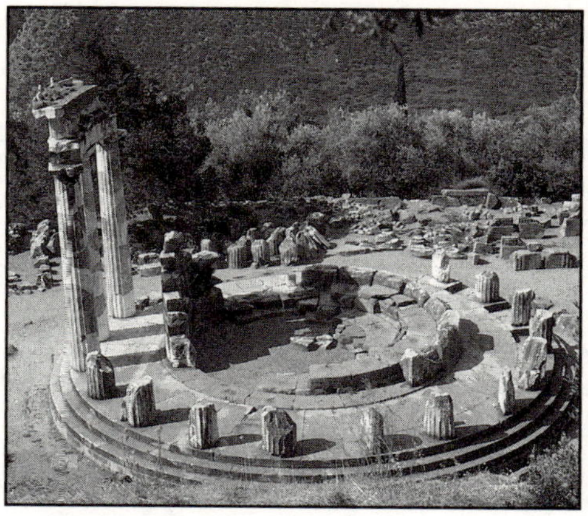

FIG. 05-71 THEODOROS OF PHOKAIA, Tholos, Delphi, Greece, ca. 375 BCE. (page 138)

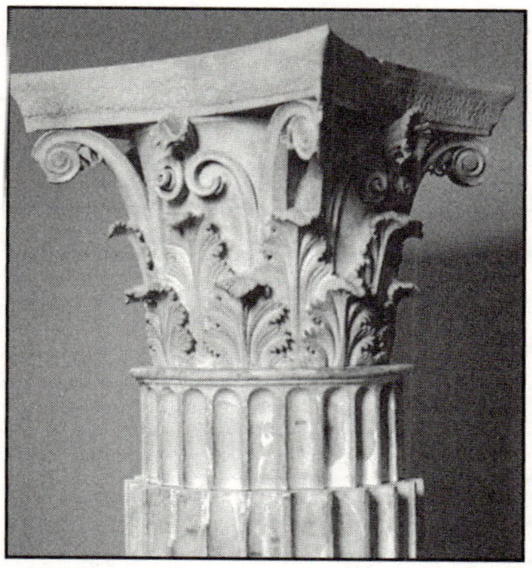

FIG. 05-72 POLYKLEITOS THE YOUNGER, Corinthian capital, from the tholos, Epidauros, Greece, ca. 350 BCE. Archaeological Museum, Epidauros. (page 139)

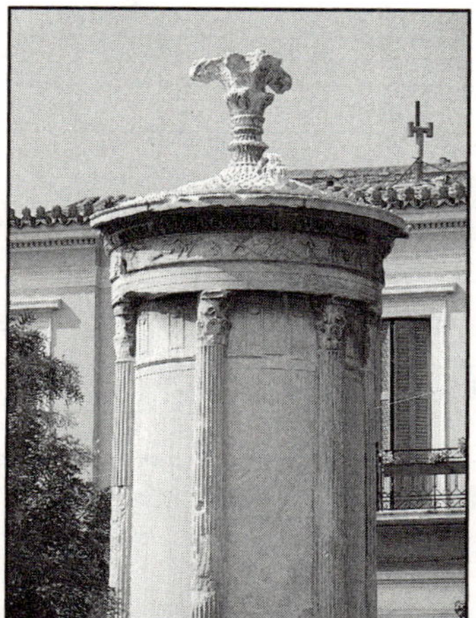

FIG. 05-73 Choragic Monument of Lysikrates, Athens, Greece, 334 BCE. (page 139)

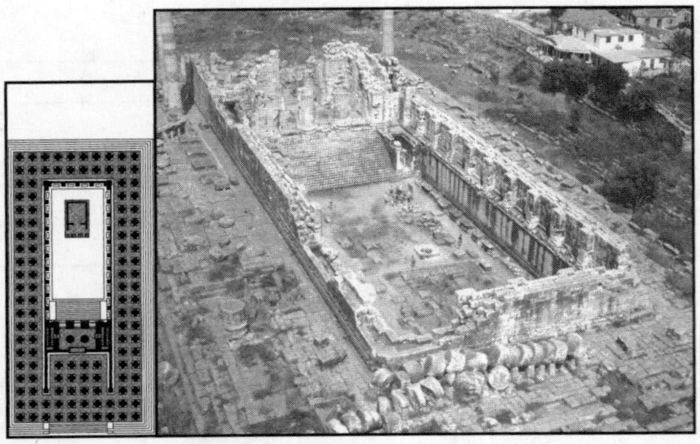

FIG. 05-74 PAIONIOS OF EPHESOS AND DAPHNIS OF MILETOS, Temple of Apollo, Didyma, Turkey, begun 313 BCE. Plan *(left)* and aerial view *(right)*. (page 140)

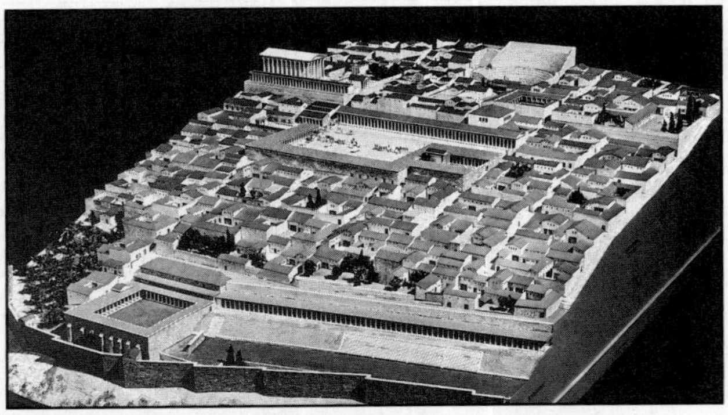

FIG. 05-75 Model of the city of Priene, Turkey, fourth century BCE and later. Staatliche Museen, Berlin. (page 141)

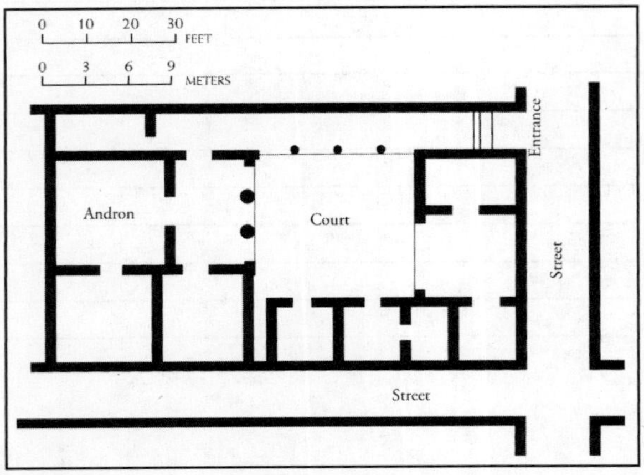

FIG. 05-76 Plan of House XXXII, Priene, Turkey, fourth century BCE. (page 141)

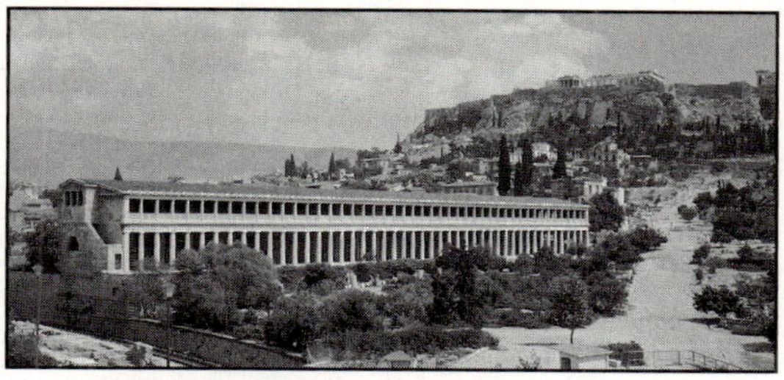

FIG. 05-77 Stoa of Attalos II, Agora, Athens, Greece, ca. 150 BCE (Acropolis in the background). (page 142)

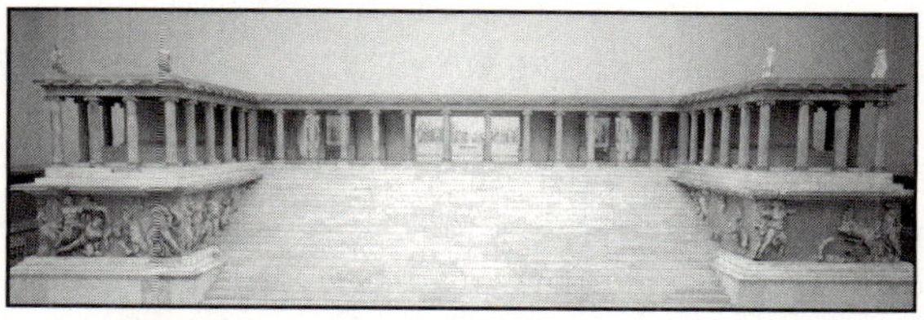

FIG. 05-78 Reconstructed west front of the Altar of Zeus, from Pergamon, Turkey, ca. 175 BCE. Staatliche Museen, Berlin. (page 142)

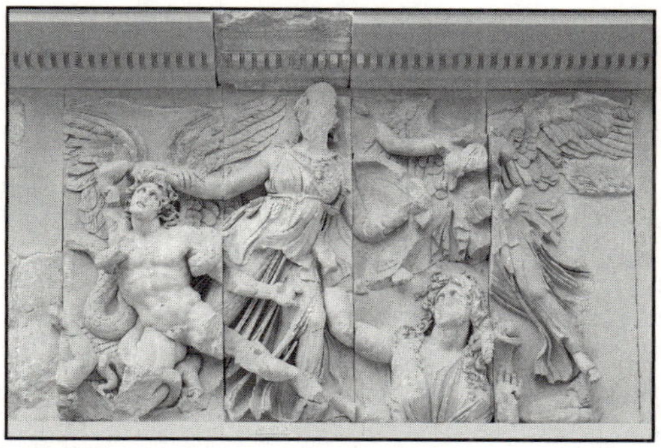

FIG. 05-79 Athena battling Alkyoneos, detail of the gigantomachy frieze, from the Altar of Zeus, Pergamon, Turkey, ca. 175 BCE. Marble, approx. 7′ 6″ high. Staatliche Museen, Berlin. (page 143)

FIG. 05-80 EPIGONOS(?), Gallic chieftain killing himself and his wife. Roman copy after a bronze original from Pergamon, Turkey, ca. 230–220 BCE, approx. 6′ 11″ high. Museo Nazionale Romano—Palazzo Altemps, Rome. (page 144)

FIG. 05-81 EPIGONOS(?), Dying Gaul. Roman copy after a bronze original from Pergamon, Turkey, ca. 230–220 BCE, approx. 3′ 1/2″ high. Museo Capitolino, Rome. (page 144)

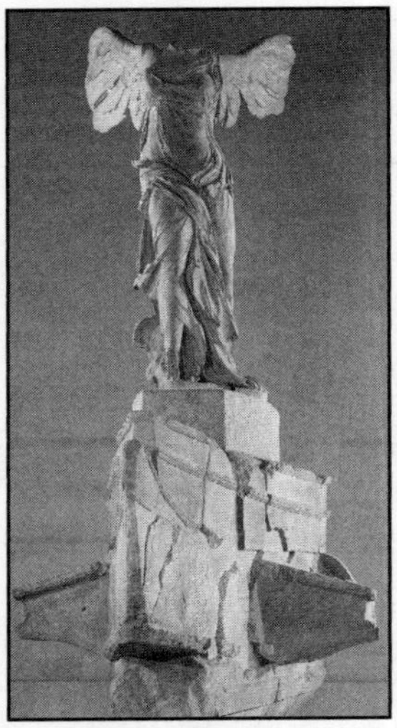

FIG. 05-82 Nike alighting on a warship *(Nike of Samothrace),* from Samothrace, Greece, ca. 190 BCE. Marble, figure approx. 8′ 1″ high. Louvre, Paris. (page 145)

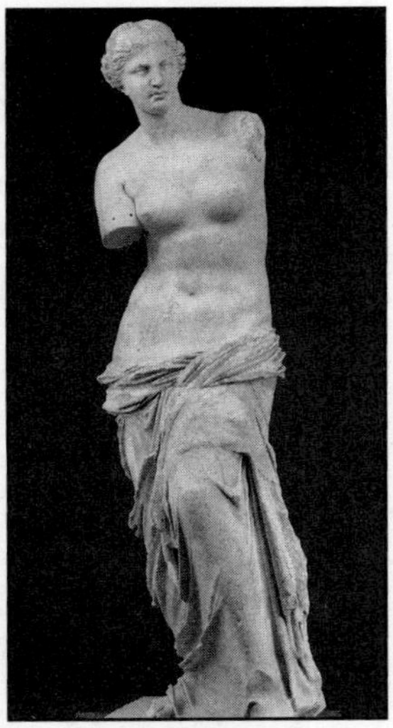

FIG. 05-83 ALEXANDROS OF ANTIOCH-ON-THE-MEANDER, Aphrodite *(Venus de Milo),* from Melos, Greece, ca. 150–125 BCE. Marble, approx. 6′ 7″ high. Louvre, Paris. (page 145)

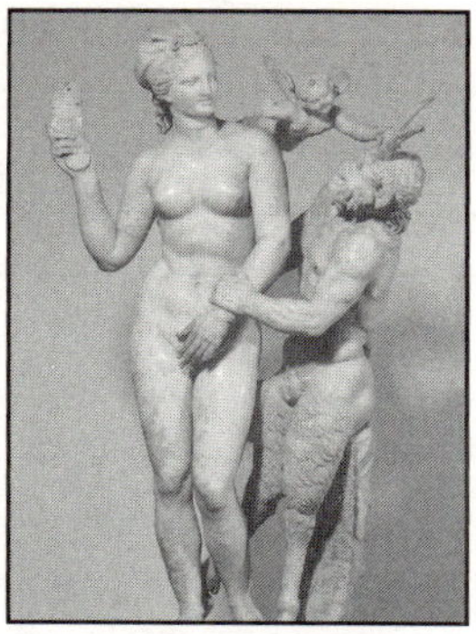

FIG. 05-84 Aphrodite, Eros, and Pan, from Delos, Greece, ca. 100 BCE. Marble, 4′ 4″ high. National Archaeological Museum, Athens. (page 146)

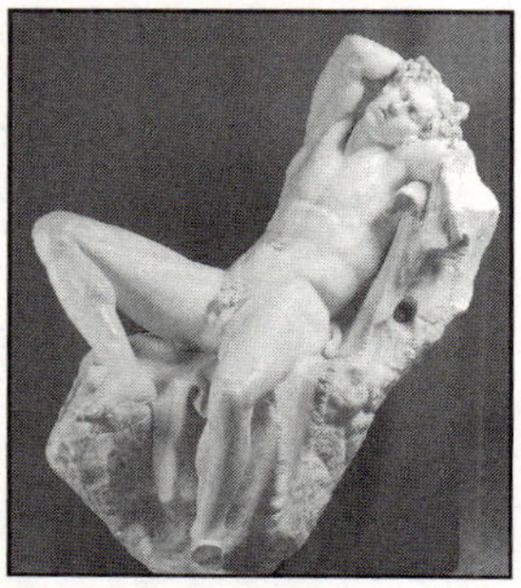

FIG. 05-85 Sleeping satyr *(Barberini Faun),* from Rome, Italy, ca. 230–200 BCE. Marble, approx. 7′ 1″ high. Glyptothek, Munich. (page 146)

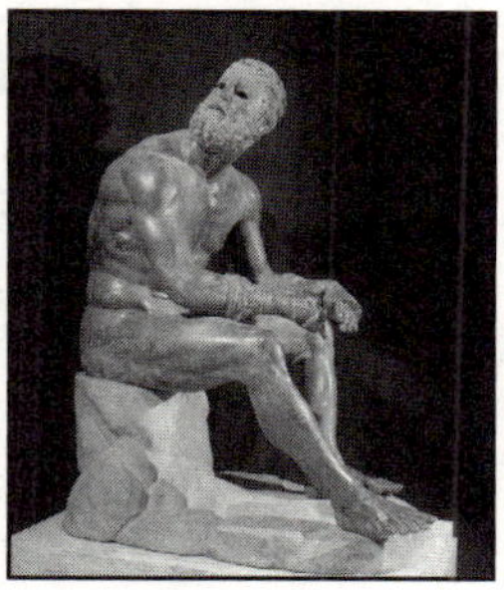

FIG. 05-86 Seated boxer, from Rome, Italy, ca. 100–50 BCE. Bronze, approx. 4′ 2 1/2″ high. Museo Nazionale Romano, Rome. (page 147)

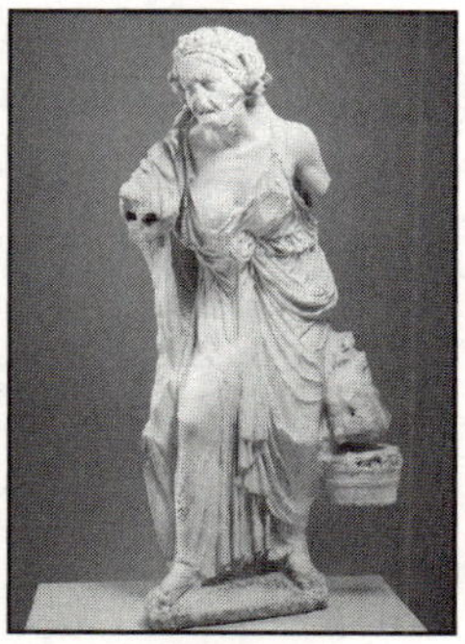

FIG. 05-87 Old market woman, ca. 150–100 BCE. Marble, approx. 4′ 1/2″ high. Metropolitan Museum of Art, New York. (page 148)

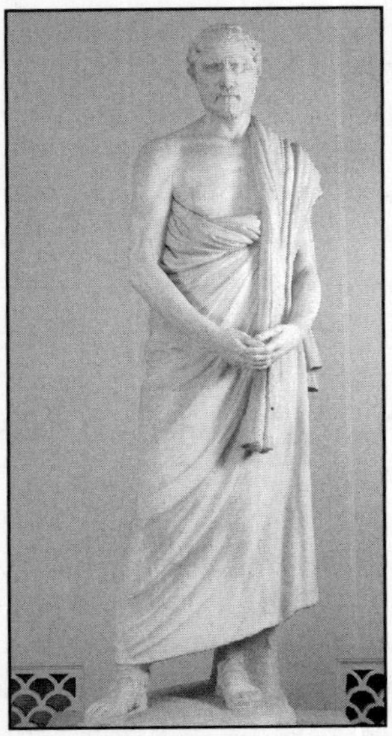

FIG. 05-88 POLYEUKTOS, Demosthenes. Roman copy after a bronze original of ca. 280 BCE. 6′ 7 1/2″ high. Ny Carlsberg Glyptotek, Copenhagen. (page 148)

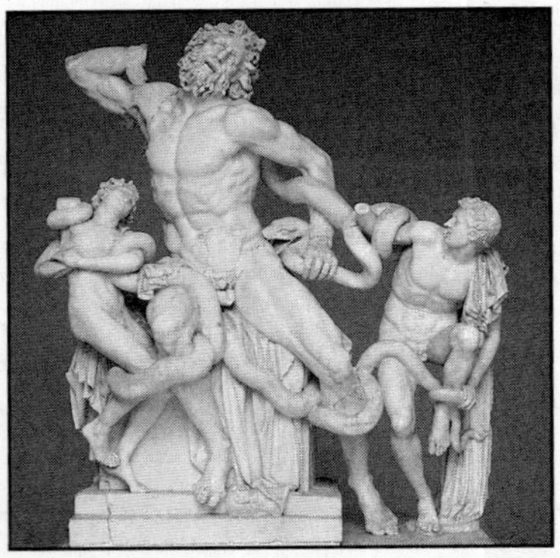

FIG. 05-89 ATHANADOROS, HAGESANDROS, and POLYDOROS OF RHODES, Laocoön and his sons, from Rome, Italy, early first century ce. Marble, approx. 7′ 10 1/2″ high. Vatican Museums, Rome. (page 149)

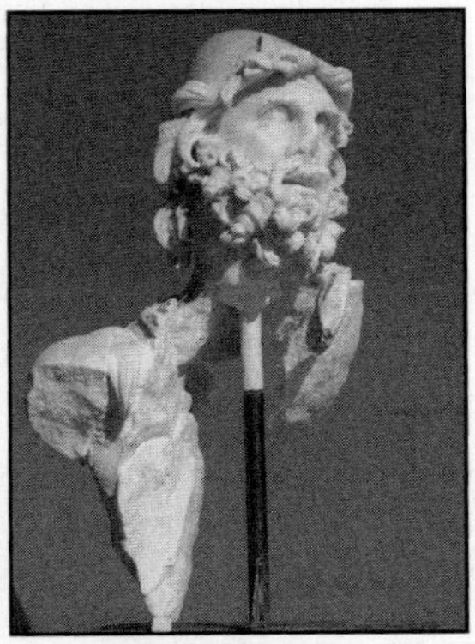

FIG. 05-90 ATHANADOROS, HAGESANDROS, and POLYDOROS OF RHODES, Odysseus, from Sperlonga, Italy, early first century ce. Marble, full figure approx. 7′ high. Museo Archeologico, Sperlonga. (page 150)

Chapter 6

Italy before the Romans:
The Art of the Etruscans

Goals

- Identify the geographic area of the Etruscan people.
- Examine the possible origins of Etruscan art and culture.
- Understand how and why the architecture and art of the Etruscans is different from that of the Greeks.
- Understand the funerary customs of the Etruscans.

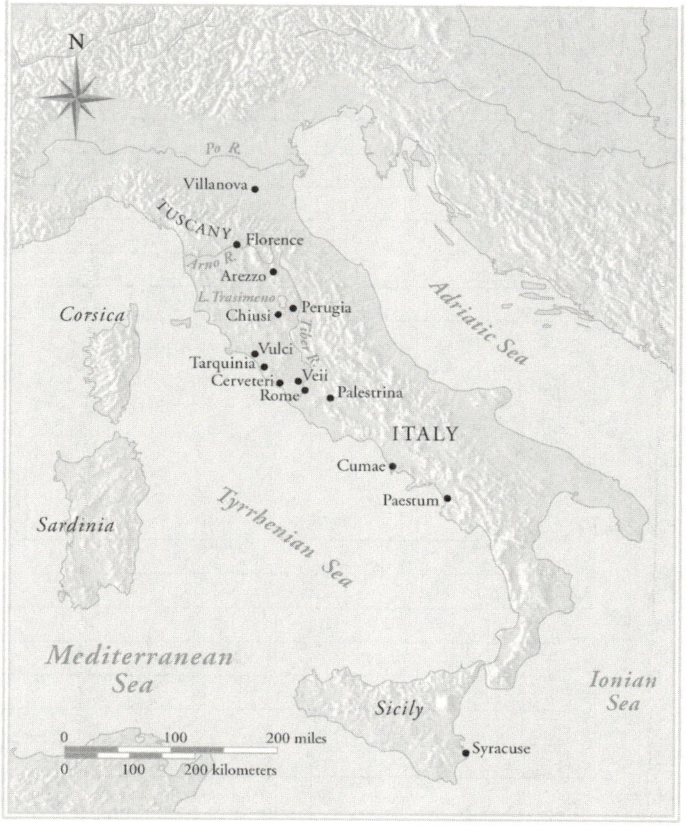

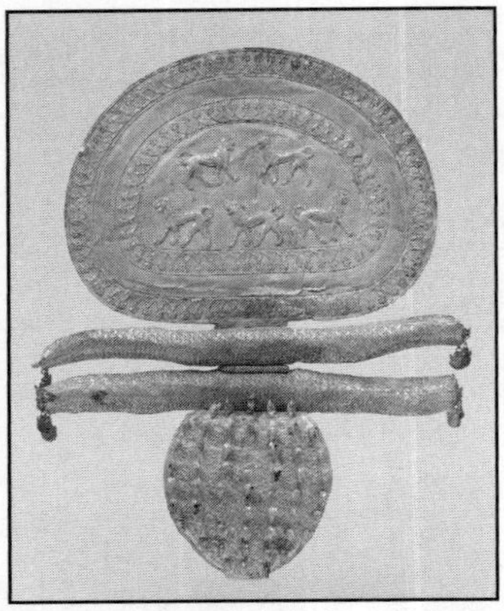

FIG. 06-01 Fibula with Orientalizing lions, from the Regolini-Galassi Tomb, Cerveteri, Italy, ca. 650–640 BCE. Gold, approx. 1′ 1/2″ high. Vatican Museums, Rome. (page 154)

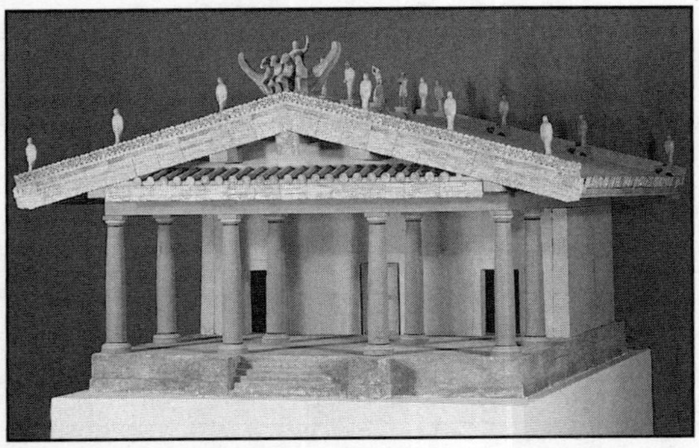

FIG. 06-02 Model of a typical Etruscan temple of the sixth century BCE, as described by Vitruvius. Istituto di Etruscologia e di Antichità Italiche, Università di Roma, Rome. (page 155)

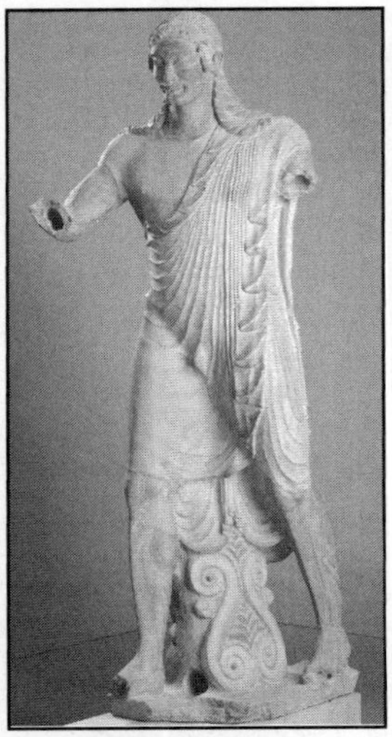

FIG. 06-03 Apulu (Apollo), from the roof of the Portonaccio Temple, Veii, Italy, ca. 510–500 BCE. Painted terracotta, approx. 5′ 11″ high. Museo Nazionale di Villa Giulia, Rome. (page 156)

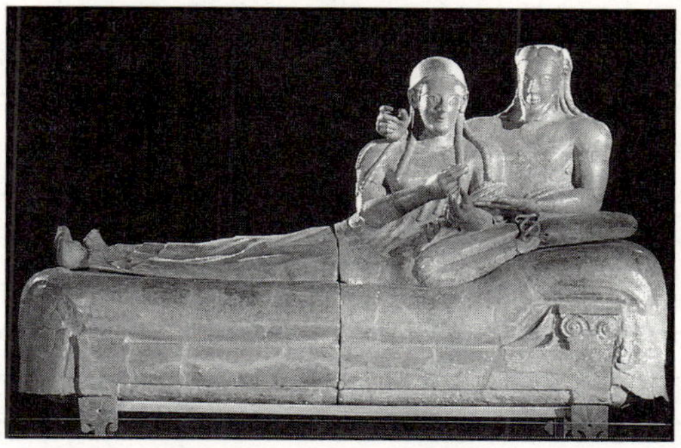

FIG. 06-04 Sarcophagus with reclining couple, from Cerveteri, Italy, ca. 520 BCE. Painted terracotta, approx. 3′ 9 1/2″ × 6′ 7″. Museo Nazionale di Villa Giulia, Rome. (page 157)

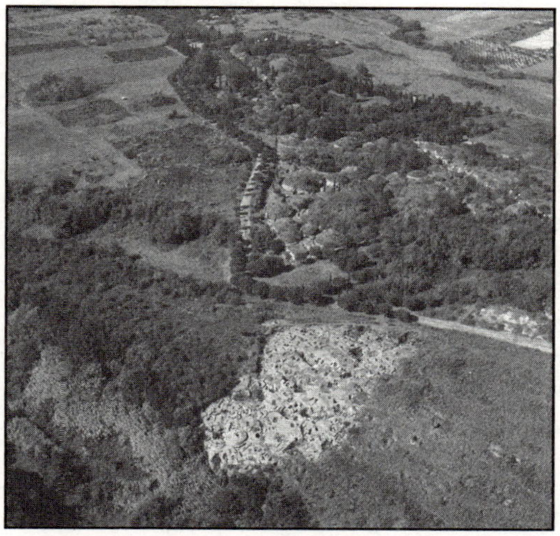

FIG. 06-05 Aerial view of Banditaccia necropolis, Cerveteri, Italy, seventh to second centuries BCE. (page 158)

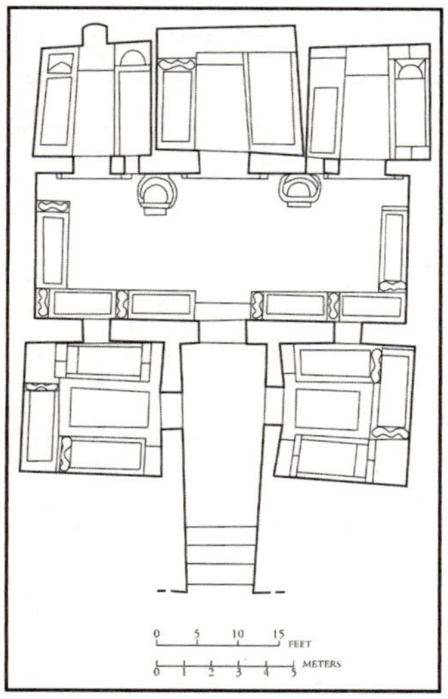

FIG. 06-06 Plan of the Tomb of the Shields and Chairs, Cerveteri, Italy, second half of the sixth century BCE. (page 158)

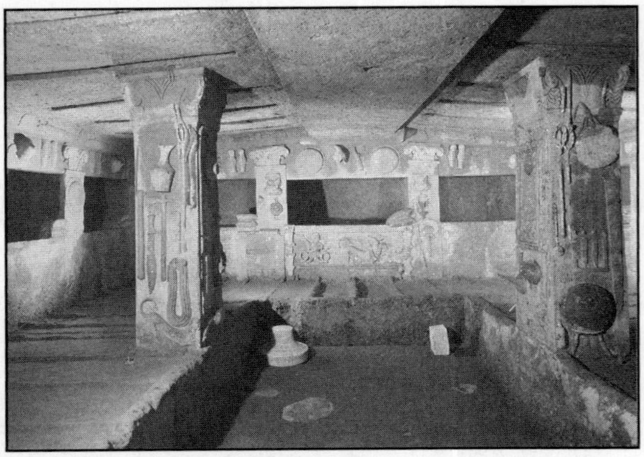

FIG. 06-07 Interior of the Tomb of the Reliefs, Cerveteri, Italy, third century BCE. (page 159)

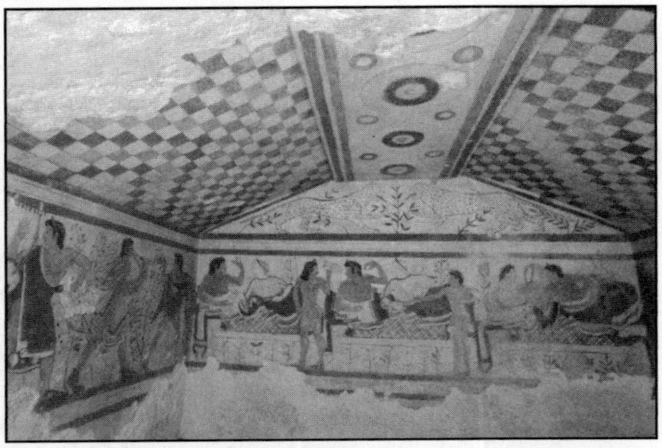

FIG. 06-08 Leopards, banqueters, and musicians, mural paintings in the Tomb of the Leopards, Tarquinia, Italy, ca. 480–470 BCE. (page 159)

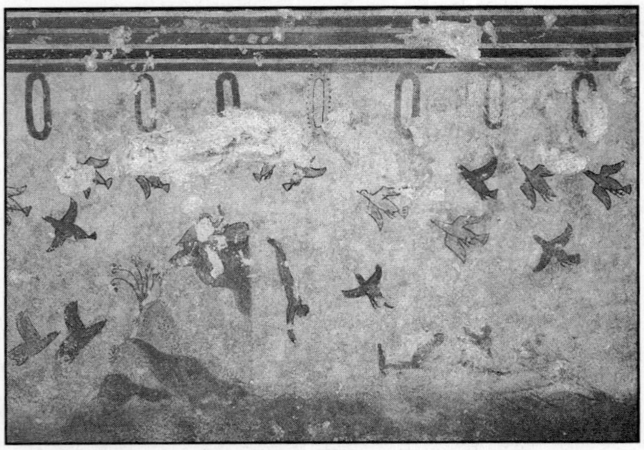

FIG. 06-09 Diving and fishing, mural painting in the Tomb of Hunting and Fishing, Tarquinia, Italy, ca. 530–520 BCE. (page 160)

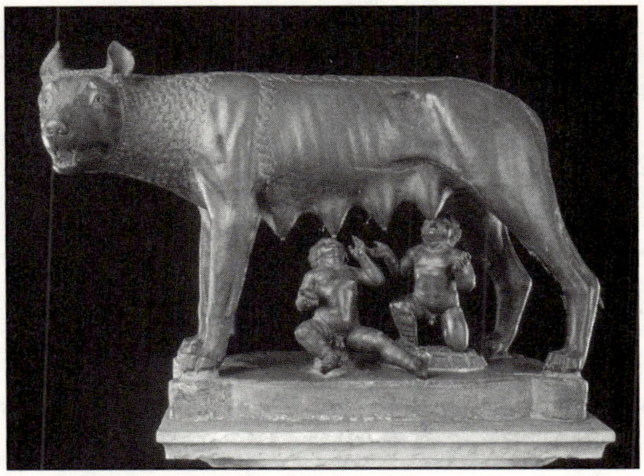

FIG. 06-10 *Capitoline Wolf,* from Rome, Italy, ca. 500–480 BCE. Bronze, approx. 2′ 7 1/2″ high. Palazzo dei Conservatori, Rome. (page 161)

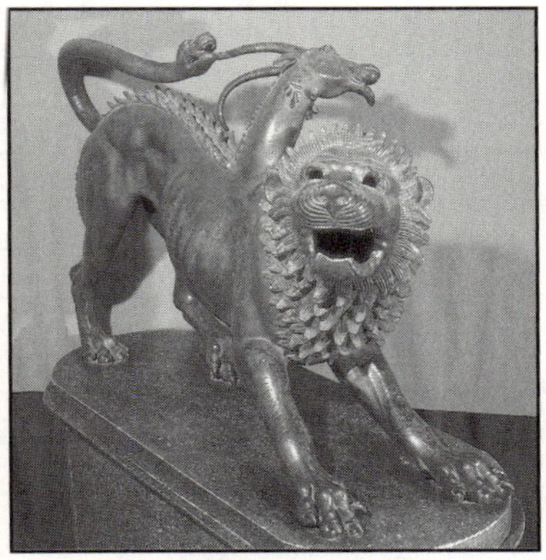

FIG. 06-11 *Chimera of Arezzo,* from Arezzo, Italy, first half of fourth century BCE. Bronze, approx. 2′ 7 1/2″ high. Museo Archeologico Nazionale, Florence. (page 162)

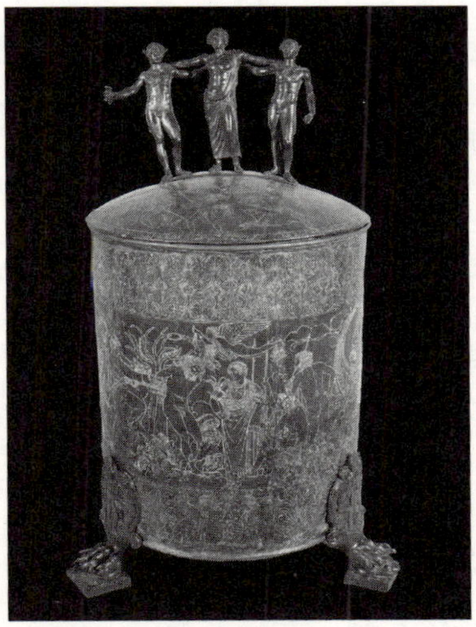

FIG. 06-12 NOVIOS PLAUTIOS, *Ficoroni Cista,* from Palestrina, Italy, late fourth century BCE. Bronze, approx. 2′ 6″ high. Museo Nazionale di Villa Giulia, Rome. (page 162)

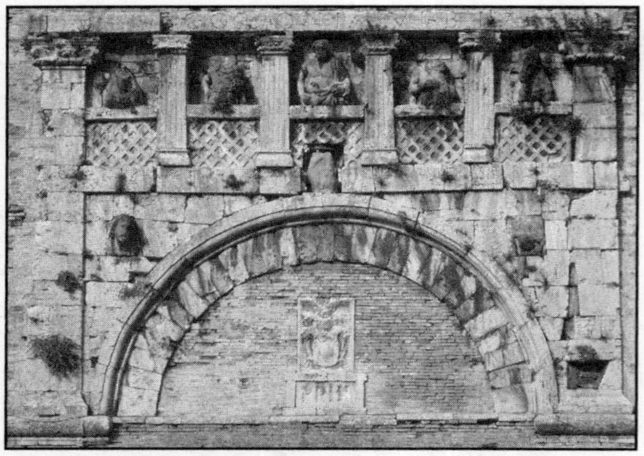

FIG. 06-13 Porta Marzia (Gate of Mars), Perugia, Italy, second century BCE. (page 163)

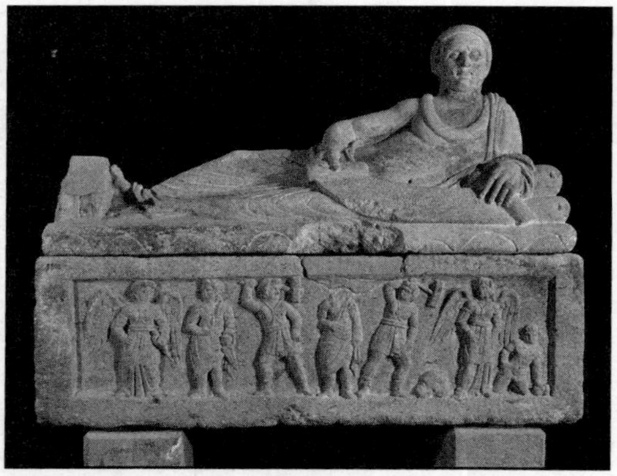

FIG. 06-14 Sarcophagus of Lars Pulena, from Tarquinia, Italy, early second century BCE. Tufa, approx. 6′ 6″ long. Museo Archeologico Nazionale, Tarquinia. (page 163)

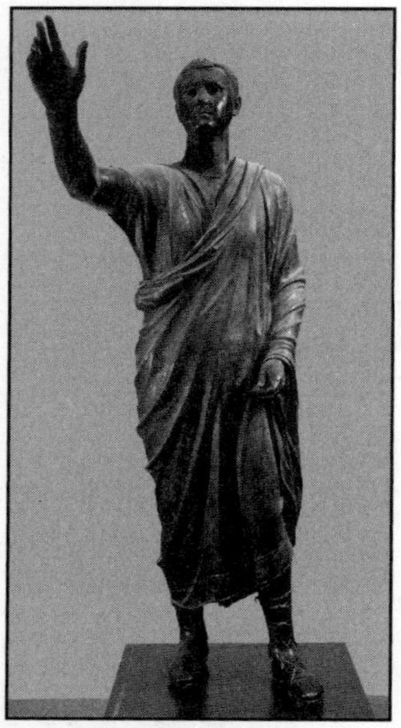

FIG. 06-15 Aule Metele *(Arringatore),* from Cortona, near Lake Trasimeno, Italy, early first century BCE. Bronze, approx. 5′ 7″ high. Museo Archeologico Nazionale, Florence. (page 164)

Chapter 7

From Seven Hills to Three Continents:
The Art of Ancient Rome

Goals

- Understand the great innovations of Roman architecture and how these innovations contributed to the expanse of the Roman Empire.
- Explore Pompeii for its information about Roman art and architecture.
- Examine the types, methods, and subject matter of Roman wall painting.
- Understand what Roman portraiture says about Roman society.
- Understand the political nature of Roman art and architecture, especially as it communicates ideas of power for the emperor and empire.
- Examine changes in Roman art and architecture as a result of expansion of the Roman Empire and the incorporation of the conquered cultures.

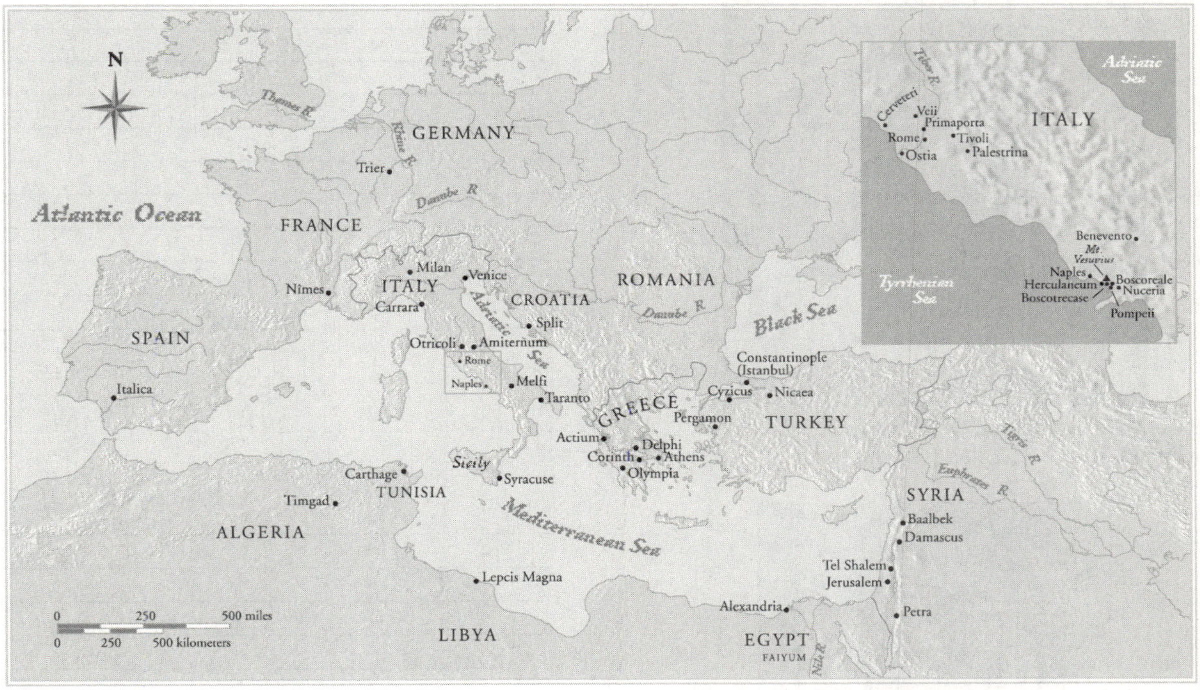

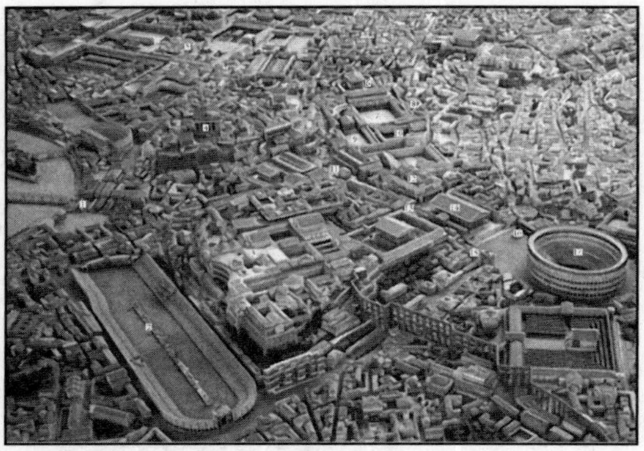

FIG. 07-01 Model of the city of Rome during the early fourth century CE. Museo della Civiltà Romana, Rome. 1) Temple of Fortuna Virilis, 2) Circus Maximus, 3) Palatine Hill, 4) Temple of Jupiter Capitolinus, 5) Pantheon 6) Column of Trajan, 7) Forum of Trajan, 8) Markets of Trajan, 9) Forum of Julius Caesar, 10) Forum of Augustus, 11) Forum Romanum, 12) Basilica Nova, 13) Arch of Titus, 14) Temple of Venus and Roma, 15) Arch of Constantine, 16) Colossus of Nero, 17) Colosseum. (page 169)

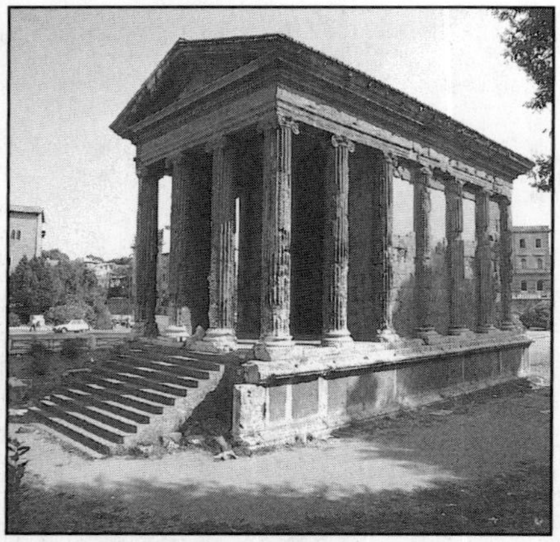

FIG. 07-02 Temple of "Fortuna Virilis" (Temple of Portunus), Rome, Italy, ca. 75 BCE. (page 171)

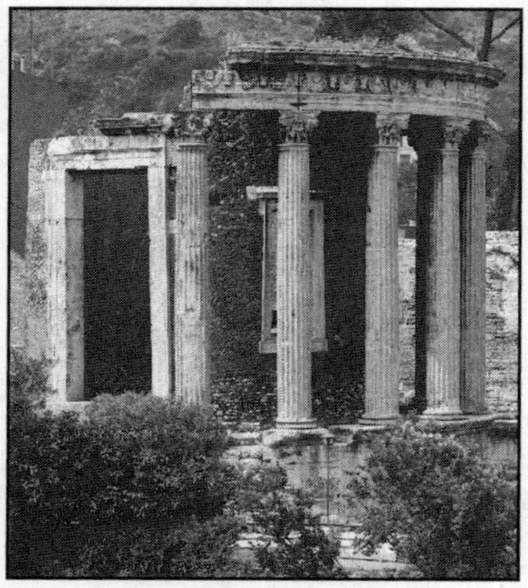

FIG. 07-03 Temple of Vesta(?), Tivoli, Italy, early first century BCE. (page 171)

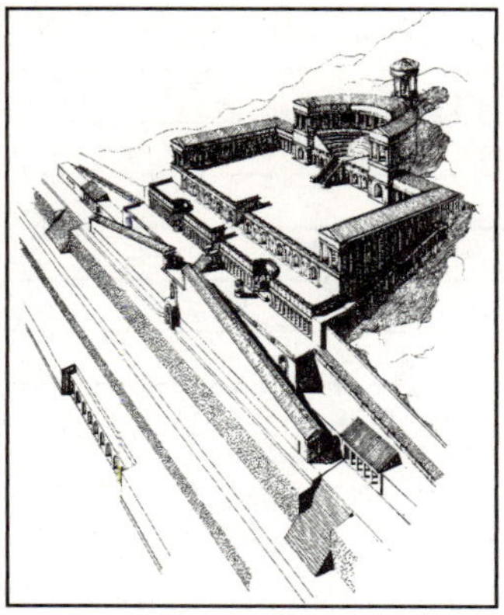

FIG. 07-04 Reconstruction drawing of the Sanctuary of Fortuna Primigenia, Palestrina, Italy, late second century BCE. (page 171)

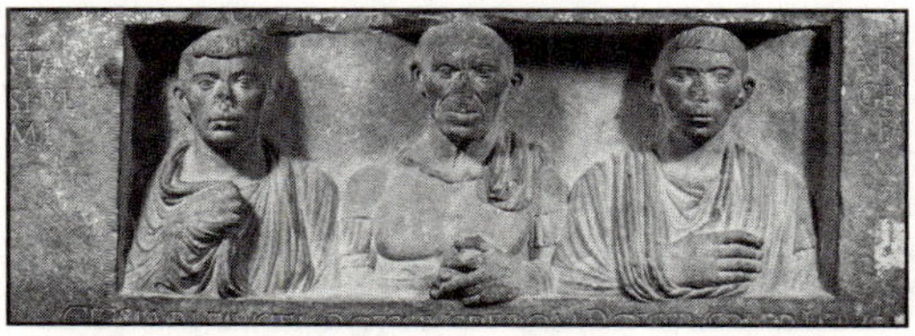

FIG. 07-05 Funerary relief with portraits of the Gessii, from Rome(?), Italy, ca. 30 BCE. Marble, approx. 2′ 1 1/2″ high. Museum of Fine Arts, Boston. (page 172)

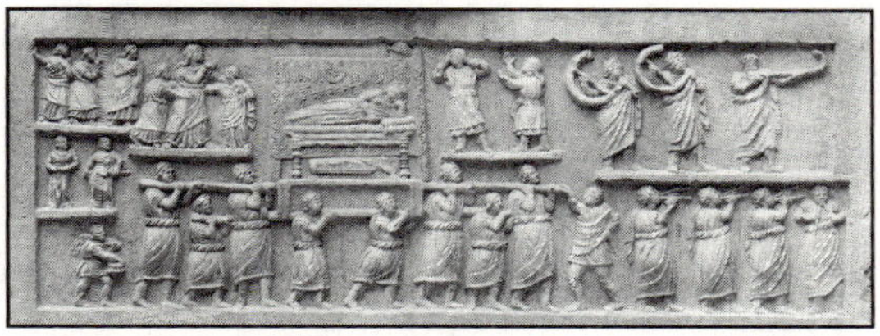

FIG. 07-06 Relief with funerary procession, from Amiternum, Italy, second half of first century BCE. Limestone, approx. 2′ 2″ high. Museo Nazionale d'Abruzzo, L'Aquila. (page 172)

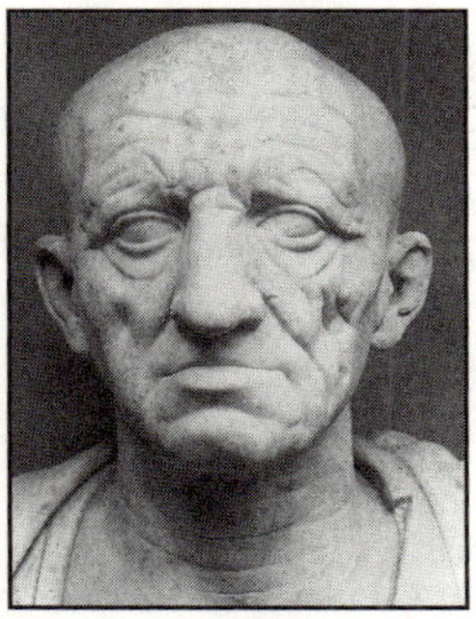

FIG. 07-07 Head of a Roman patrician, from Otricolli, Italy, ca. 75–50 BCE. Marble, approx. 1′ 2″ high. Museo Torlonia, Rome. (page 173)

FIG. 07-08 Portrait of a Roman general, from the Sanctuary of Hercules, Tivoli, Italy, ca. 75–50 BCE. Marble, approx. 6′ 2″ high. Museo Nazionale Romano-Palazzo Massimo alle Terme, Rome. (page 176)

FIG. 07-09 Denarius with portrait of Julius Caesar, 44 BCE. Silver, diameter approx. 3/4″. American Numismatic Society, New York. (page 174)

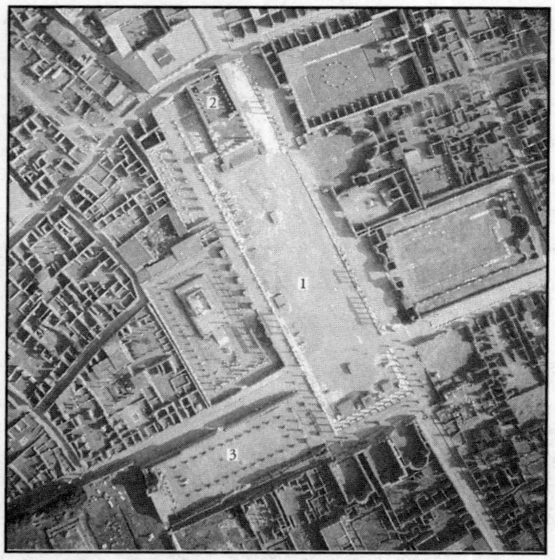

FIG. 07-10 Aerial view of the forum (1), with Temple of Jupiter (Capitolium, 2) and Basilica (3), Pompeii, Italy, second century BCE and later. (page 175)

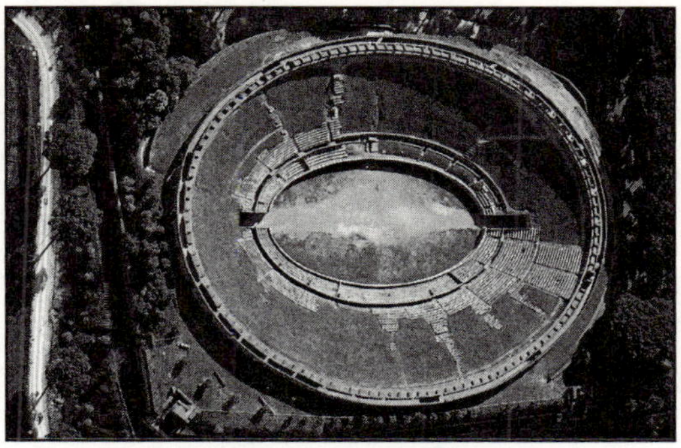

FIG. 07-11 Aerial view of the amphitheater, Pompeii, Italy, ca. 70 BCE. (page 176)

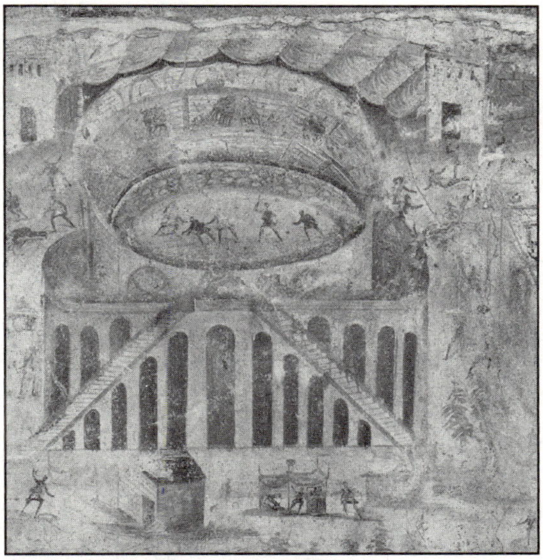

FIG. 07-12 Brawl in the Pompeii amphitheater, wall painting from House I,3,23, Pompeii, Italy, ca. 60–79 CE. Approx. 5′ 7″ × 6′ 1″. Museo Nazionale, Naples. (page 176)

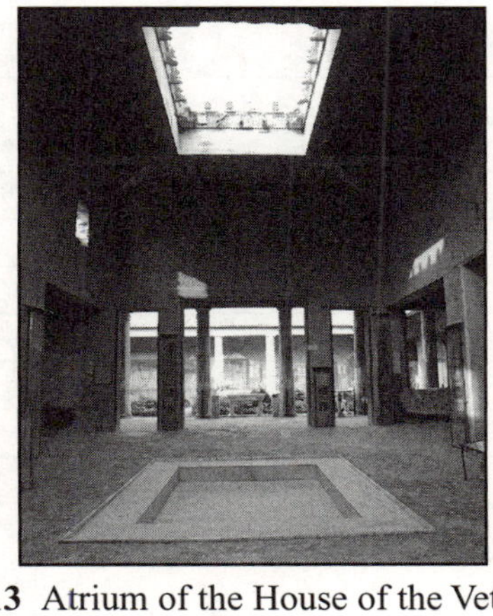

FIG. 07-13 Atrium of the House of the Vettii, Pompeii, Italy, second century BCE, rebuilt 62–79 CE. (page 176)

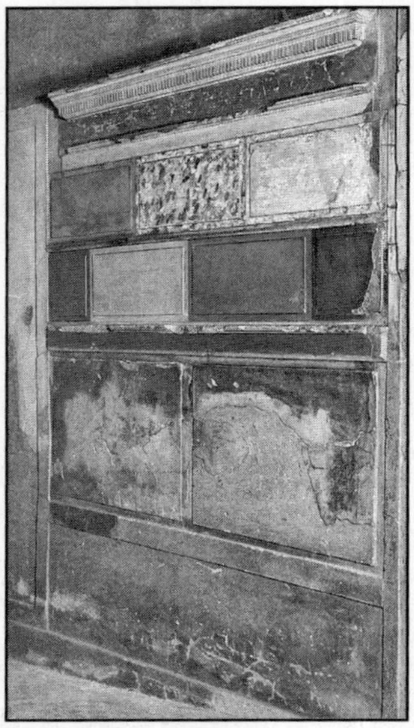

FIG. 07-14 First Style wall painting in the fauces of the Samnite House, Herculaneum, Italy, late second century BCE. (page 178)

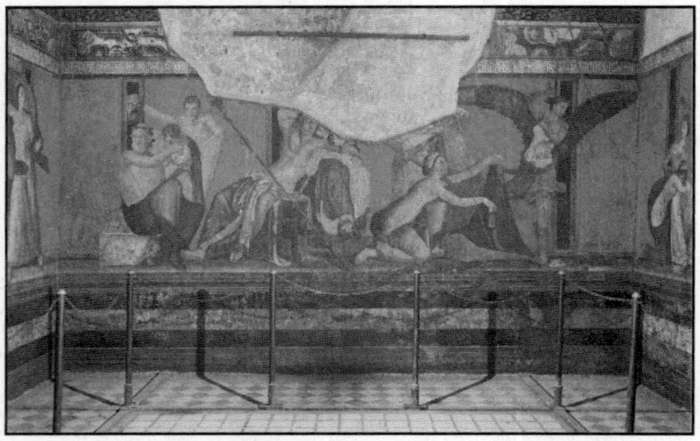

FIG. 07-15 Dionysiac mystery frieze, Second Style wall paintings in Room 5 of the Villa of the Mysteries, Pompeii, Italy, ca. 60–50 BCE. Frieze approx. 5′ 4″ high. (page 179)

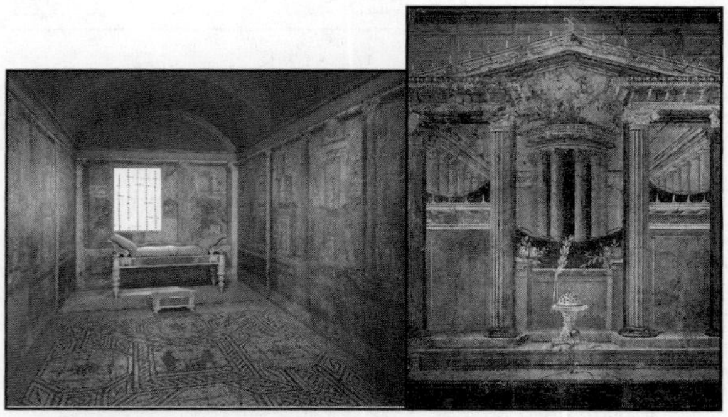

FIG. 07-16 Second Style wall paintings (general view, left, and detail of tholos, right) from Cubiculum M of the Villa of Publius Fannius Synistor, Boscoreale, Italy, ca. 50–40 BCE. Approx. 8′ 9″ high. Metropolitan Museum of Art, New York. (page 179)

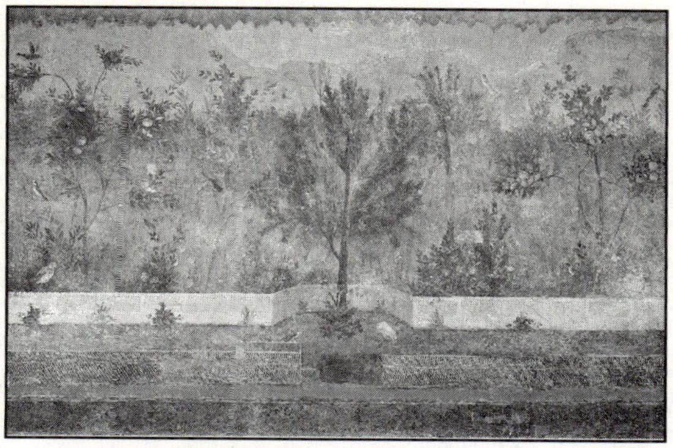

FIG. 07-17 Gardenscape, Second Style wall painting, from the Villa of Livia, Primaporta, Italy, ca. 30–20 BCE. Approx. 6′ 7″ high. Museo Nazionale Romano-Palazzo Massimo alle Terme, Rome. (page 180)

FIG. 07-18 Detail of a Third Style wall painting, from Cubiculum 15 of the Villa of Agrippa Postumus, Boscotrecase, Italy, ca. 10 BCE. Approx. 7′ 8″ high. Metropolitan Museum of Art, New York. (page 181)

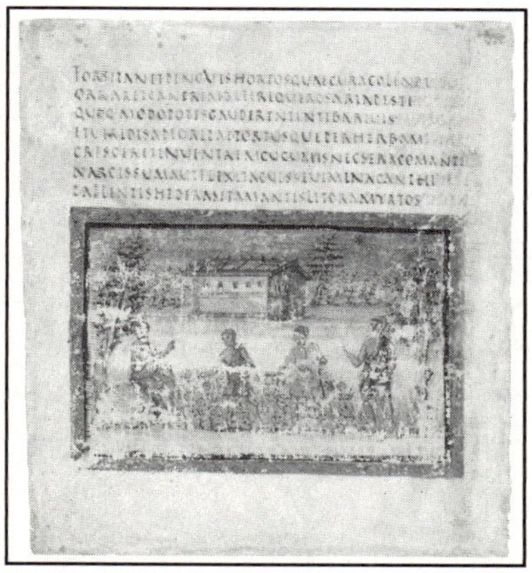

FIG. 07-19 The old farmer of Corycus, folio 7 verso of the *Vatican Vergil,* ca. 400–420 CE. Tempera on parchment, approx. 1′ 1/2″ × 1′. Biblioteca Apostolica Vaticana, Rome. (page 181)

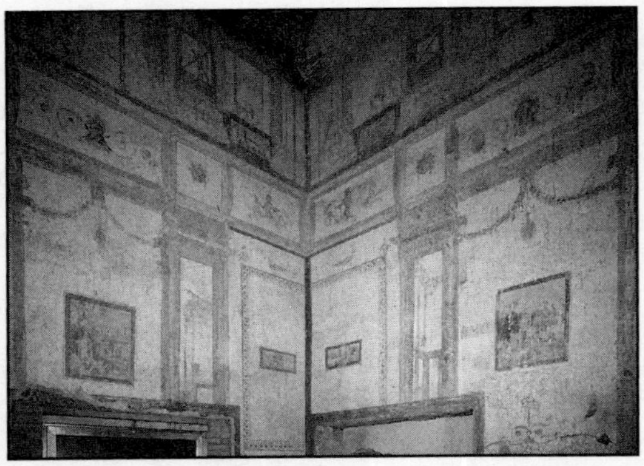

FIG. 07-20 Fourth Style wall paintings in Room 78 of the Domus Aurea (Golden House) of Nero, Rome, Italy, 64–68 CE. (page 182)

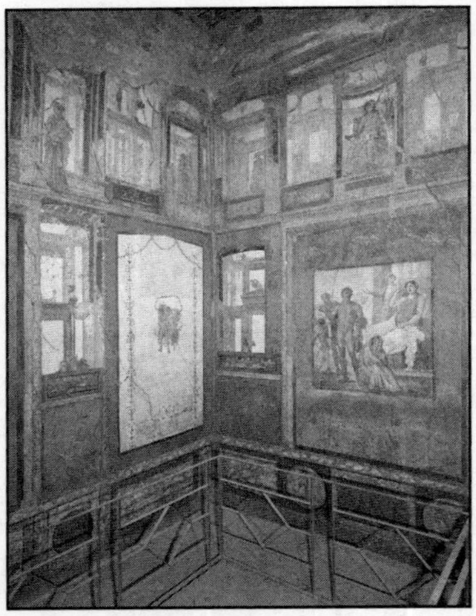

FIG. 07-21 Fourth Style wall paintings in the Ixion Room (Triclinium P) of the House of the Vettii, Pompeii, Italy, ca. 70–79 CE. (page 183)

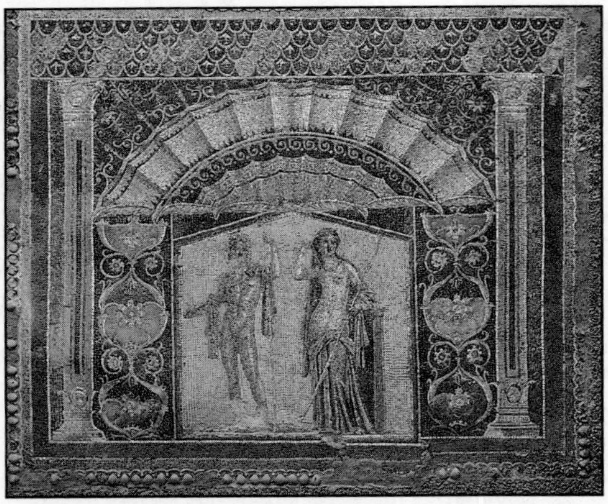

FIG. 07-22 Neptune and Amphitrite, wall mosaic in the summer triclinium of the House of Neptune and Amphitrite, Herculaneum, Italy, ca. 62–79 CE. (page 184)

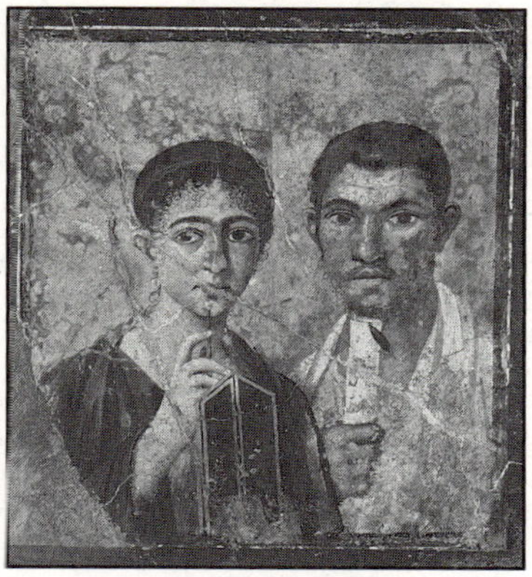

FIG. 07-23 Portrait of a husband and wife, wall painting from House VII,2,6, Pompeii, Italy, ca. 70–79 CE. Approx. 1′ 11″ × 1′ 8 1/2″. Museo Nazionale, Naples. (page 184)

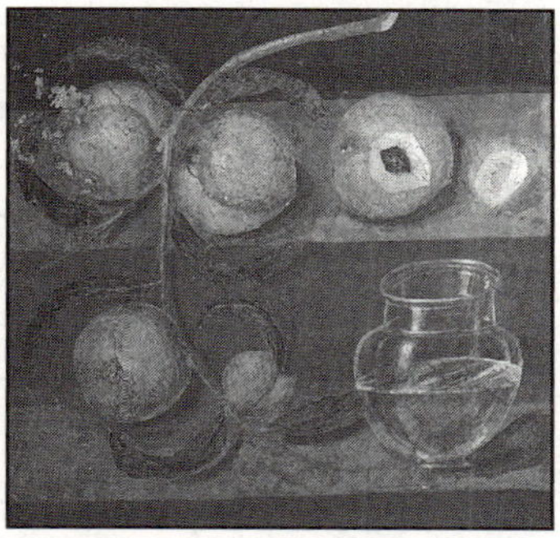

FIG. 07-24 Still life with peaches, detail of a Fourth Style wall painting, from Herculaneum, Italy, ca. 62–79 CE. Approx. 1′ 2″ × 1′ 1 1/2″. Museo Nazionale, Naples. (page 184)

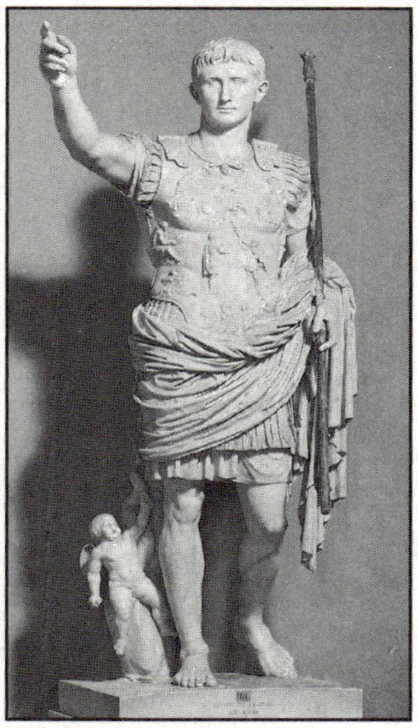

FIG. 07-25 Portrait of Augustus as general, from Primaporta, Italy, early first century ce copy of a bronze original of ca. 20 BCE. Marble, 6′ 8″ high. Vatican Museums, Rome. (page 186)

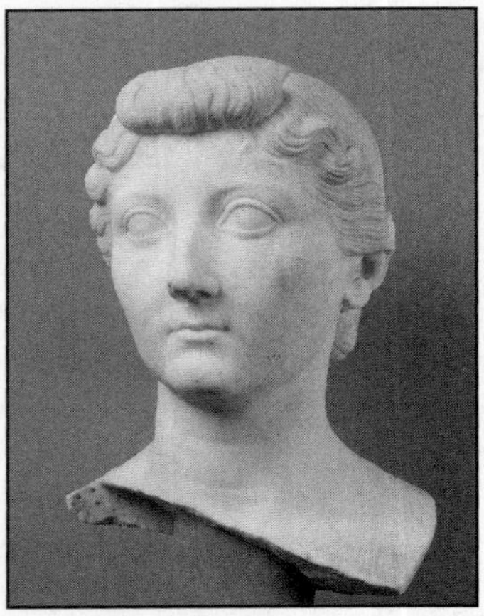

FIG. 07-26 Portrait bust of Livia, from Faiyum, Egypt, early first century CE. Marble, approx. 1′ 1 1/2″ high. Ny Carlsberg Glyptotek, Copenhagen. (page 186)

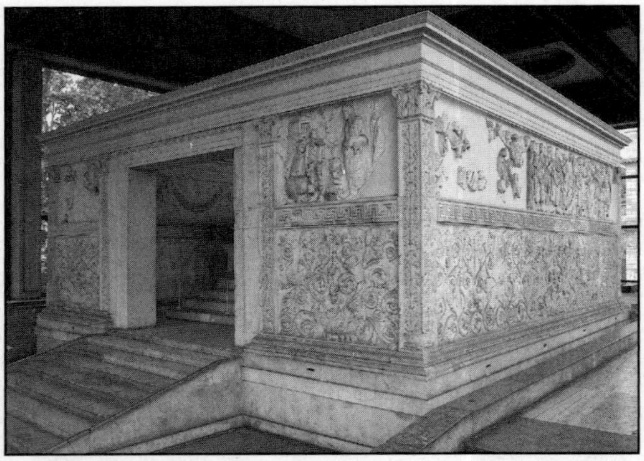

FIG. 07-27 Ara Pacis Augustae (Altar of Augustan Peace), view from the southwest, Rome, Italy, 13–9 BCE. (page 187)

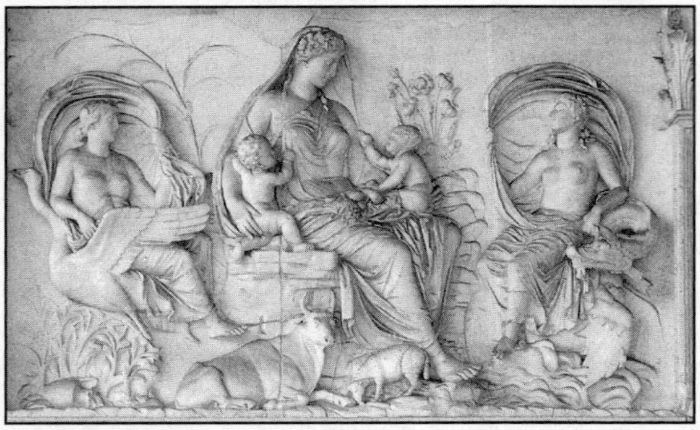

FIG. 07-28 Female personification (Tellus?), panel from the east facade of the Ara Pacis Augustae, Rome, Italy, 13–9 BCE. Marble, approx. 5′ 3″ high. (page 187)

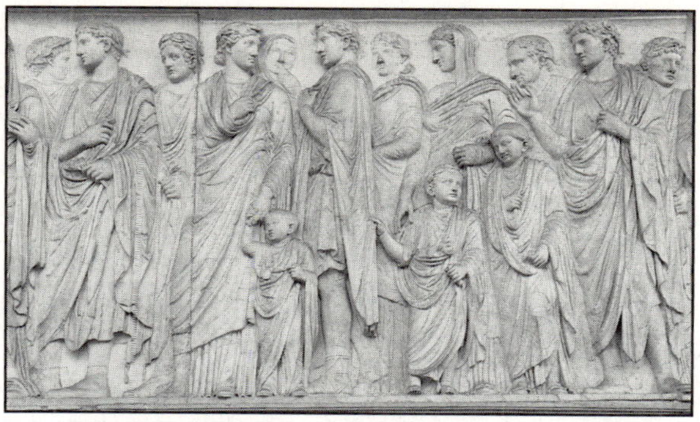

FIG. 07-29 Procession of the imperial family, detail of the south frieze of the Ara Pacis Augustae, Rome, Italy, 13–9 BCE. Marble, approx. 5′ 3″ high. (page 187)

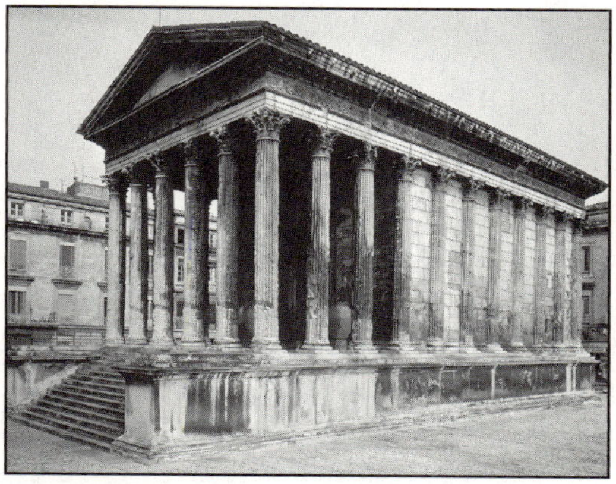

FIG. 07-30 Maison Carrée, Nîmes, France, ca. 1–10 CE. (page 188)

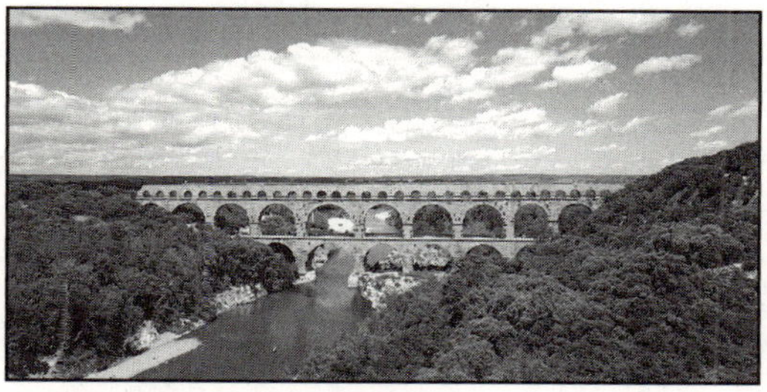

FIG. 07-31 Pont-du-Gard, Nîmes, France, ca. 16 BCE. (page 189)

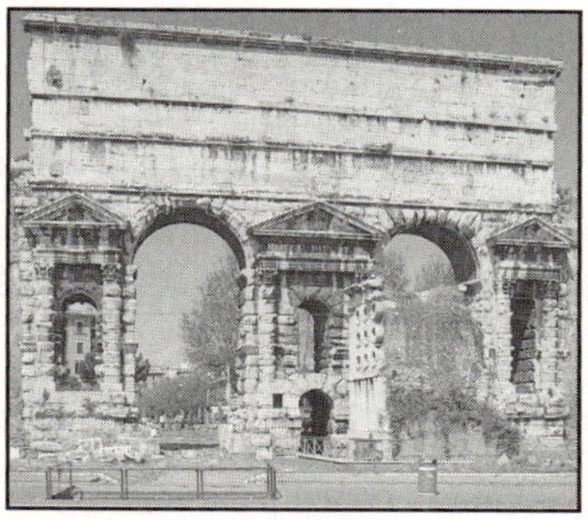

FIG. 07-32 Porta Maggiore, Rome, Italy, ca. 50 CE. (page 189)

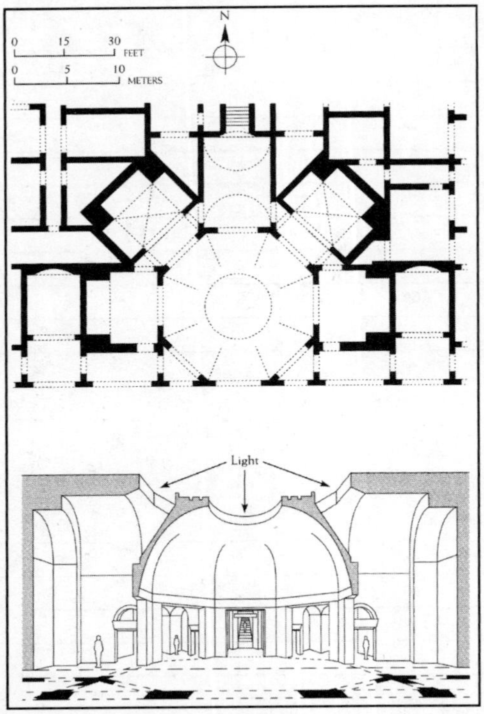

FIG. 07-33 SEVERUS and CELER, plan *(above)* and section *(below)* of the octagonal hall of the Domus Aurea (Golden House) of Nero, Rome, Italy, 64–68 CE. (page 190)

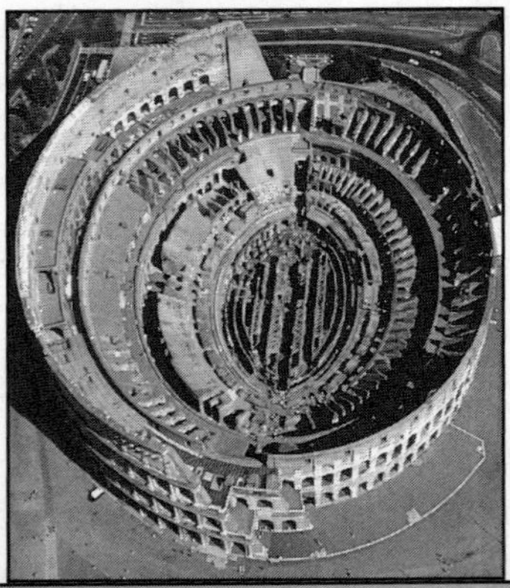

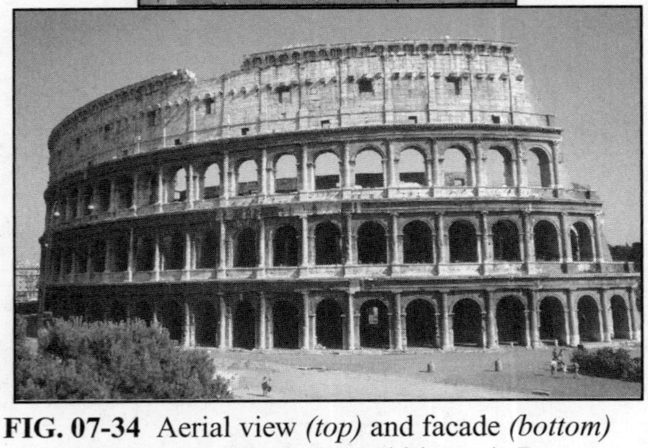

FIG. 07-34 Aerial view *(top)* and facade *(bottom)* of the Colosseum (Flavian Amphitheater), Rome, Italy, ca. 70–80 CE. (page 191)

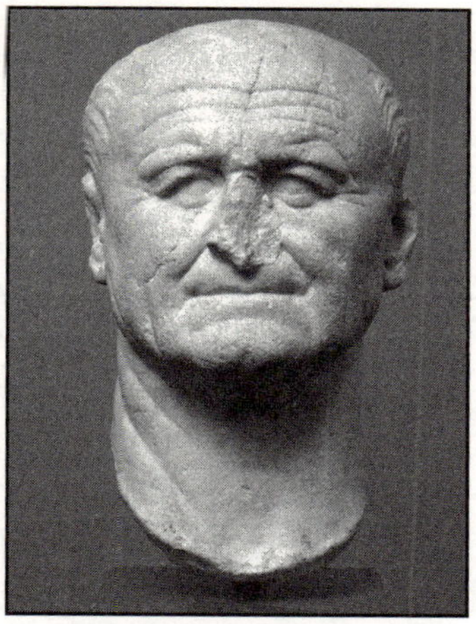

FIG. 07-35 Portrait of Vespasian, ca. 75–79 CE. Marble, approx. 1′ 4″ high. Ny Carlsberg Glyptotek, Copenhagen. (page 192)

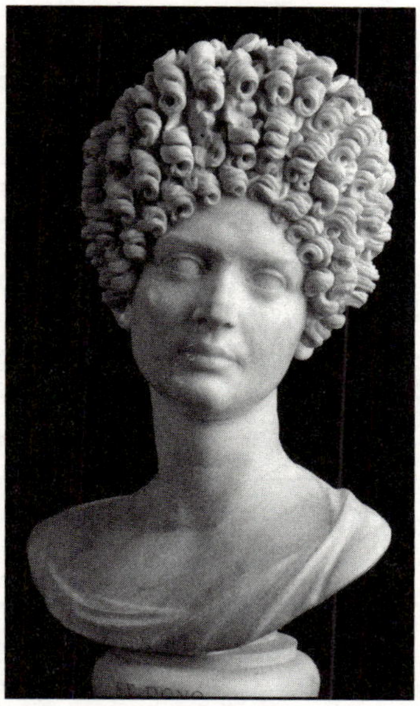

FIG. 07-36 Portrait bust of a Flavian woman, from Rome, Italy, ca. 90 CE. Marble, approx. 2′ 1″ high. Museo Capitolino, Rome. (page 192)

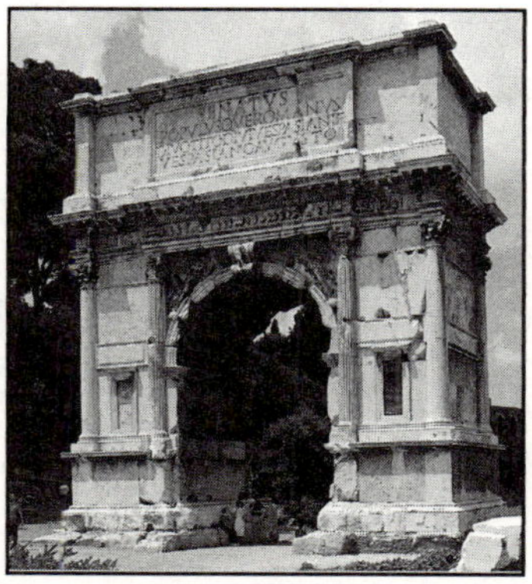

FIG. 07-37 Arch of Titus, Rome, Italy, after 81 CE. (page 193)

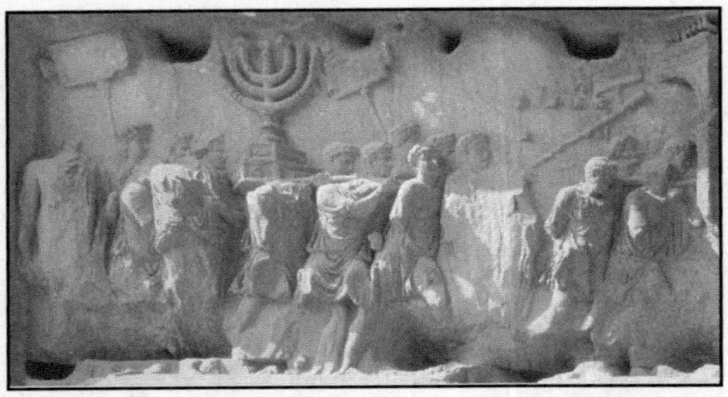

FIG. 07-38 Spoils of Jerusalem, relief panel in the passageway of the Arch of Titus, Rome, Italy, after 81 CE. Marble, approx. 7′ 10″ high. (page 193)

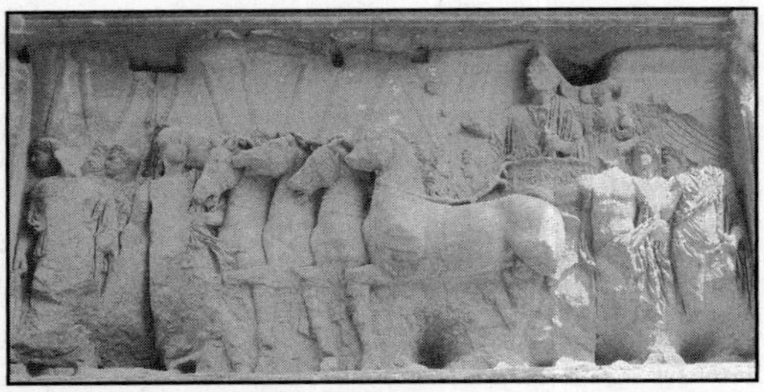

FIG. 07-39 Triumph of Titus, relief panel in the passageway of the Arch of Titus, Rome, Italy, after 81 CE. Marble, approx. 7′ 10″ high. (page 194)

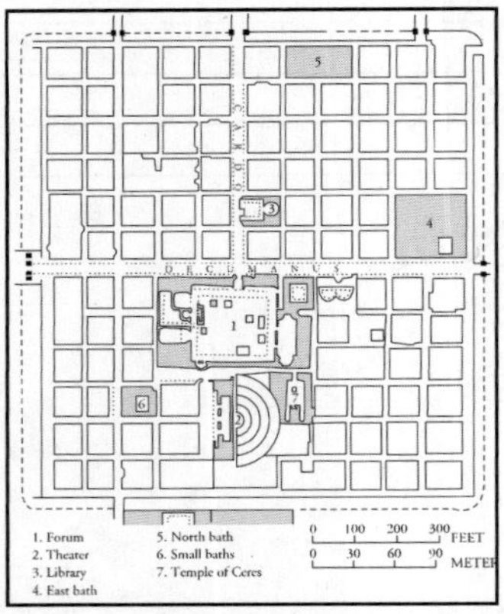

FIG. 07-40 Plan of Timgad (Thamugadi), Algeria, founded 100 CE. (page 195)

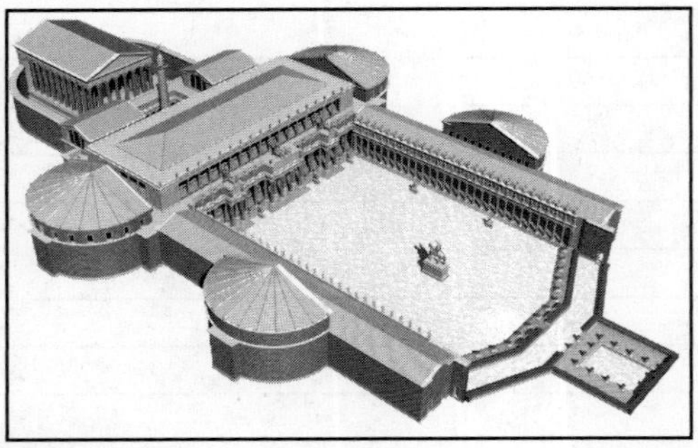

FIG. 07-41 APOLLODORUS OF DAMASCUS, model of Forum of Trajan, Rome, Italy, dedicated 112 CE. Museo della Civiltà. (page 195)

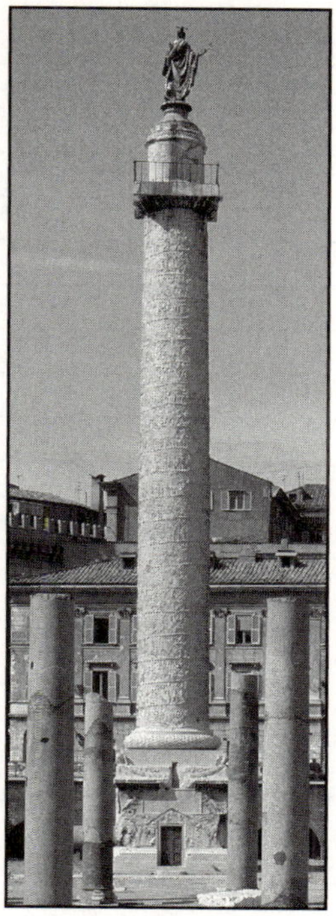

FIG. 07-42 Column of Trajan, Forum of Trajan, Rome, Italy, dedicated 112 CE. (page 196)

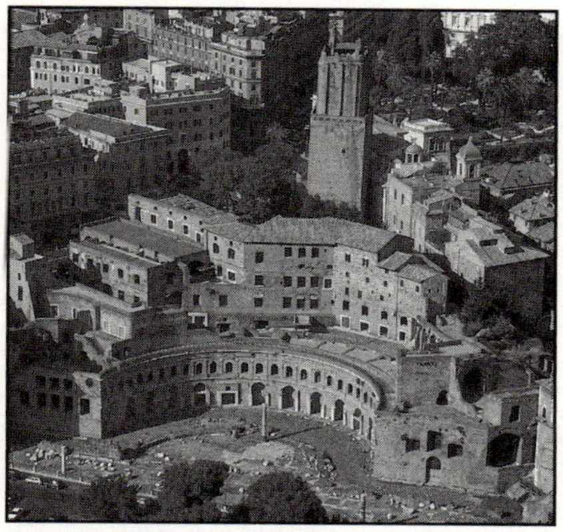

FIG. 07-43 APOLLODORUS OF DAMASCUS, aerial view of Markets of Trajan, Rome, Italy, ca. 100–112 CE. (page 197)

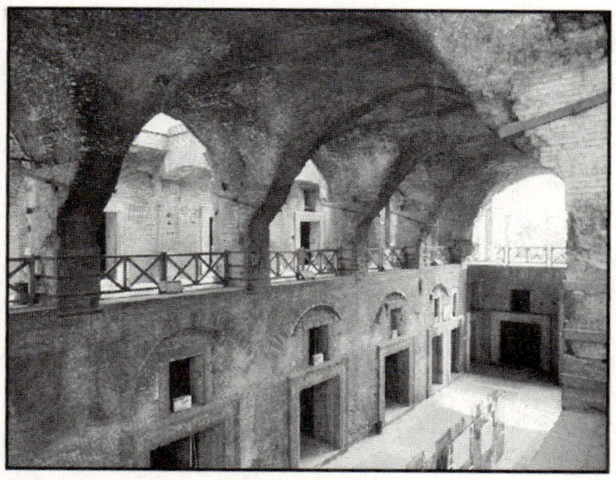

FIG. 07-44 APOLLODORUS OF DAMASCUS, interior of the great hall, Markets of Trajan, Rome, Italy, ca. 100–112 CE. (page 197)

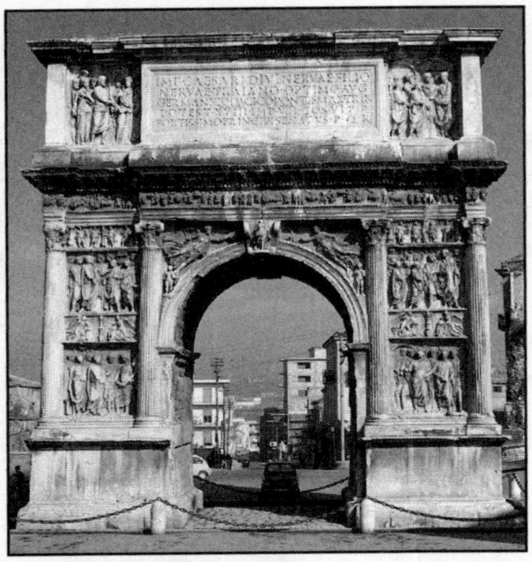

FIG. 07-45 Arch of Trajan, Benevento, Italy, ca. 114–118 CE. (page 198)

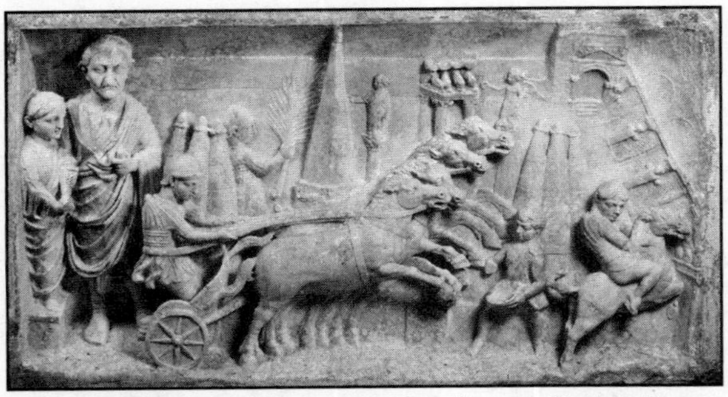

FIG. 07-46 Funerary relief of a circus official, from Ostia, Italy, ca. 110–130 CE. Marble, approx. 1′ 8″ high. Vatican Museums, Rome. (page 198)

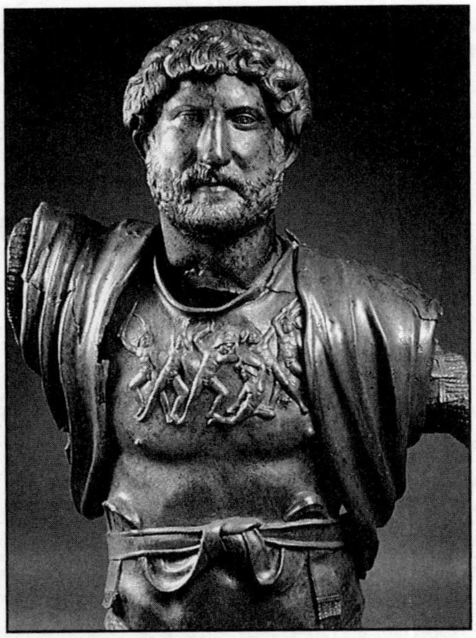

FIG. 07-47 Portrait bust of Hadrian as general, from Tel Shalem, Israel, ca. 130–138 CE. Bronze, approx. 2′ 11″ high. Israel Museum, Jerusalem. (page 199)

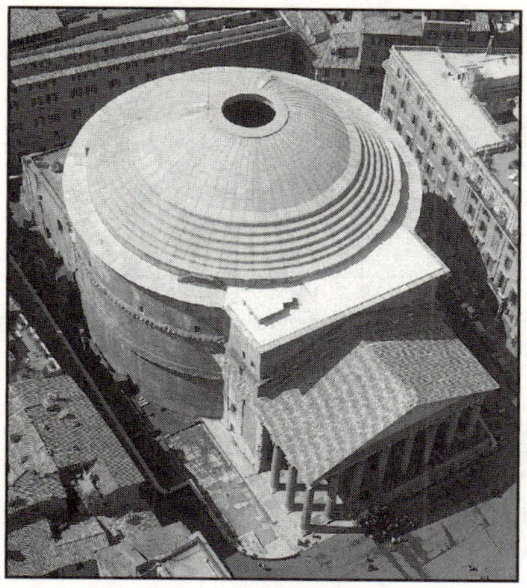

FIG. 07-48 Aerial view of the Pantheon, Rome, Italy, 118–125 CE. (page 199)

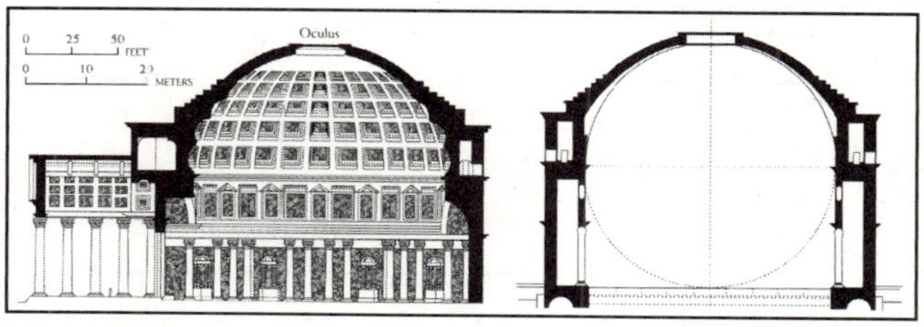

FIG. 07-49 Longitudinal and lateral sections of the Pantheon, Rome, Italy, 118–125 CE. (page 200)

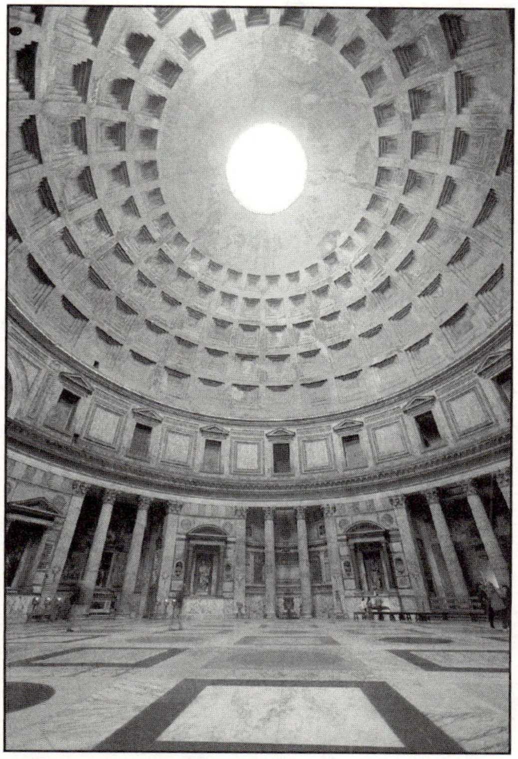

FIG. 07-50 Interior of the Pantheon, Rome, Italy, 118–125 CE. (page 200)

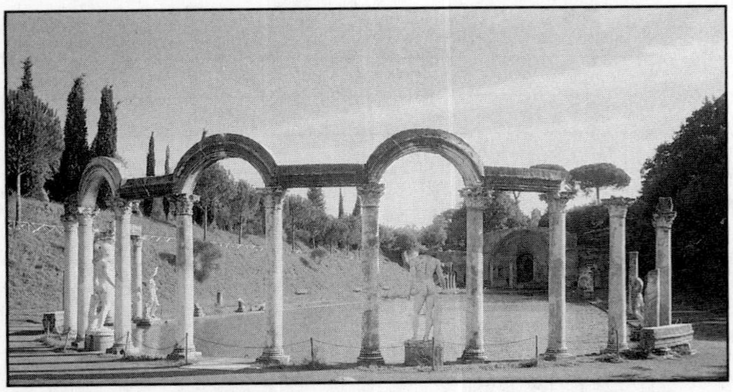

FIG. 07-51 Canopus and Serapeum, Hadrian's Villa, Tivoli, Italy, ca. 125–128 CE. (page 201)

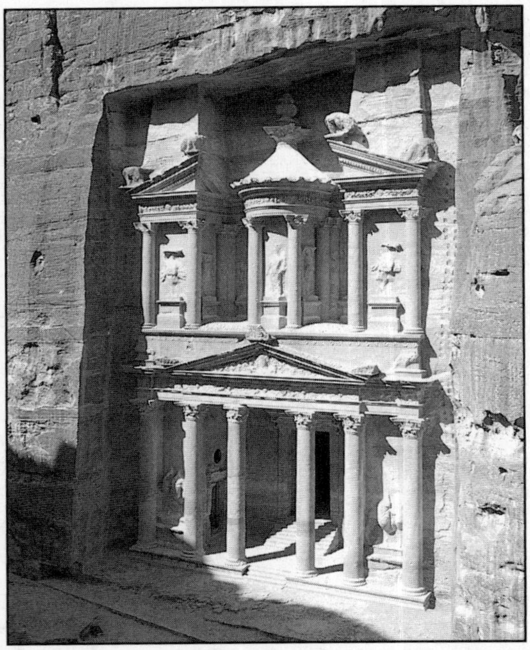

FIG. 07-52 Al-Khazneh ("Treasury"), Petra, Jordan, second century CE. (page 202)

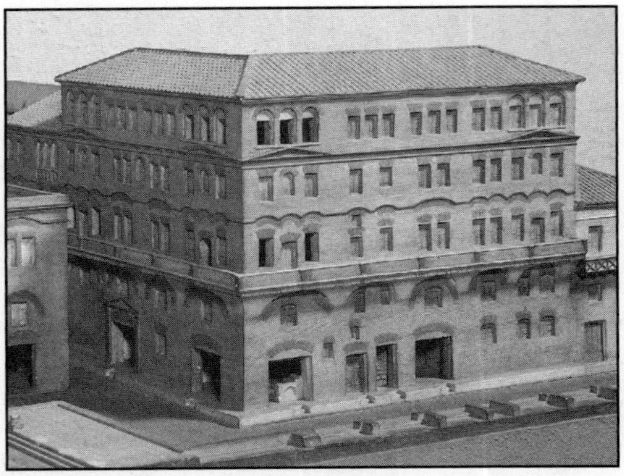

FIG. 07-53 Model of an insula, Ostia, Italy, second century CE. Museo della Civiltà Romana, Rome. (page 202)

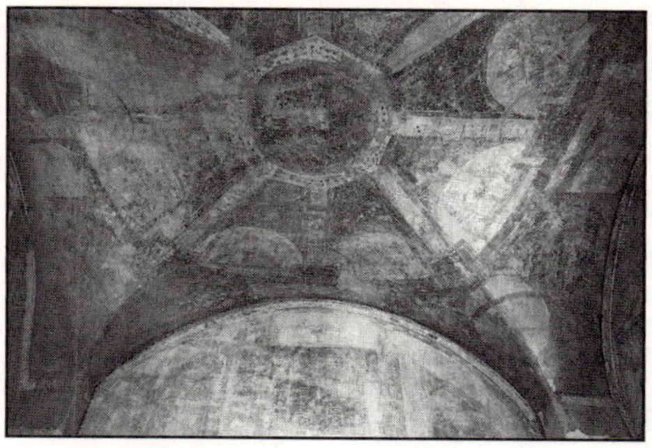

FIG. 07-54 Ceiling and wall paintings in Room IV of the Insula of the Painted Vaults, Ostia, Italy, early third century CE. (page 203)

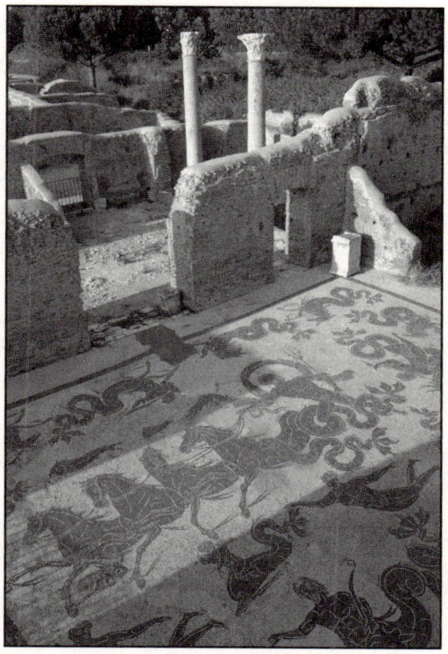

FIG. 07-55 Neptune and creatures of the sea, floor mosaic in the Baths of Neptune, Ostia, Italy, ca. 140 CE. (page 203)

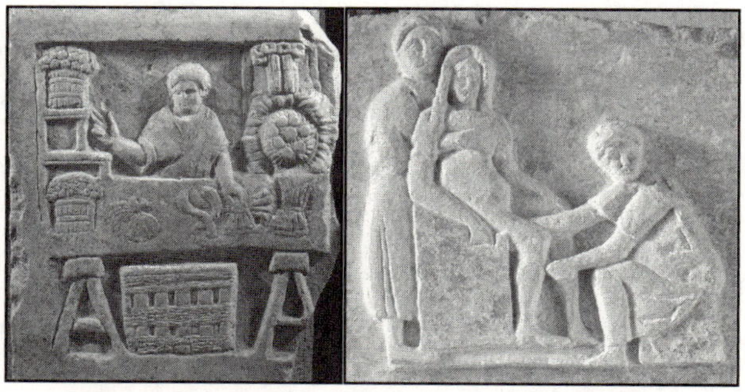

FIG. 07-56 Funerary reliefs of a vegetable vendor *(left)* and a midwife *(right),* from Ostia, Italy, second half of second century ce. Painted terracotta, approx. 1′ 5″ and 11″ high, respectively. Museo Ostiense, Ostia. (page 204)

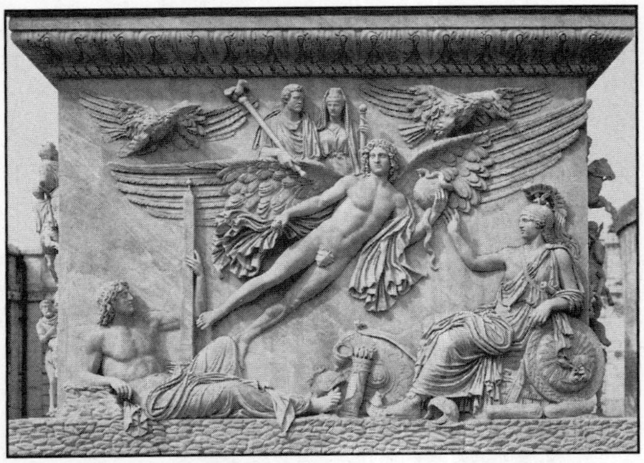

FIG. 07-57 Apotheosis of Antoninus Pius and Faustina, pedestal of the Column of Antoninus Pius, Rome, Italy, ca. 161 CE. Marble, approx. 8′ 1 1/2″ high. Vatican Museums, Rome. (page 204)

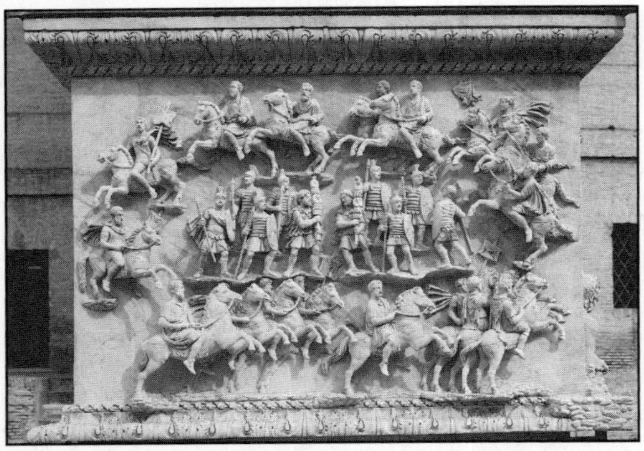

FIG. 07-58 Decursio, pedestal of the Column of Antoninus Pius, Rome, Italy, ca. 161 CE. Marble, approx. 8′ 1 1/2″ high. Vatican Museums, Rome. (page 205)

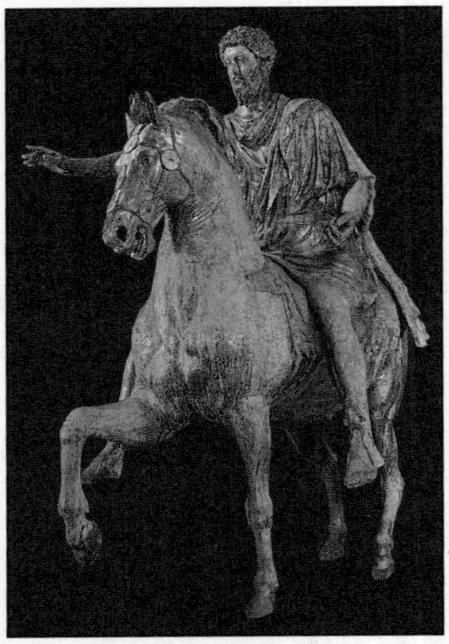

FIG. 07-59 Equestrian statue of Marcus Aurelius, from Rome, Italy, ca. 175 CE. Bronze, approx. 11′ 6″ high. Musei Capitolini, Rome. (page 206)

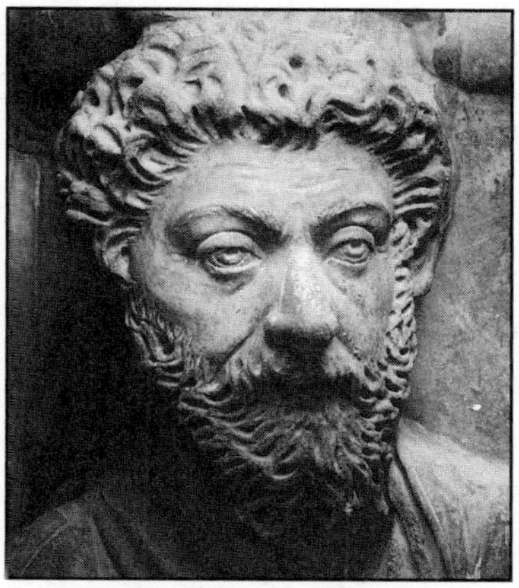

FIG. 07-60 Portrait of Marcus Aurelius, detail of a relief from a lost arch, Rome, Italy, ca. 175–180 CE. Marble, approx. life-size. Palazzo dei Conservatori, Rome. (page 206)

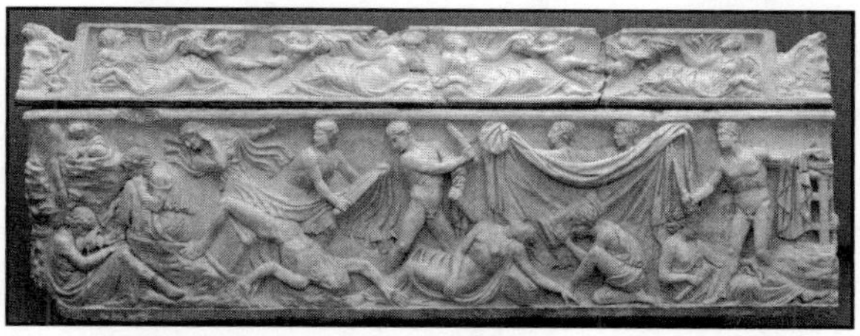

FIG. 07-61 Sarcophagus with the myth of Orestes, ca. 140–150 CE. Marble, 2′ 7 1/2″ high. Cleveland Museum of Art, Cleveland. (page 207)

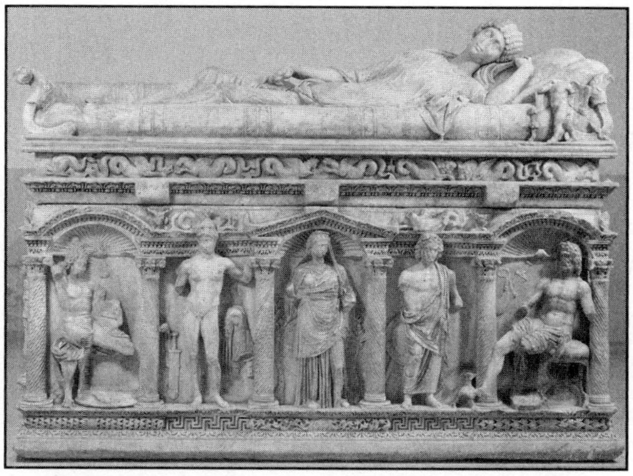

FIG. 07-62 Asiatic sarcophagus with kline portrait of a woman, from Rapolla, near Melfi, Italy, ca. 165–170 CE. Marble, approx. 5′ 7″ high. Museo Nazionale Archeologico del Melfese, Melfi. (page 207)

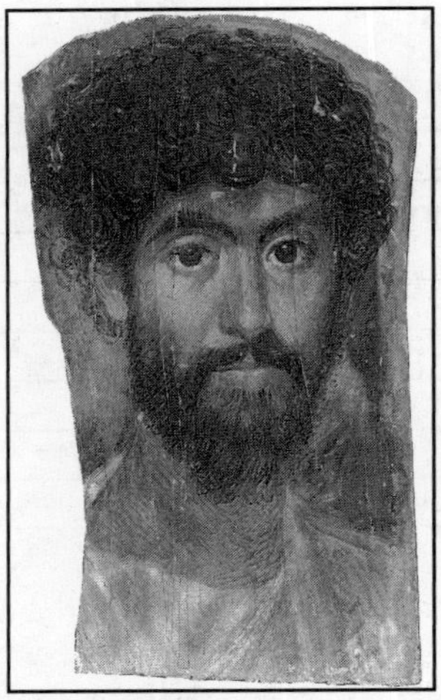

FIG. 07-63 Mummy portrait of a man, from Faiyum, Egypt, ca. 160–170 CE. Encaustic on wood, approx. 1′ 2″ high. Albright-Knox Art Gallery, Buffalo. (page 208)

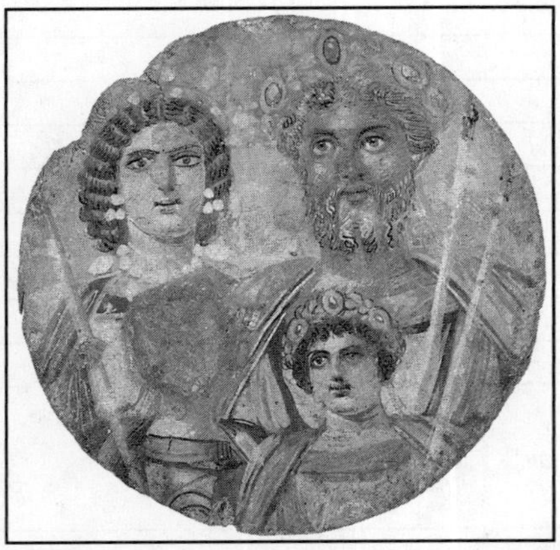

FIG. 07-64 Painted portrait of Septimius Severus and his family, from Egypt, ca. 200 CE. Tempera on wood, approx. 1′ 2″ diameter. Staatliche Museen, Berlin. (page 209)

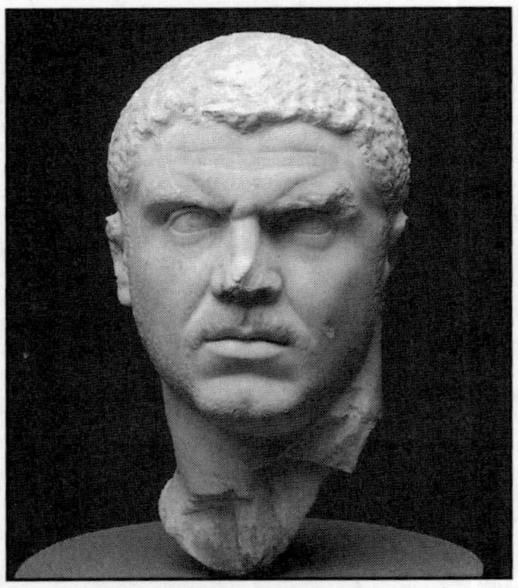

FIG. 07-65 Portrait of Caracalla, ca. 211–217 CE. Marble, approx. 1′ 2″ high. Metropolitan Museum of Art, New York. (page 209)

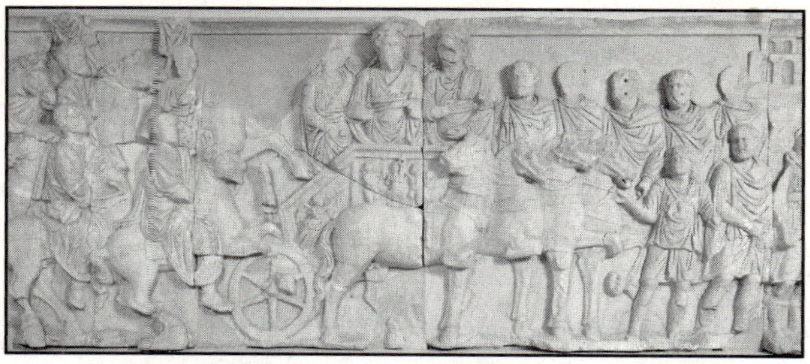

FIG. 07-66 Chariot procession of Septimius Severus, relief from the Arch of Septimius Severus, Lepcis Magna, Libya, 203 CE. Marble, approx. 5′ 6″ high. Castle Museum, Tripoli. (page 210)

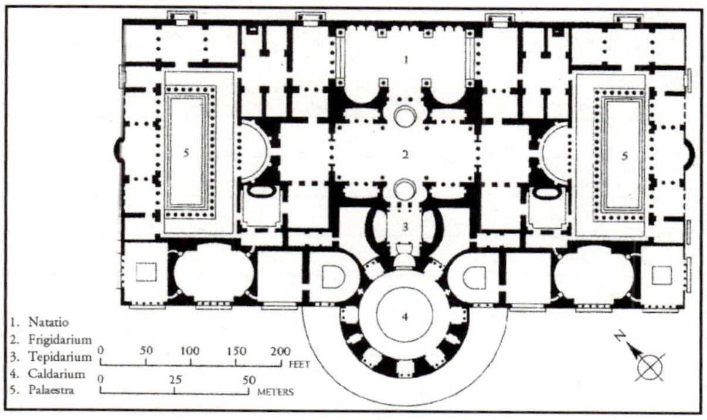

FIG. 07-67 Plan of the central section of the Baths of Caracalla, Rome, Italy, 212–216 CE. 1) Natatio, 2) Frigidarium, 3) Tepidarium, 4) Caldarium, 5) Palaestra. The bathing, swimming, and exercise areas were surrounded by landscaped gardens, lecture halls, and other rooms, all enclosed within a great concrete perimeter wall. (page 210)

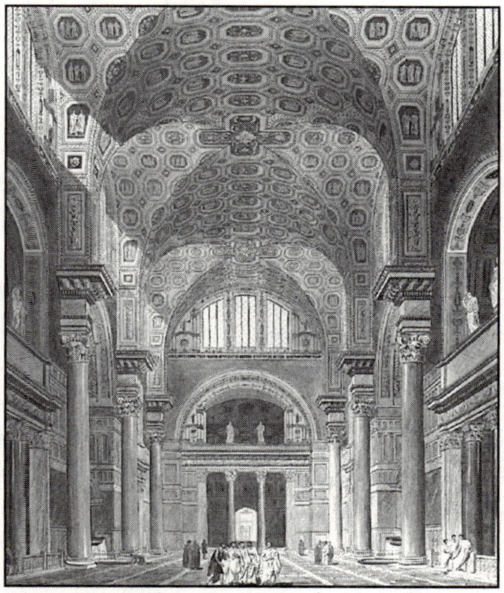

FIG. 07-68 Reconstruction drawing of the central hall *(frigidarium)* of the Baths of Caracalla, Rome, Italy, 212–216 CE. (page 211)

FIG. 07-69 Portrait bust of Trajan Decius, 249–251 CE. Marble, full bust approx. 2′ 7″ high. Museo Capitolino, Rome. (page 211)

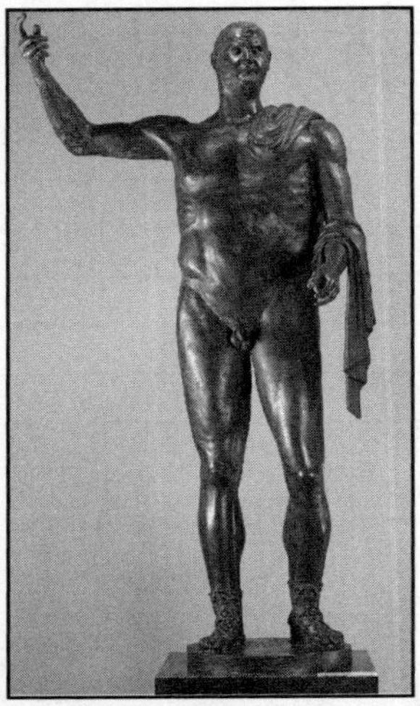

FIG. 07-70 Heroic portrait of Trebonianus Gallus, from Rome, Italy, 251–253 CE. Bronze, approx. 7′ 11″ high. Metropolitan Museum of Art, New York. (page 212)

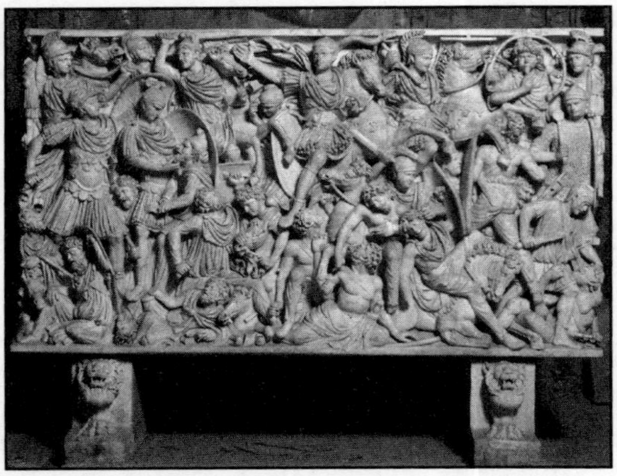

FIG. 07-71 Battle of Romans and barbarians *(Ludovisi Battle Sarcophagus),* from Rome, Italy, ca. 250–260 CE. Marble, approx. 5′ high. Museo Nazionale Romano-Palazzo Altemps, Rome. (page 212)

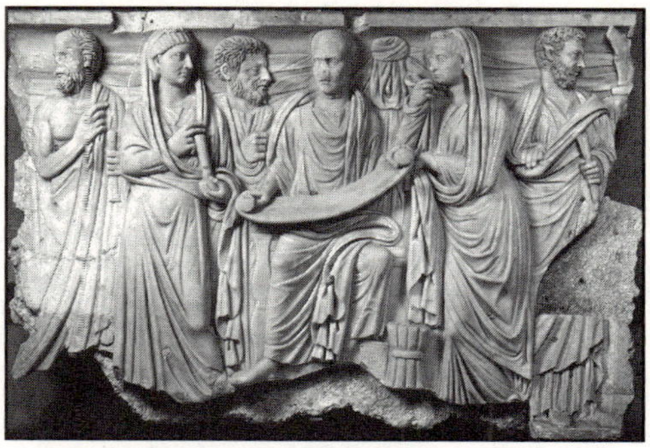

FIG. 07-72 Sarcophagus of a philosopher, ca. 270–280 CE. Marble, approx. 4′ 11″ high. Vatican Museums, Rome. (page 213)

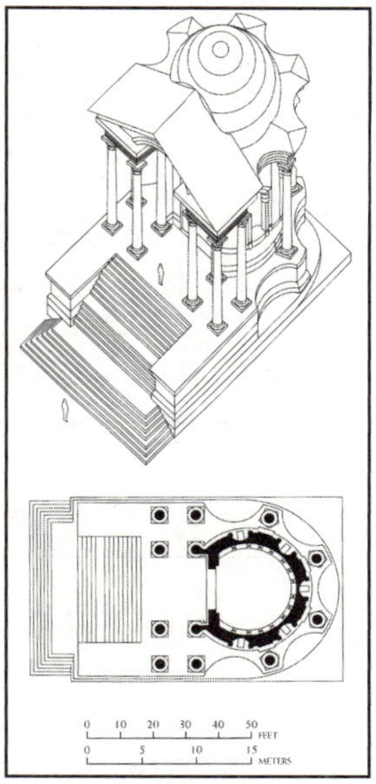

FIG. 07-73 Restored view *(top)* and plan *(bottom)* of the Temple of Venus, Baalbek, Lebanon, third century CE. (page 213)

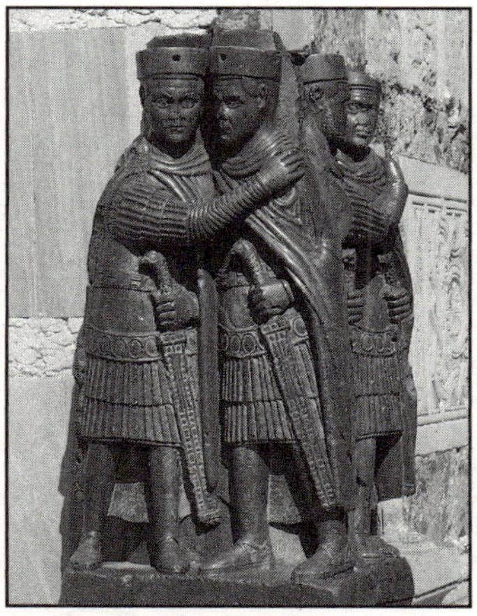

FIG. 07-74 Portraits of the four tetrarchs, from Constantinople, ca. 305 CE. Porphyry, approx. 4′ 3″ high. Saint Mark's, Venice. (page 214)

FIG. 07-75 Model of the Palace of Diocletian, Split, Croatia, ca. 300–305 CE. Museo della Civiltà Romana, Rome. (page 214)

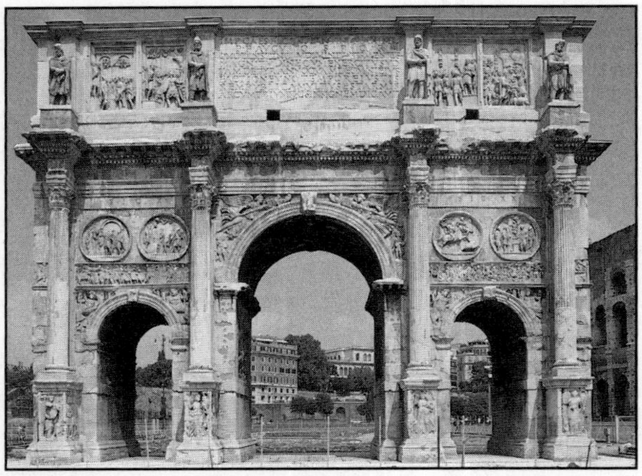

FIG. 07-76 Arch of Constantine (south side), Rome, Italy, 312–315 CE. (page 215)

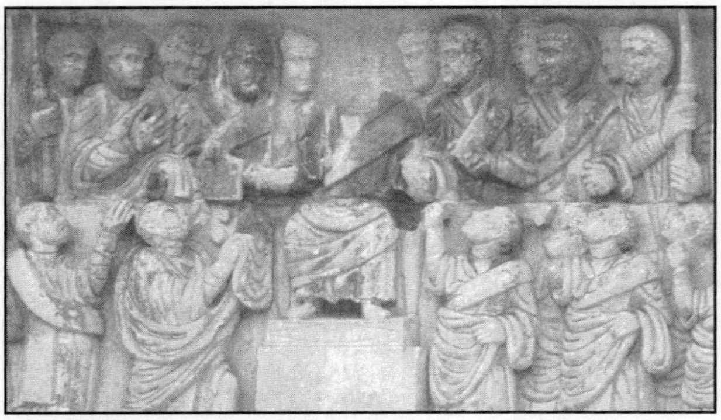

FIG. 07-77 Distribution of largess, detail of the north frieze of the Arch of Constantine, Rome, Italy, 312–315 CE. Marble, approx. 3′ 4″ high.

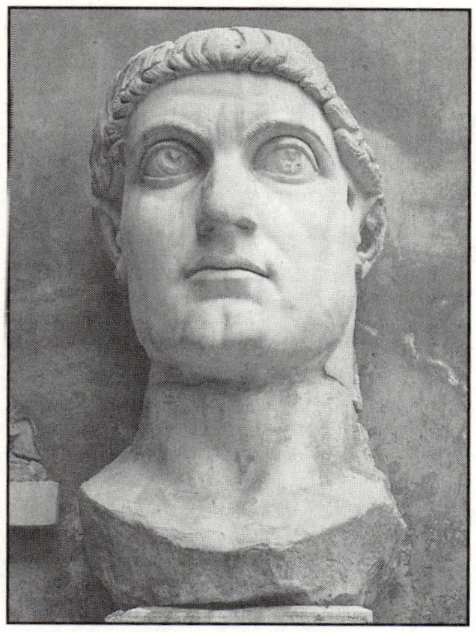

FIG. 07-78 Portrait of Constantine, from the Basilica Nova, Rome, Italy, ca. 315–330 CE. Marble, approx. 8′ 6″ high. Palazzo dei Conservatori, Rome. (page 216)

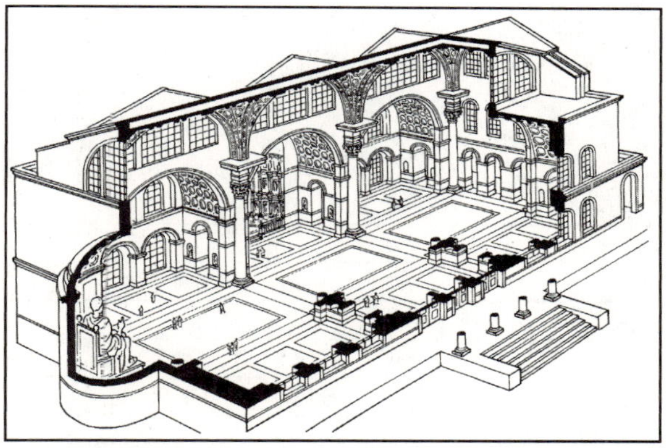

FIG. 07-79 Reconstruction drawing of the Basilica Nova (Basilica of Constantine), Rome, Italy, ca. 306–312 CE. (page 217)

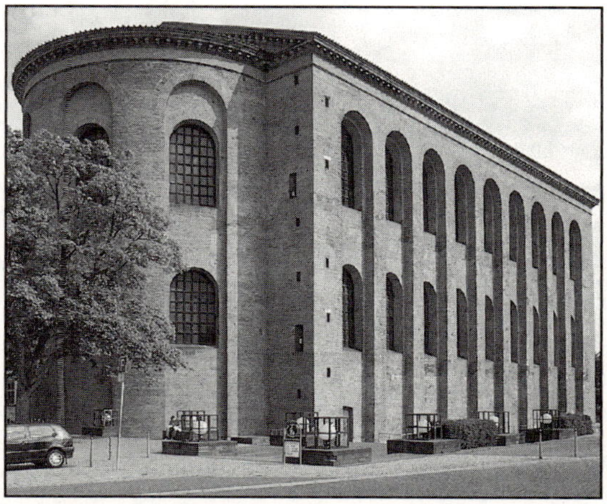

FIG. 07-80 Aula Palatina (exterior), Trier, Germany, early fourth century CE. (page 217)

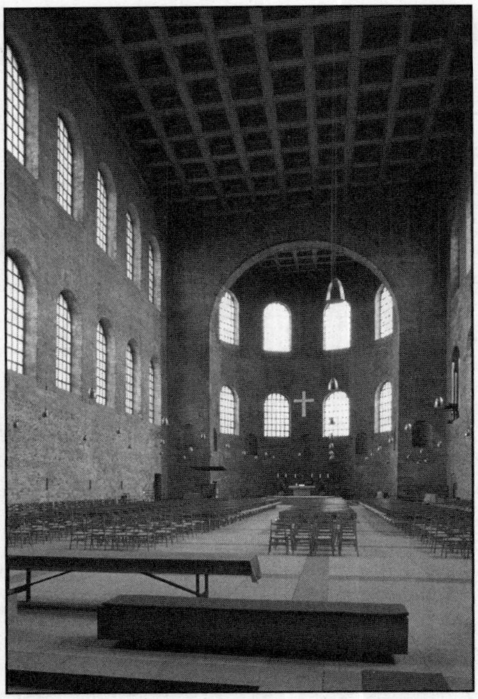

FIG. 07-81 Aula Palatina (interior), Trier, Germany, early fourth century CE. (page 218)

FIG. 07-82 Coins with portraits of Constantine. Nummus *(top),* 307 CE. Billon, diameter approx. 1″. American Numismatic Society, New York. Medallion *(bottom),* ca. 315 CE. Silver, diameter approx. 1″. Staatliche Münzsammlung, Munich. (page 218)

Chapter 8

Pagans, Christians, and Jews:
The Art of Late Antiquity

Goals

- Understand the influence of religion in the art of the Roman Empire in Late Antiquity.
- Examine the art forms and architecture of Late Antiquity.
- Understand the concept of "synchronism" in early Christian art.
- Understand the different media used to create early Christian art.
- Know and cite artistic and architectural terminology from the period.

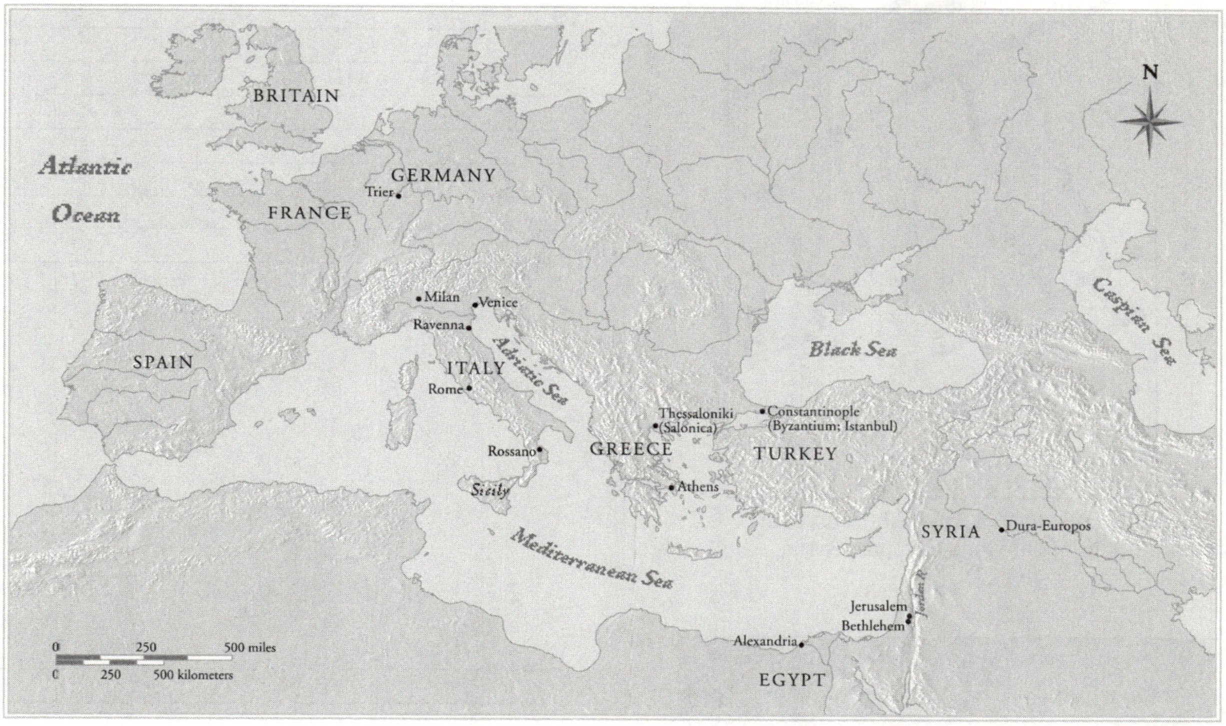

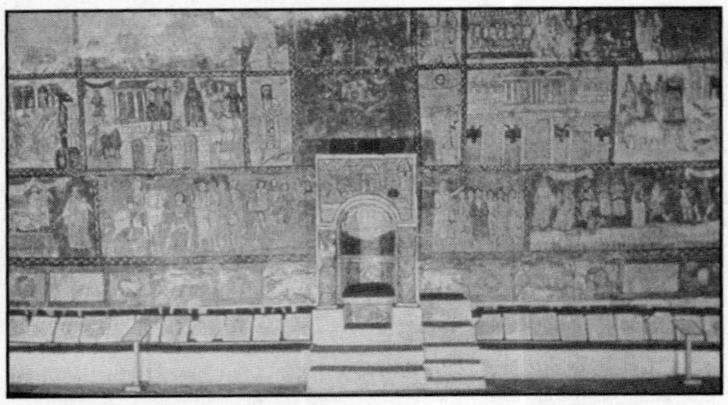

FIG. 08-01 Interior of the synagogue at Dura-Europos, Syria, with wall paintings of Old Testament themes, ca. 245–256. Tempera on plaster. Reconstruction in National Museum, Damascus. (page 223)

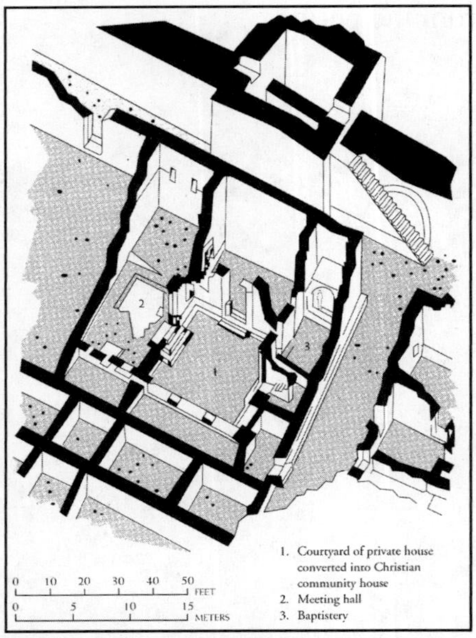

FIG. 08-02 Reconstruction of the Christian community house at Dura-Europos, Syria, ca. 240–256. (page 223)

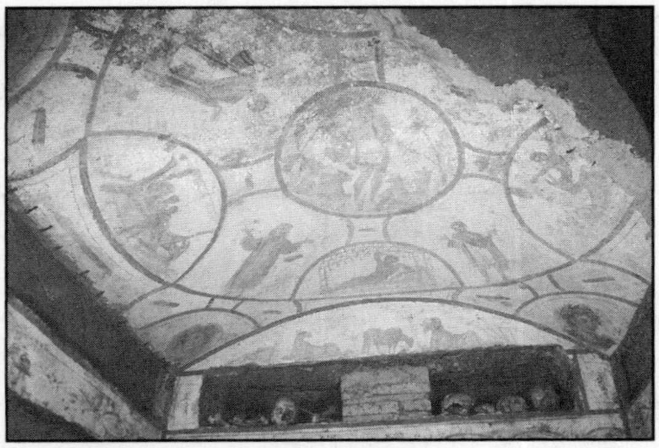

FIG. 08-03 The Good Shepherd, the story of Jonah, and orants, painted ceiling of a cubiculum in the Catacomb of Saints Peter and Marcellinus, Rome, Italy, early fourth century. (page 224)

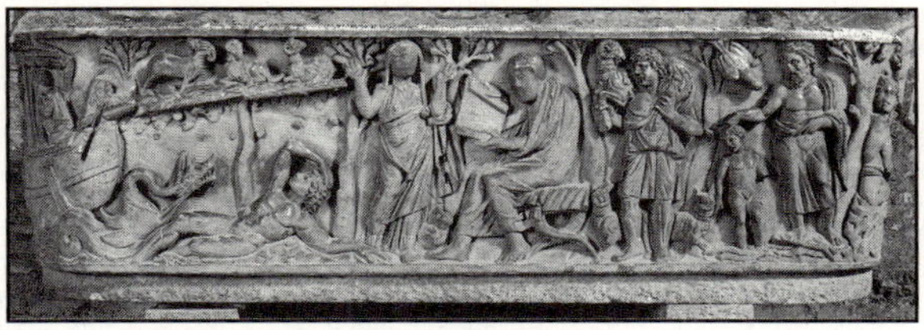

FIG. 08-04 Sarcophagus with philosopher, orant, and Old and New Testament scenes, Santa Maria Antiqua, Rome, Italy, ca. 270. Marble, 1′ 11 1/4″ × 7′ 2″. (page 226)

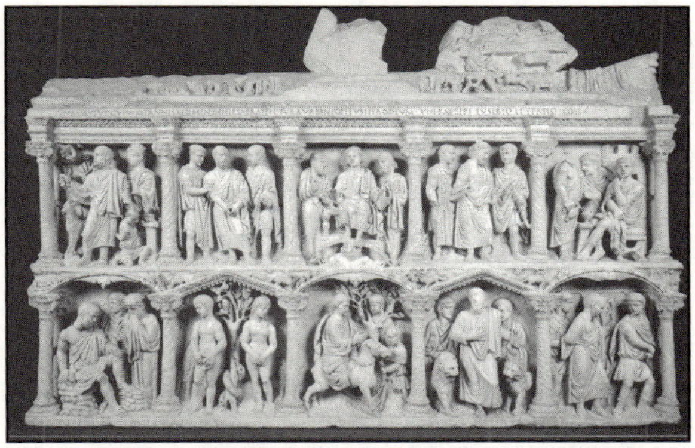

FIG. 08-05 Sarcophagus of Junius Bassus, from Rome, Italy, ca. 359. Marble, 3′ 10 1/2″ × 8′. Museo Storico del Tesoro della Basilica di San Pietro, Rome. (page 226)

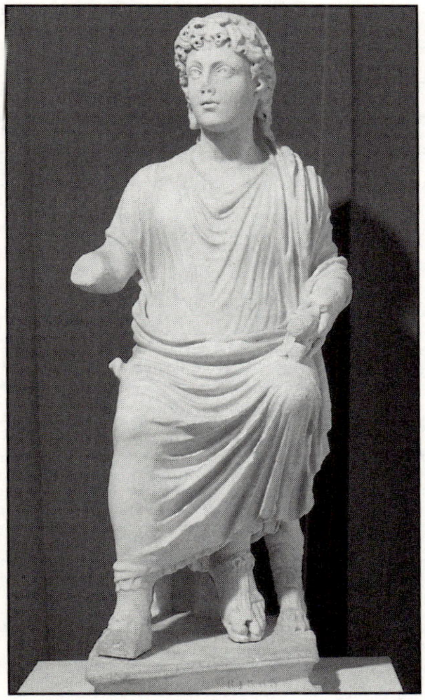

FIG. 08-06 Christ seated, from Civita Latina, Italy, ca. 350–375. Marble, approx. 2′ 4 1/2″ high. Museo Nazionale Romano—Palazzo Massimo alle Terme, Rome. (page 227)

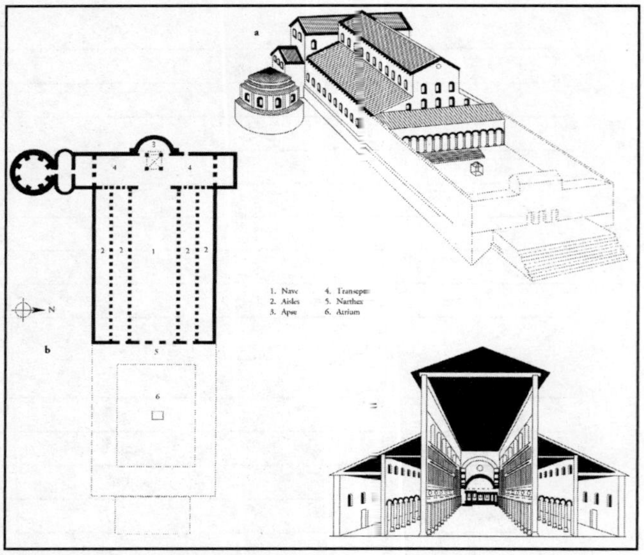

FIG. 08-07 Restored view (*a*), plan (*b*), and section (*c*) of Old Saint Peter's, Rome, Italy, begun ca. 320. (The restoration of the forecourt is conjectural.) (page 230)

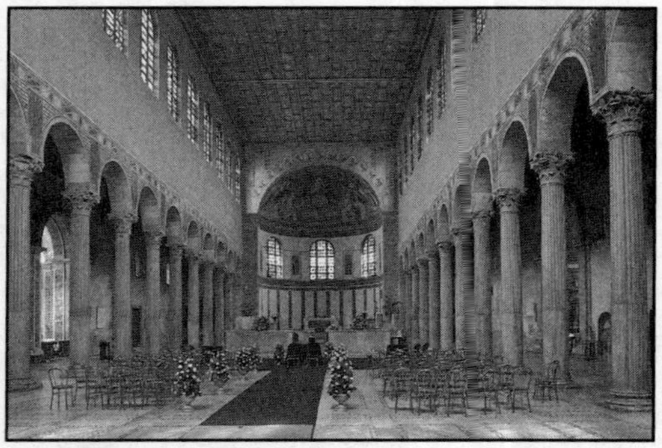

FIG. 08-08 Interior of Santa Sabina, Rome, Italy, 422–432. (page 231)

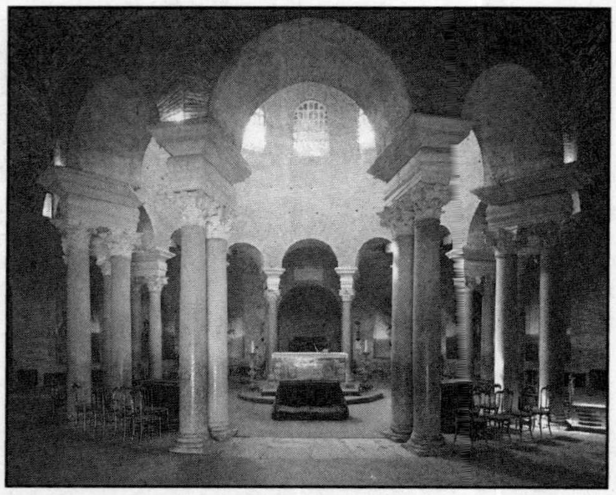

FIG. 08-09 Interior of Santa Costanza, Rome, Italy, ca. 337–351. (page 232)

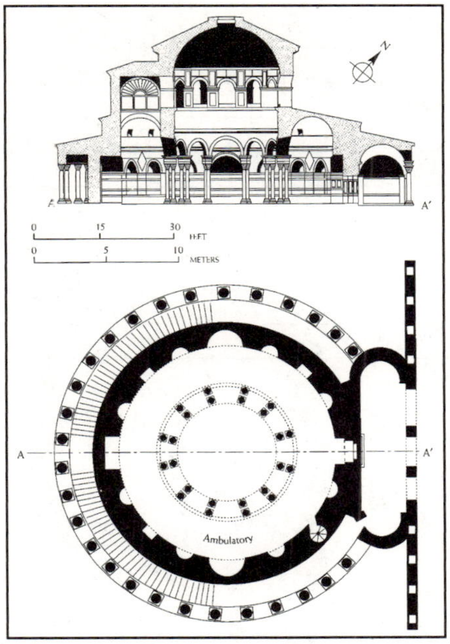

FIG. 08-10 Longitudinal section *(top)* and plan *(bottom)* of Santa Costanza, Rome, Italy, ca. 337–351. (page 232)

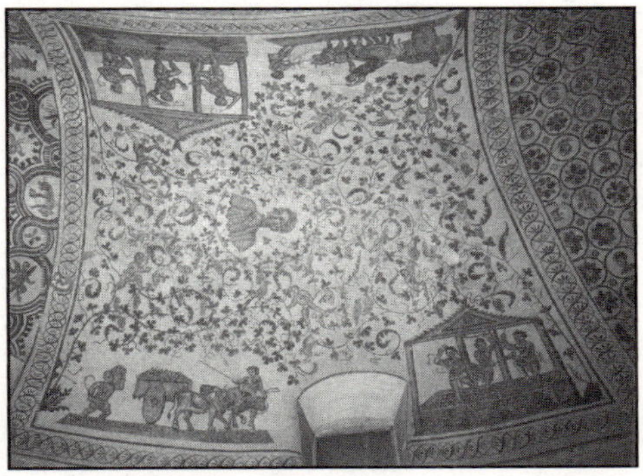

FIG. 08-11 Detail of vault mosaic in the ambulatory of Santa Costanza, Rome, Italy, ca. 337–351. (page 233)

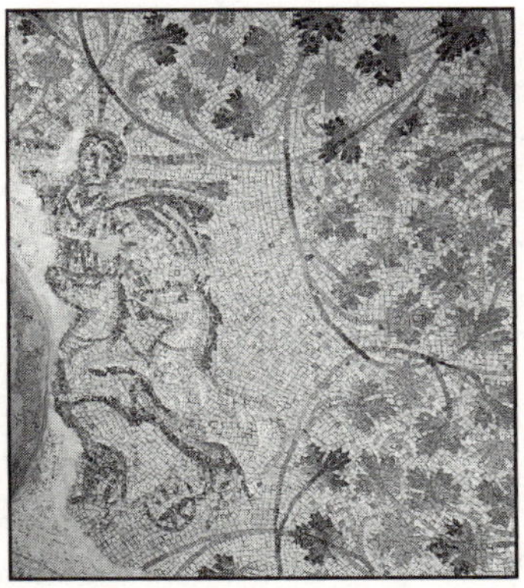

FIG. 08-12 Christ as Sol Invictus, detail of a vault mosaic in the Mausoleum of the Julii, Rome, Italy, late third century. (page 233)

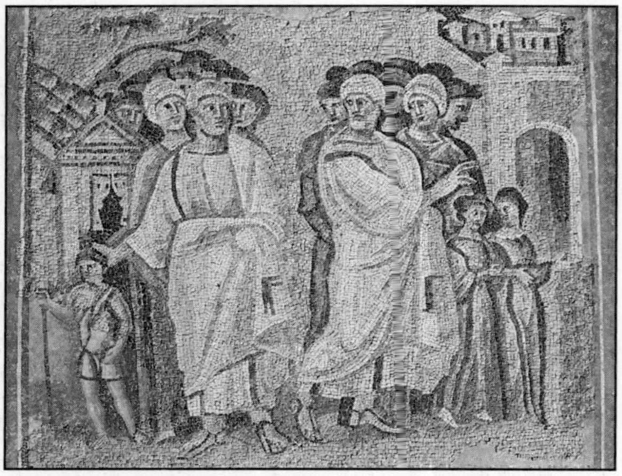

FIG. 08-13 The parting of Lot and Abraham, mosaic in the nave of Santa Maria Maggiore, Rome, Italy, 432–440. (page 234)

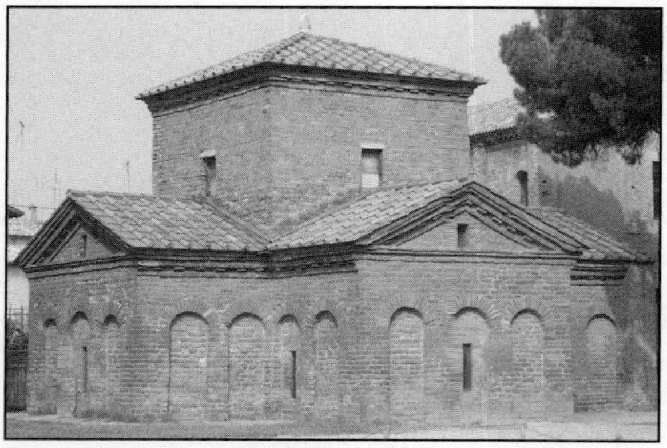

FIG. 08-14 Mausoleum of Galla Placidia, Ravenna, Italy, ca. 425. (page 235)

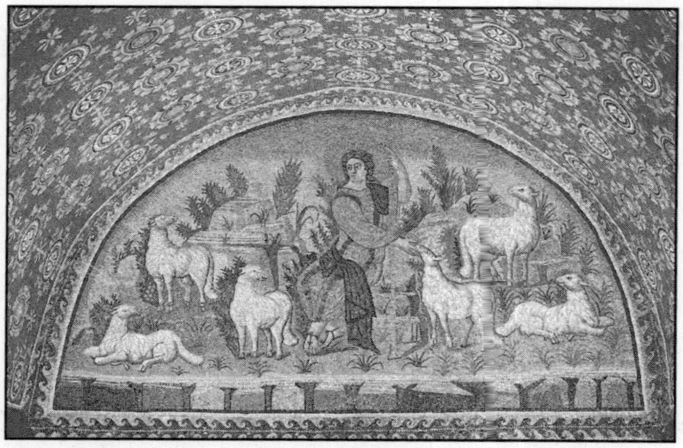

FIG. 08-15 Christ as the Good Shepherd, mosaic from the entrance wall of the Mausoleum of Galla Placidia, Ravenna, Italy, ca. 425. (page 236)

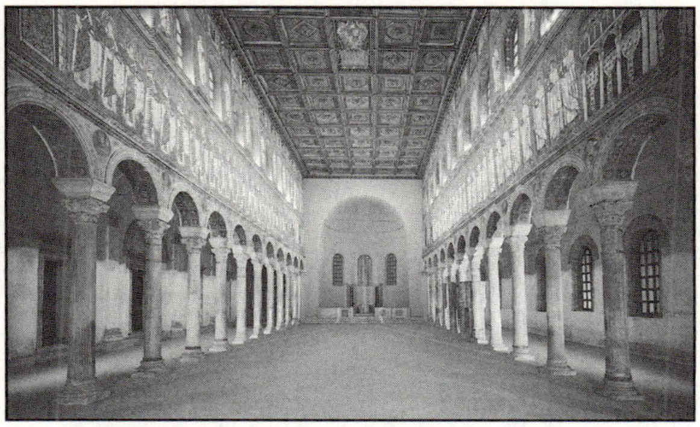

FIG. 08-16 Interior of Sant'Apollinare Nuovo, Ravenna, Italy, dedicated 504. (page 237)

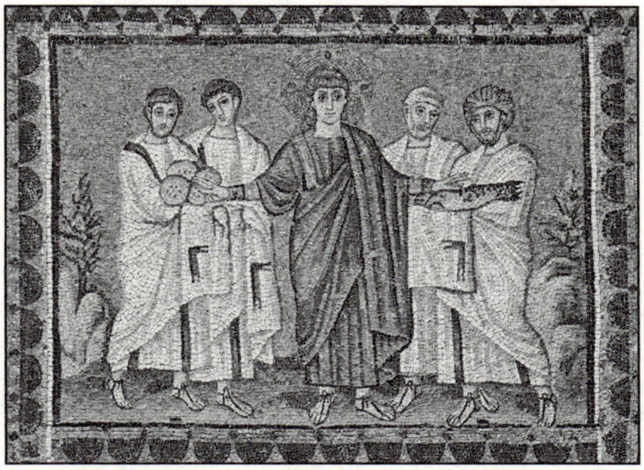

FIG. 08-17 Miracle of the loaves and fishes, mosaic from the top register of the nave wall (above the clerestory windows) of Sant'Apollinare Nuovo, Ravenna, Italy, ca. 504. (page 237)

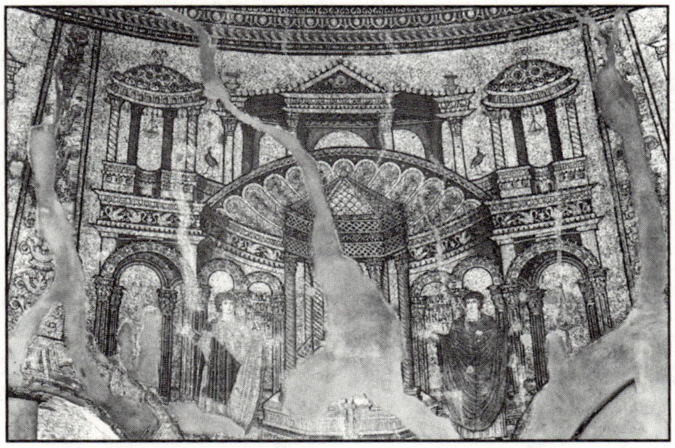

FIG. 08-18 Saints Onesiphorus and Porphyrius, detail of the dome mosaic, Church of Saint George, Thessaloniki, Greece, ca. 390–450. (page 238)

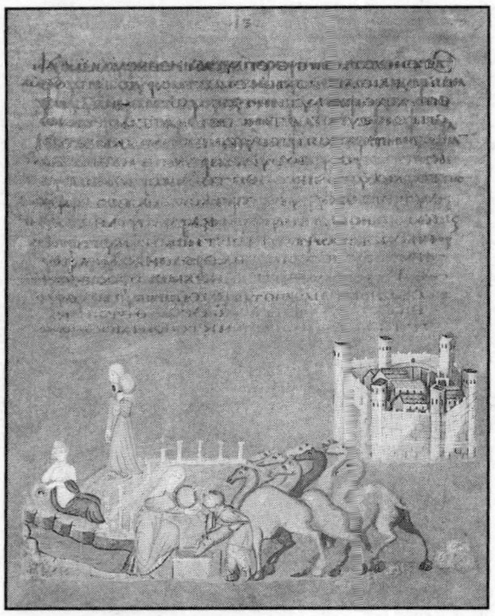

FIG. 08-19 Rebecca and Eliezer at the well, folio 7 recto of the *Vienna Genesis,* early sixth century. Tempera, gold, and silver on purple vellum, approx. 1′ 1/4″ × 9 1/4″. Österreichische Nationalbibliothek, Vienna. (page 239)

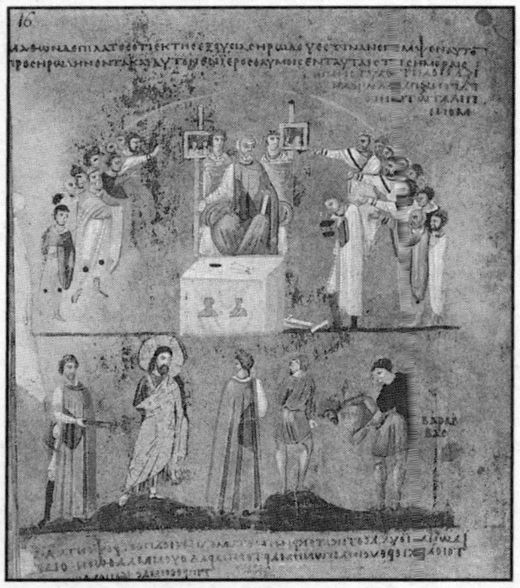

FIG. 08-20 Christ before Pilate, folio 8 verso of the *Rossano Gospels,* early sixth century. Tempera on purple vellum, approx. 11″ × 10 1/4″. Museo Diocesano d'Arte Sacra, Rossano. (page 240)

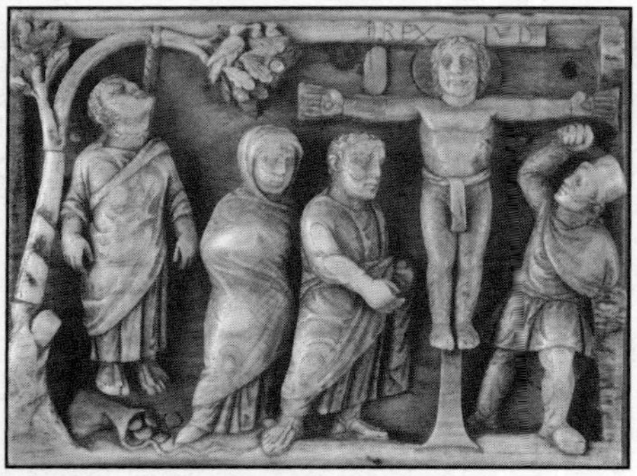

FIG. 08-21 Suicide of Judas and Crucifixion of Christ, plaque from a box, ca. 420. Ivory, 3″ × 3 7/8″. British Museum, London. (page 241)

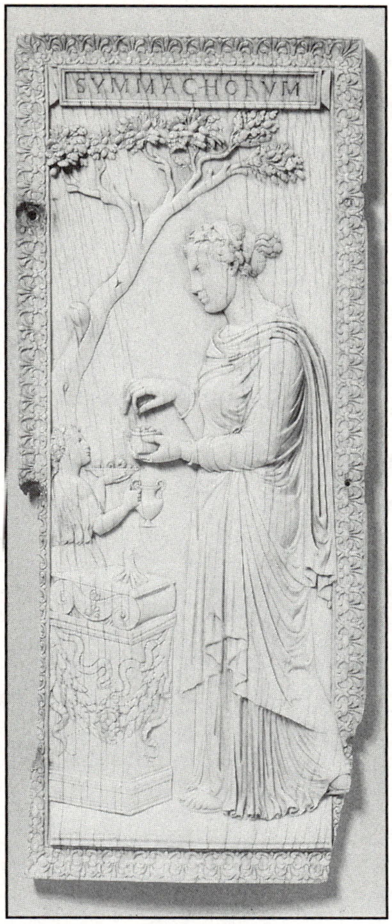

FIG. 08-22 Woman sacrificing at an altar, right leaf of the Diptych of the Nicomachi and the Symmachi, ca. 400. Ivory, 11 3/4″ × 5 1/2″. Victoria & Albert Museum, London. (page 242)

Chapter 9

Rome in the East:
The Art of Byzantium

Goals

- Understand Constantine's move to the east and the extent of the Roman Empire in the east.
- Understand the cultural mix of Roman, Christian, and eastern influences in the art of Byzantium.
- Define distinct characteristics in art from various periods of the Byzantine Empire.
- Define distinct characteristics in architecture of this period.

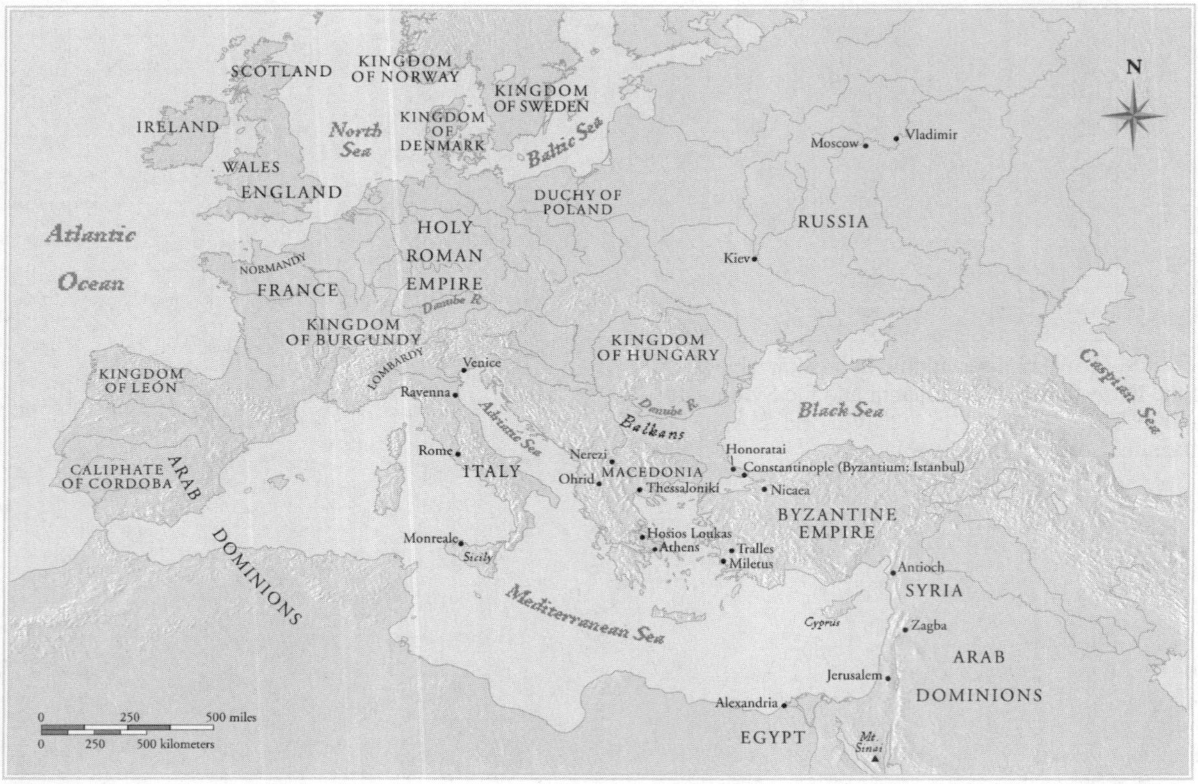

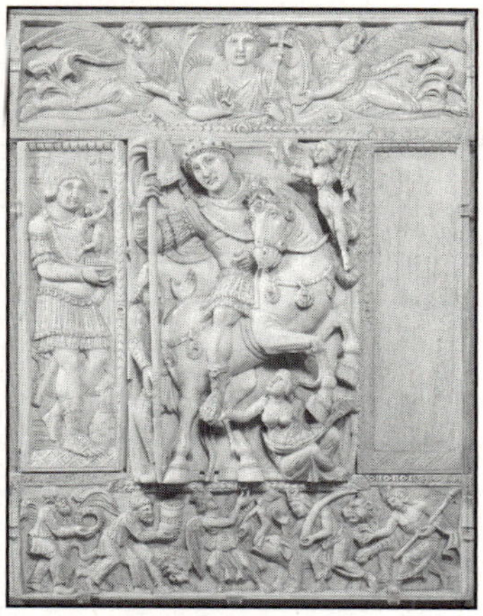

FIG. 09-01 Justinian as world conqueror *(Barberini Ivory),* mid-sixth century. Ivory, 1′ 1 1/2″ × 10 1/2″. Louvre, Paris. (page 248)

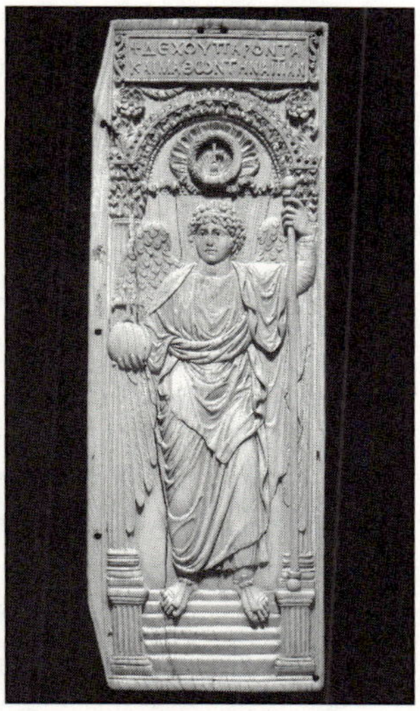

FIG. 09-02 Saint Michael the Archangel, right leaf of a diptych, early sixth century. Ivory, approx. 1′ 5″ × 5 1/2″. British Museum, London. (page 248)

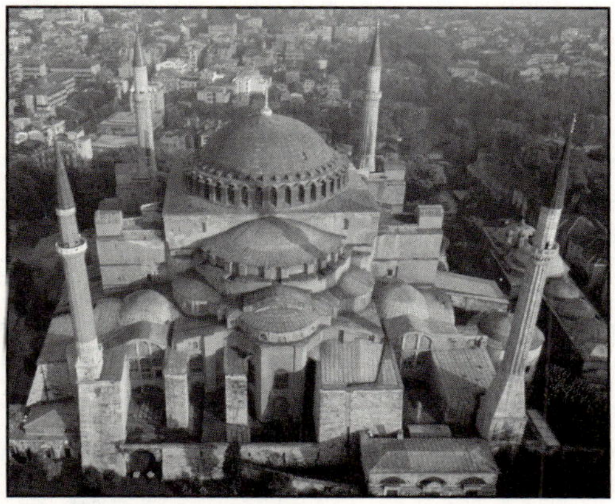

FIG. 09-03 Anthemius of Tralles and Isidorus of Miletus, Hagia Sophia (view facing north), Constantinople (Istanbul), Turkey, 532–537. (page 249)

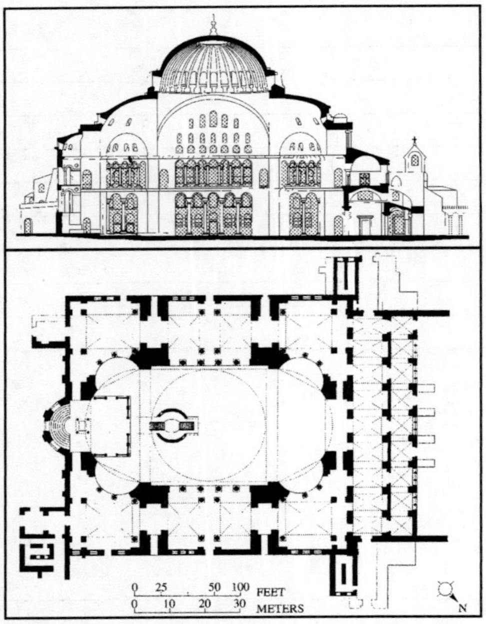

FIG. 09-04 Anthemius of Tralles and Isidorus of Miletus, longitudinal section *(left)* and plan *(right)* of Hagia Sophia, Constantinople (Istanbul), Turkey, 532–537 (after drawings by Van Nice and Antoniades). (page 250)

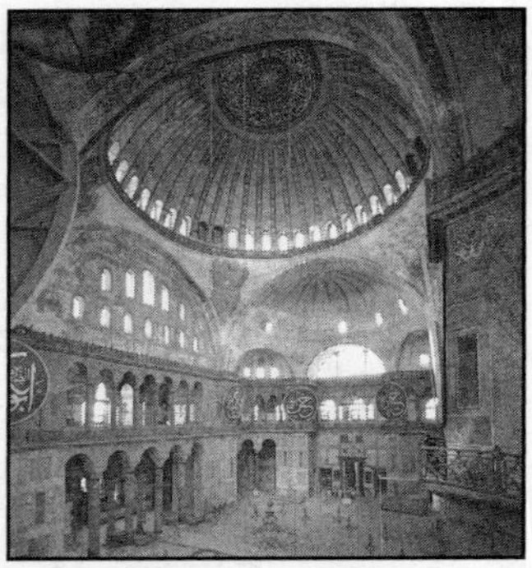

FIG. 09-05 Anthemius of Tralles and Isidorus of Miletus, interior of Hagia Sophia (view facing southwest), Constantinople (Istanbul), Turkey, 532–537. (page 250)

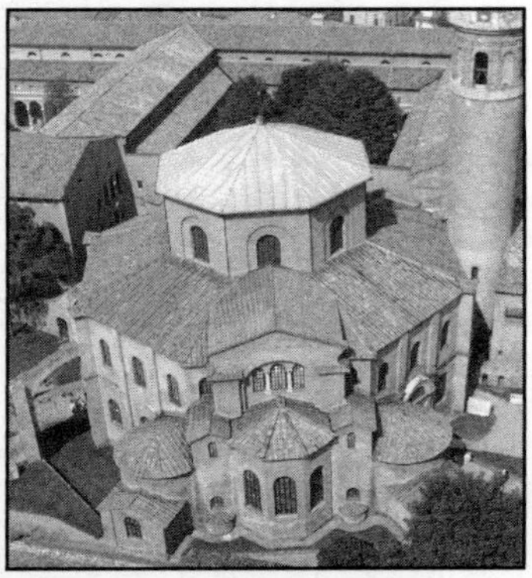

FIG. 09-06 Aerial view of San Vitale (view facing northwest), Ravenna, Italy, 526–547. (page 252)

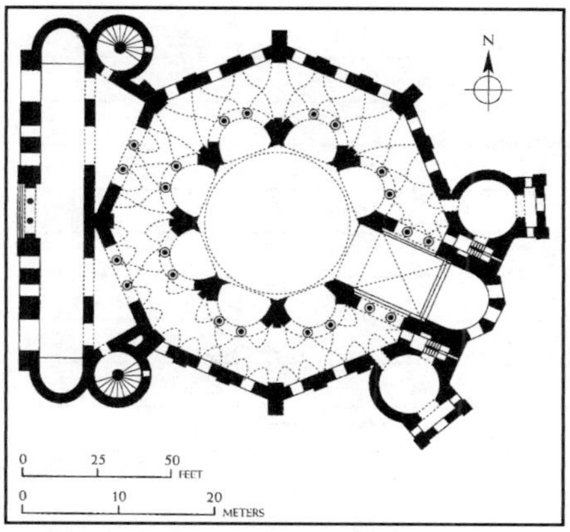

FIG. 09-07 Plan of San Vitale, Ravenna, Italy, 526–547. (page 252)

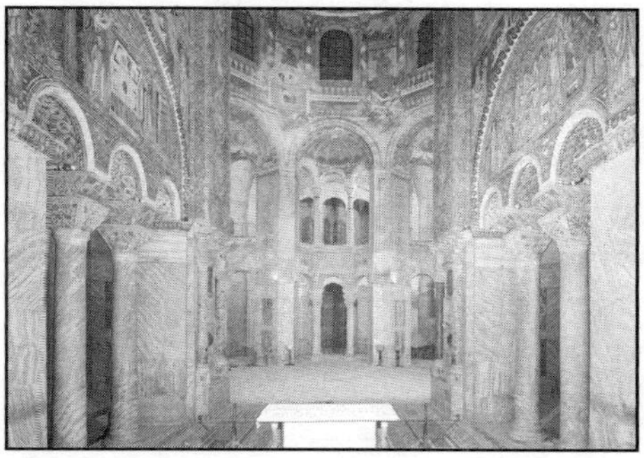

FIG. 09-08 Interior of San Vitale (view from the apse into the choir), Ravenna, Italy, 526–547. (page 253)

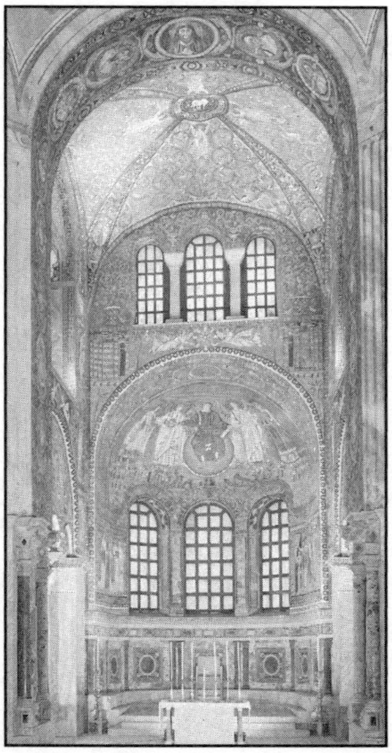

FIG. 09-09 Choir and apse of San Vitale with mosaic of Christ between two angels, Saint Vitalis, and Bishop Ecclesius, Ravenna, Italy, 526–547. (page 254)

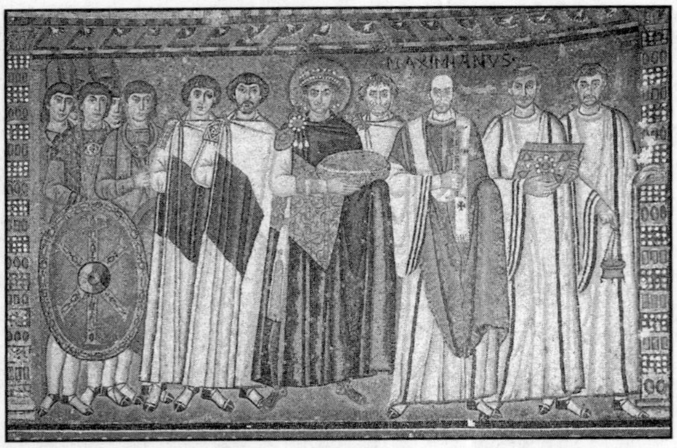

FIG. 09-10 Justinian, Bishop Maximianus, and attendants, mosaic from the north wall of the apse, San Vitale, Ravenna, Italy, ca. 547. (page 255)

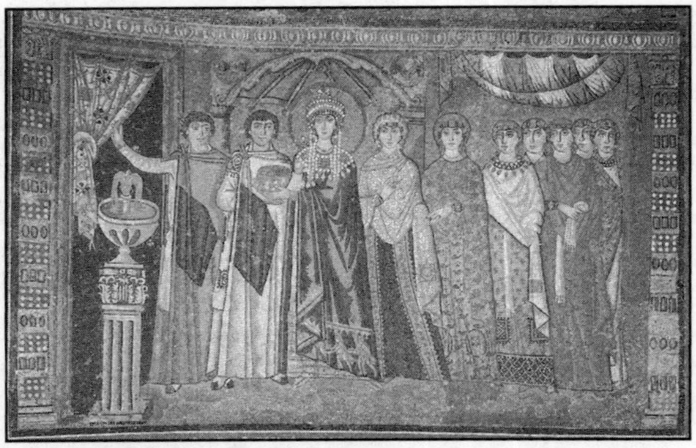

FIG. 09-11 Theodora and attendants, mosaic from the south wall of the apse, San Vitale, Ravenna, Italy, ca. 547. (page 255)

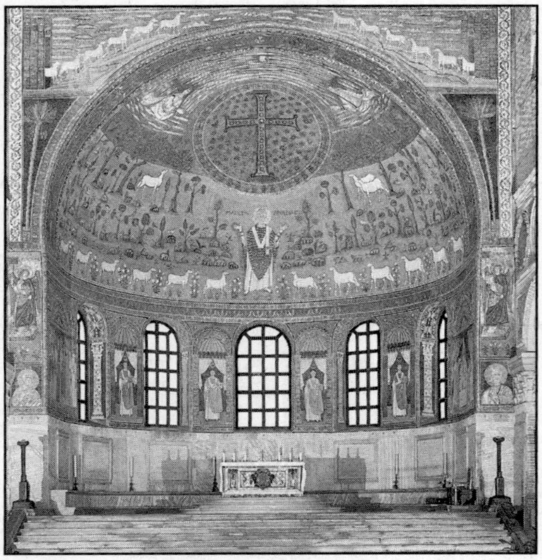

FIG. 09-12 Saint Apollinaris amid sheep, apse mosaic, Sant'Apollinare in Classe, Ravenna, Italy, ca. 533–549. (page 257)

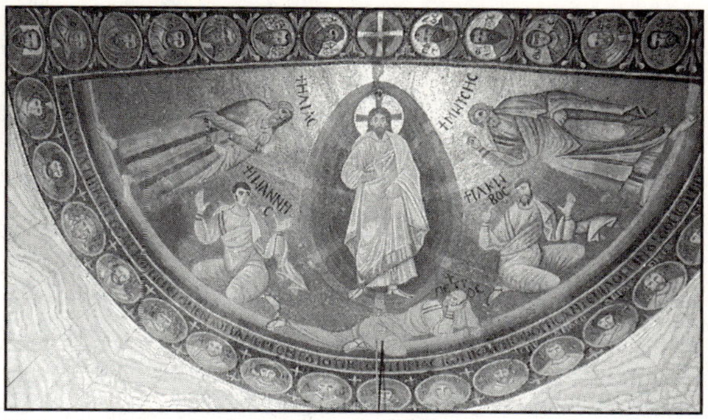

FIG. 09-13 Transfiguration of Jesus, apse mosaic, Church of the Virgin, monastery of Saint Catherine, Mount Sinai, Egypt, ca. 548–565. (page 258)

FIG. 09-14 Anicia Juliana between Magnanimity and Prudence, folio 6 verso of the *Vienna Dioskorides,* from Honoratai, near Constantinople (Istanbul), Turkey, ca. 512. Tempera on parchment, approx. 1′3″ × 1′11″. Österreichische Nationalbibliothek, Vienna. (page 259)

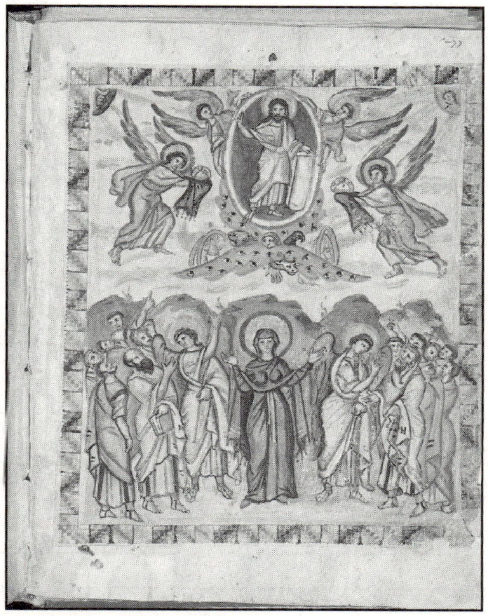

FIG. 09-15 Ascension of Christ, folio 13 verso of the *Rabbula Gospels,* from Zagba, Syria, 586. Approx. 1′ 1″ × 10 1/2″. Biblioteca Medicea-Laurenziana, Florence. (page 259)

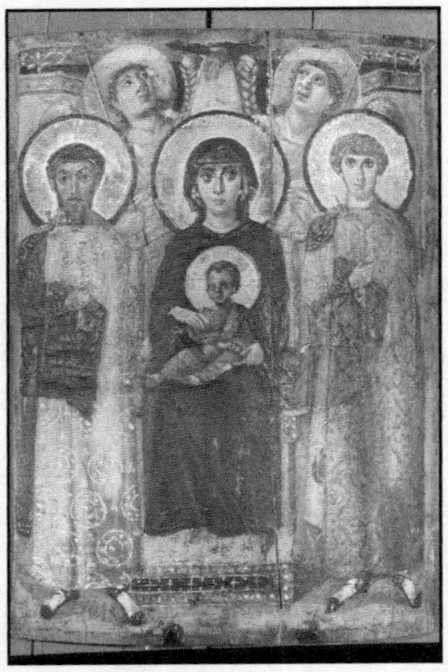

FIG. 09-16 Virgin (Theotokos) and Child between Saints Theodore and George, icon, sixth or early seventh century. Encaustic on wood, 2′ 3″ × 1′ 7 3/8″. Monastery of Saint Catherine, Mount Sinai, Egypt. (page 260)

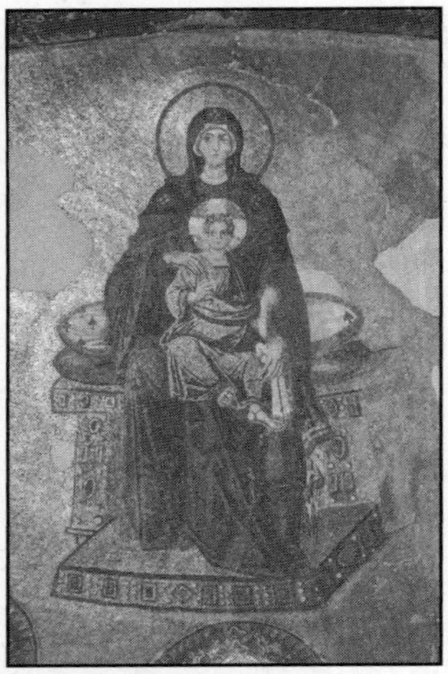

FIG. 09-17 Virgin (Theotokos) and Child enthroned, apse mosaic, Hagia Sophia, Constantinople (Istanbul), Turkey, dedicated 867. (page 262)

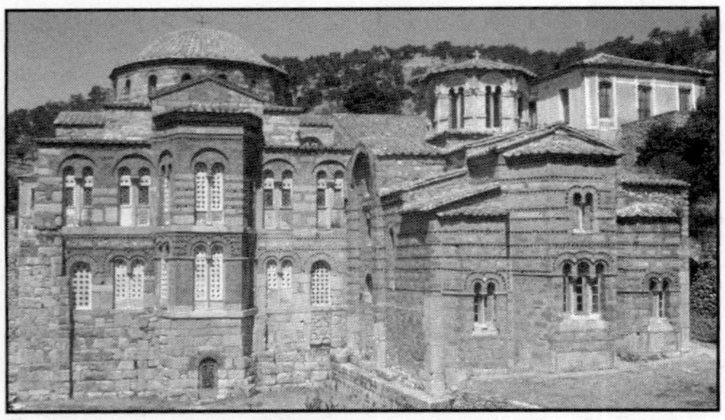

FIG. 09-18 Monastery churches at Hosios Loukas, Greece (view from the east). Katholikon *(left),* first quarter of 11th century, and Church of the Theotokos *(right),* second half of 10th century. (page 262)

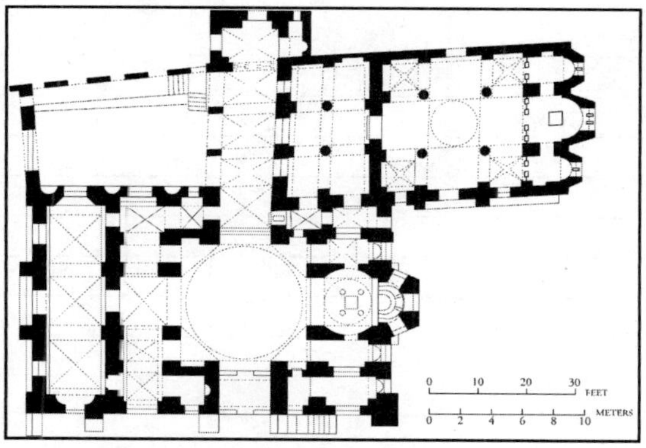

FIG. 09-19 Plans of Church of the Theotokos *(top)* and Katholikon *(bottom),* Hosios Loukas, Greece, second half of 10th and first quarter of 11th century. (page 263)

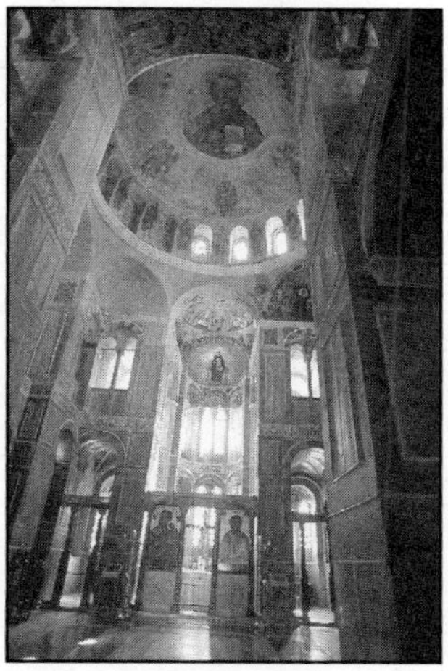

FIG. 09-20 Interior of Katholikon (view facing east), Hosios Loukas, Greece, first quarter of 11th century. (page 263)

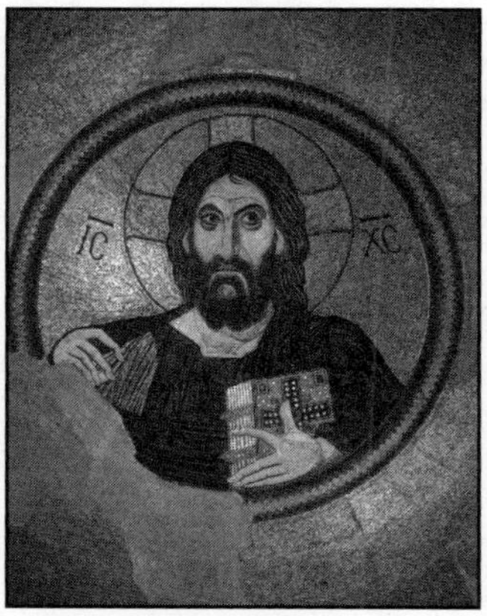

FIG. 09-21 Christ as Pantokrator, dome mosaic in the Church of the Dormition, Daphni, Greece, ca. 1090–1100. (page 264)

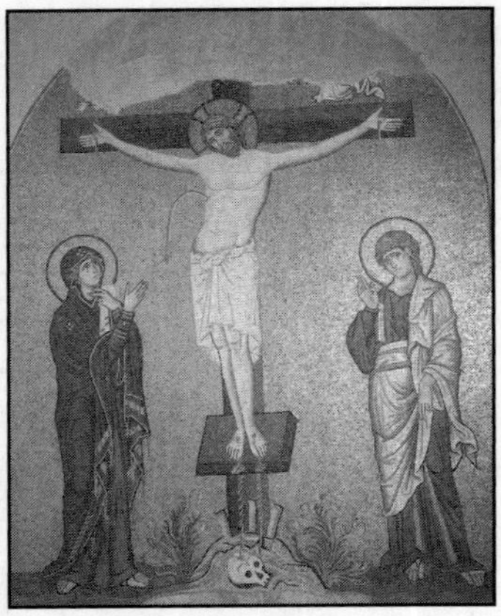

FIG. 09-22 Crucifixion, mosaic in the Church of the Dormition, Daphni, Greece, ca. 1090–1100. (page 265)

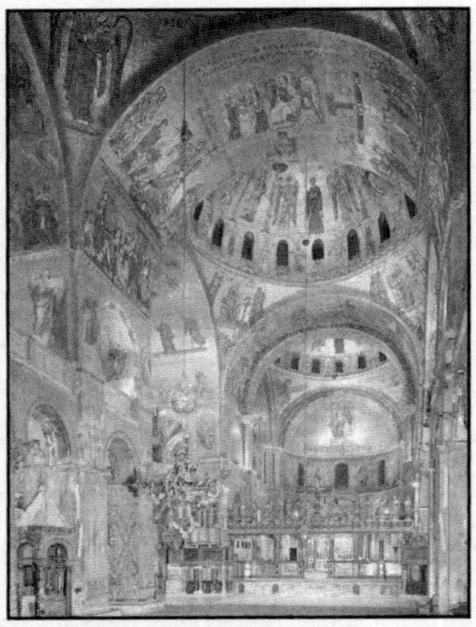

FIG. 09-23 Interior of Saint Mark's (view facing east), Venice, Italy, begun 1063. (page 266)

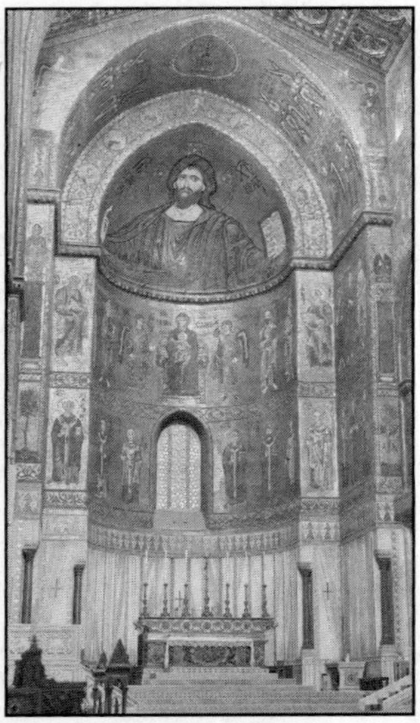

FIG. 09-24 Pantokrator, Theotokos and Child, angels, and saints, apse mosaic in the cathedral at Monreale, Italy, ca. 1180–1190. (page 267)

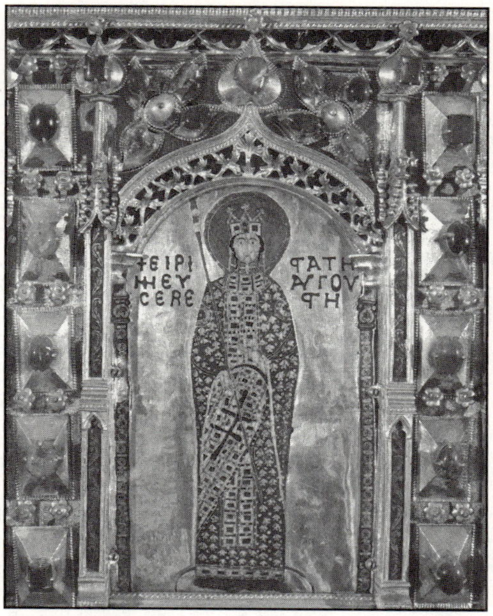

FIG. 09-25 Empress Irene, detail of the *Pala d'Oro,* Saint Mark's, Venice, Italy, ca. 1105. Gold cloisonné inlaid with precious stones, detail approx. 7″ × 4 1/2″. (page 267)

FIG. 09-26 Christ enthroned with saints *(Harbaville Triptych),* ca. 950. Ivory, central panel 9 1/2″ × 5 1/2″. Louvre, Paris. (page 268)

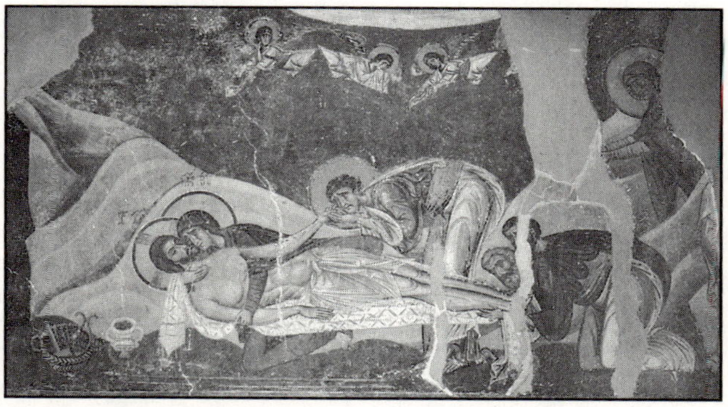

FIG. 09-27 Lamentation over the Dead Christ, wall painting, Saint Pantaleimon, Nerezi, Macedonia, 1164. (page 269)

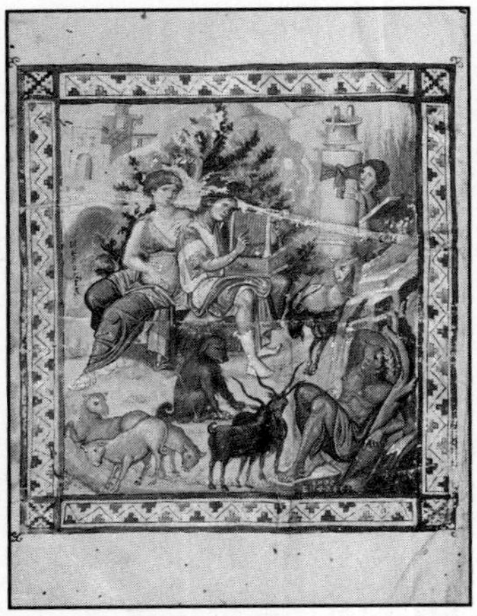

FIG. 09-28 David composing the Psalms, folio 1 verso of the *Paris Psalter,* ca. 950–970. Tempera on vellum, 1′ 2 1/8″ × 10 1/4″. Bibliothèque Nationale, Paris. (page 269)

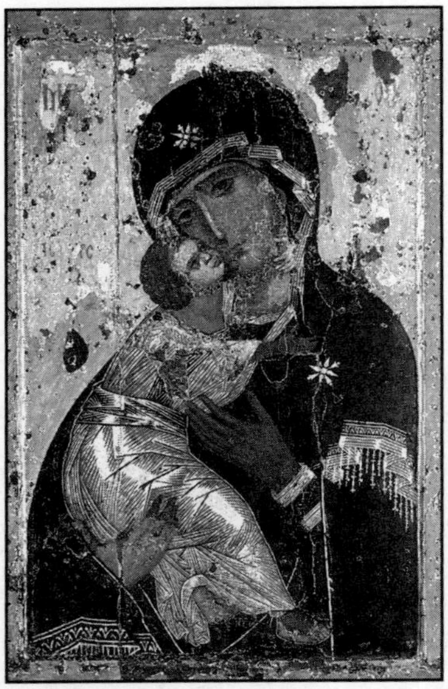

FIG. 09-29 Virgin (Theotokos) and Child, icon *(Vladimir Virgin),* late 11th to early 12th century. Tempera on wood, original panel approx. 2′ 6 1/2″ × 1′ 9″. Tretyakov Gallery, Moscow. (page 270)

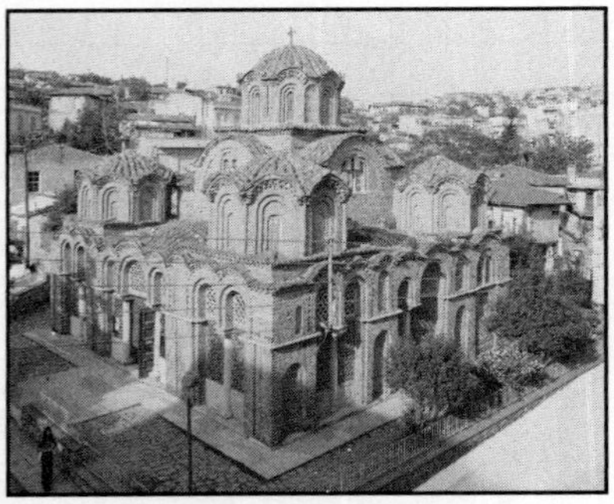

FIG. 09-30 Church of Saint Catherine, Thessaloniki, Greece, ca. 1280. (page 271)

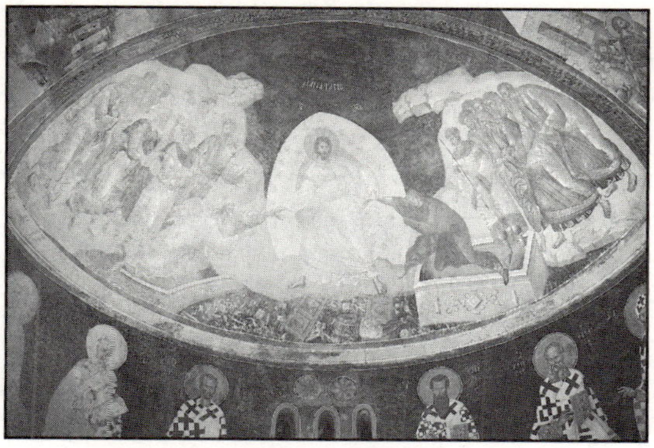

FIG. 09-31 Anastasis, apse fresco in the *parekklesion* of the Church of Christ in Chora (now the Kariye Museum), Constantinople (Istanbul), Turkey, ca. 1310–1320. (page 271)

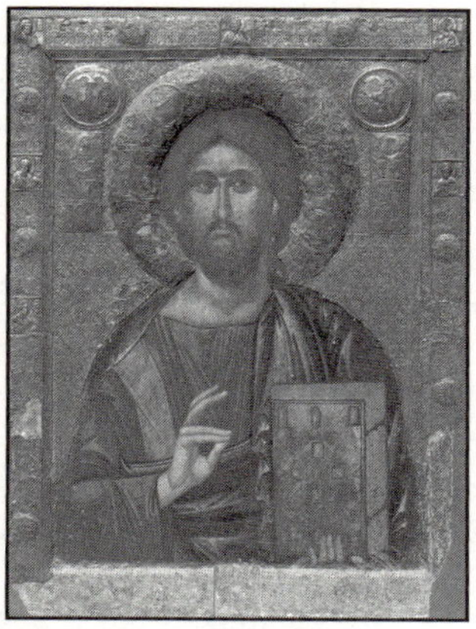

FIG. 09-32 Christ as Savior of Souls, icon from the church of Saint Clement, Ohrid, Macedonia, early 14th century. Tempera, linen, and silver on wood, 3′1/4″ × 2′ 2 1/2″. Icon Gallery of Saint Clement, Ohrid. (page 272)

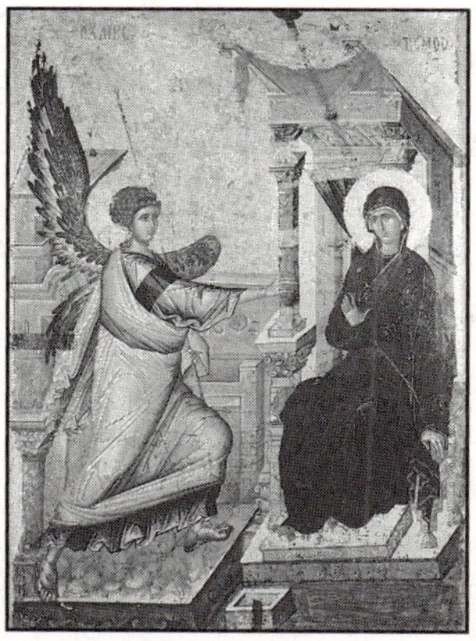

FIG. 09-33 Annunciation, reverse of two-sided icon from the church of Saint Clement, Ohrid, Macedonia, early 14th century. Tempera and linen on wood, 3′ 1/4″ × 2′ 2 3/4″. Icon gallery of Saint Clement, Ohrid. (page 272)

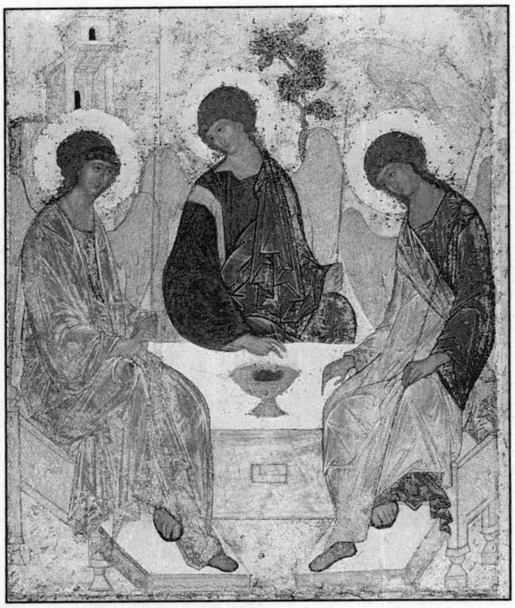

FIG. 09-34 ANDREI RUBLYEV, Three angels (Old Testament Trinity), ca. 1410. Tempera on wood, 4′ 8″ × 3′ 9″. Tretyakov Gallery, Moscow. (page 273)

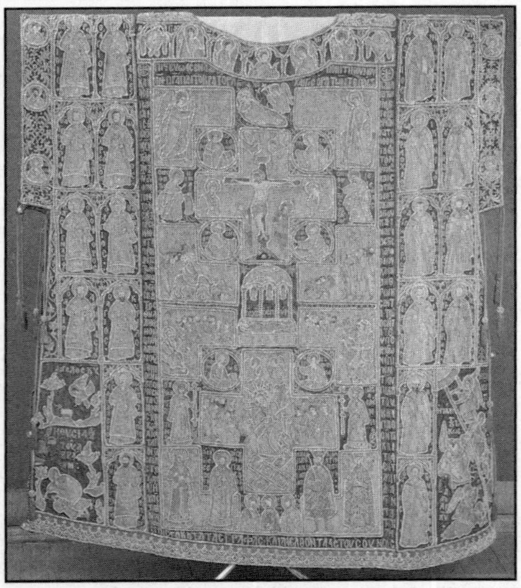

FIG. 09-35 Large sakkos of Photius, ca. 1417. Satin embroidered with gold and silver thread and silk with pearl ornament, approx. 4′ 5″ long. Kremlin Armory, Moscow. (page 274)

Chapter 10

In Praise of Allah:
The Art of the Islamic World

Goals

- Examine the origins and roots of the Islamic faith that are manifest in art and architecture.
- Understand the near Eastern artistic traditions that shape original forms in the art of Islam.
- Understand and cite architectural developments and the terminology of Islamic religious, funerary, and other structures.
- Examine the media, techniques, and designs that are specific to the art of Islam, particularly in the "luxury" arts.
- Understand the contributions of Islamic art and ideas to later western art and culture.

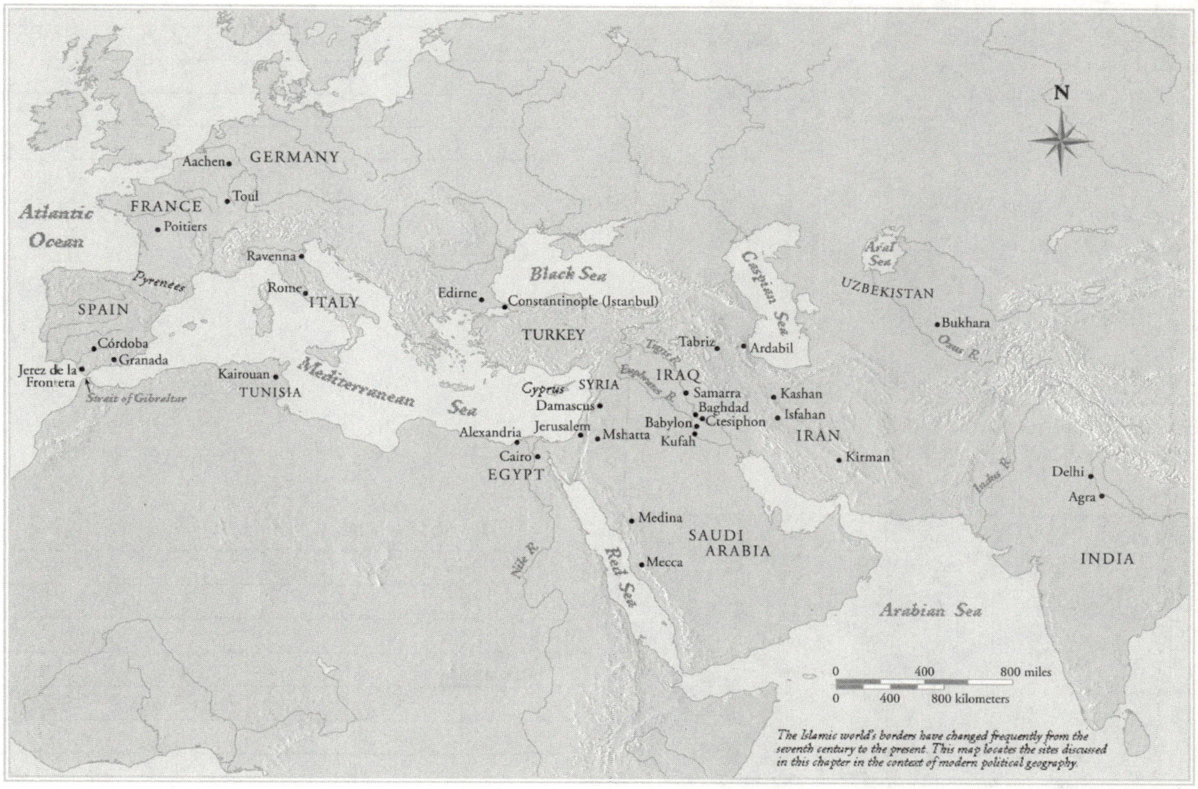

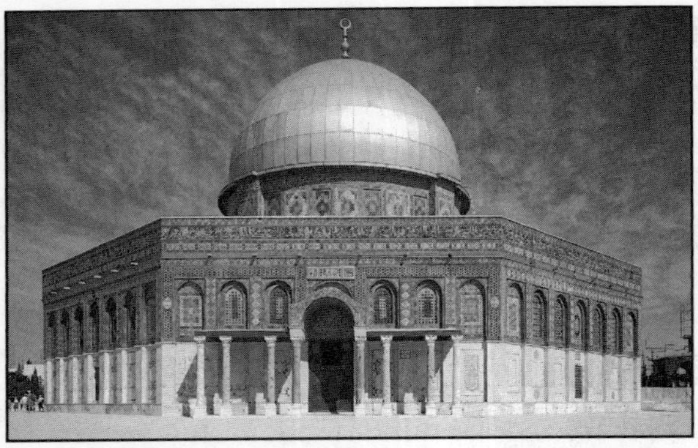

FIG. 10-01 Dome of the Rock, Jerusalem, 687–692. (page 279)

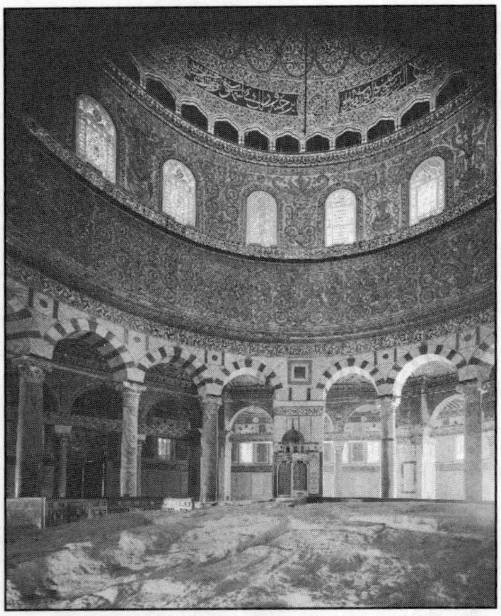

FIG. 10-02 Interior of the Dome of the Rock, Jerusalem, 687–692. (page 280)

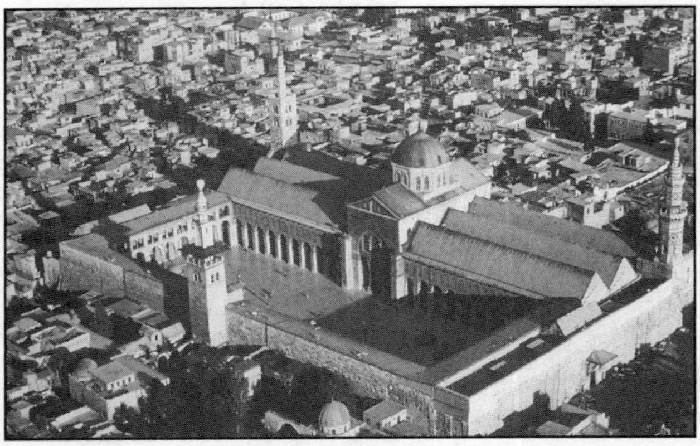

FIG. 10-03 Aerial view of the Great Mosque, Damascus, Syria, 706–715. (page 280)

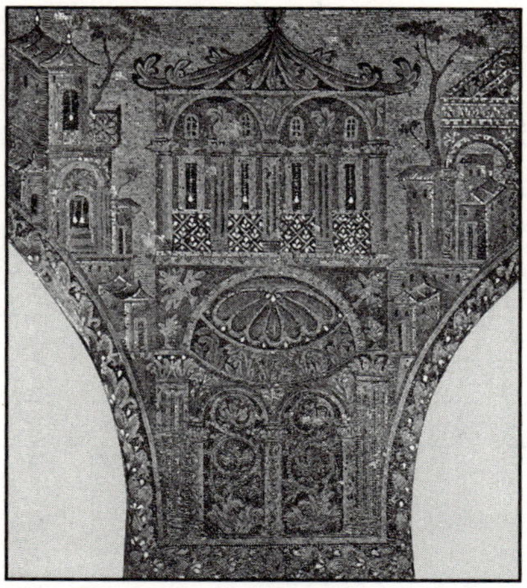

FIG. 10-04 Detail of a mosaic in the courtyard arcade of the Great Mosque, Damascus, Syria, 706–715. (page 281)

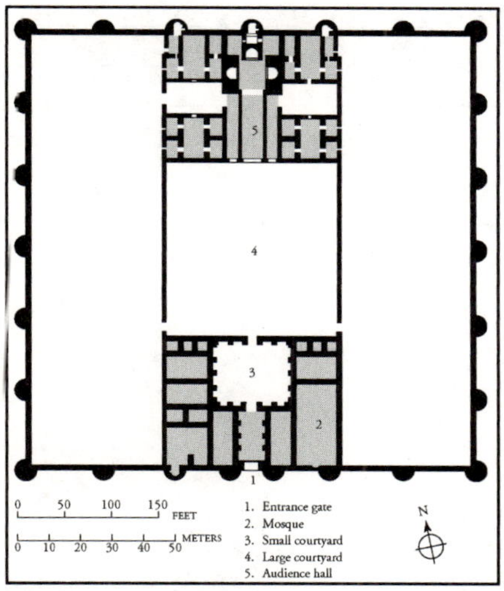

FIG. 10-05 Plan of the Umayyad palace, Mshatta, Jordan, ca. 740–750 (after Alberto Berengo Gardin). (page 282)

FIG. 10-06 Frieze of the Umayyad palace, Mshatta, Jordan, ca. 740–750. Limestone, 16′ 7″ high. Museum für Islamische Kunst, Staatliche Museen, Berlin. (page 283)

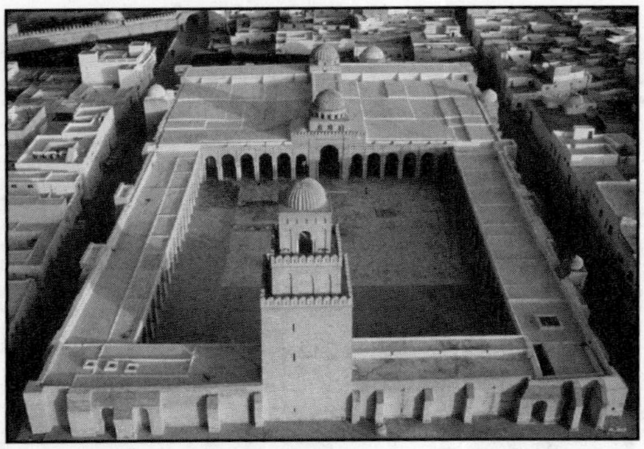

FIG. 10-07 Aerial view of the Great Mosque, Kairouan, Tunisia, ca. 836–875. (page 283)

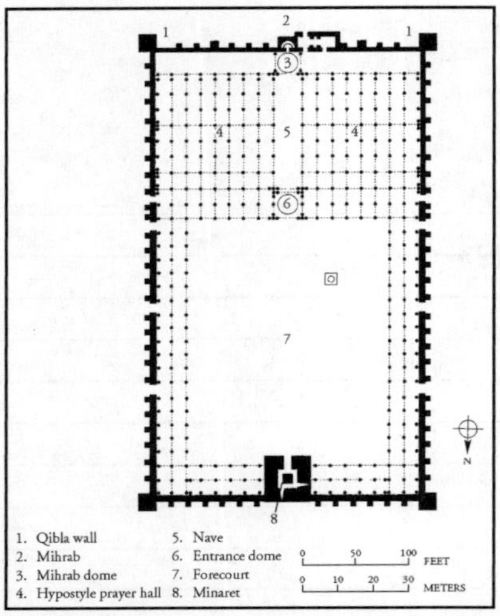

FIG. 10-08 Plan of the Great Mosque, Kairouan, Tunisia, ca. 836–875. (page 283)

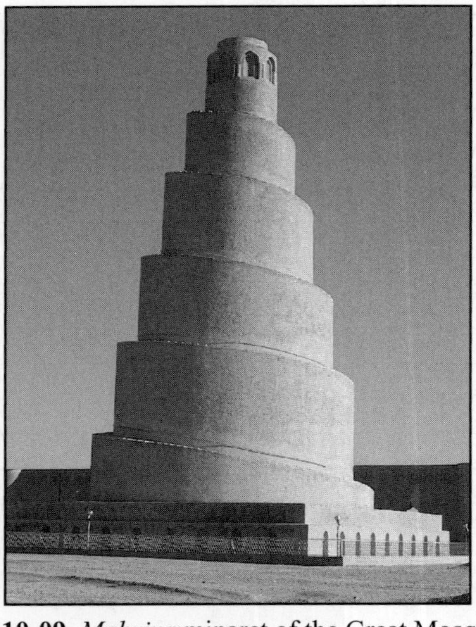

FIG. 10-09 *Malwiya* minaret of the Great Mosque, Samarra, Iraq, 848–852. (page 284)

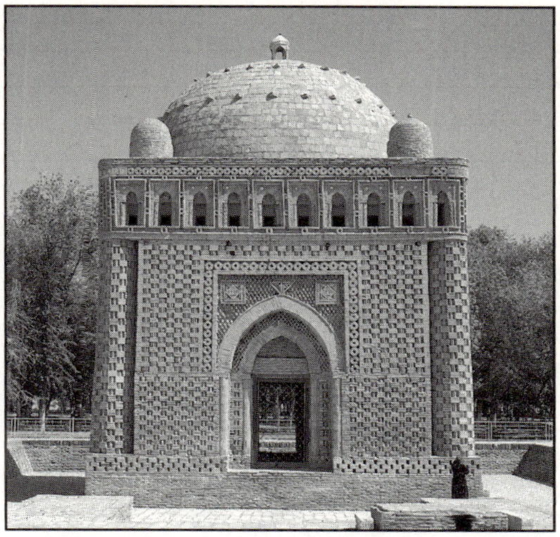

FIG. 10-10 Mausoleum of the Samanids, Bukhara, Uzbekistan, early tenth century. (page 284)

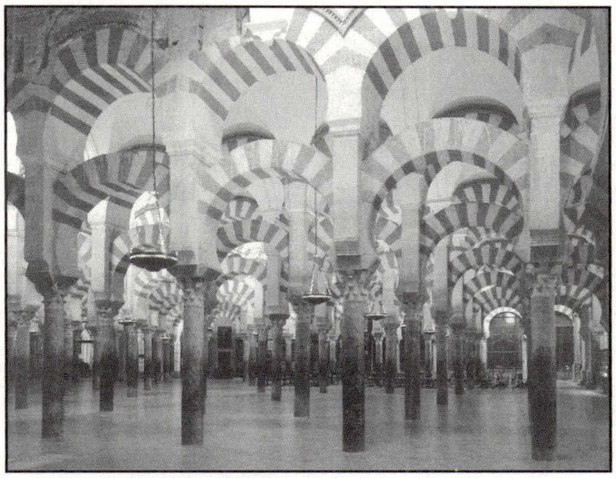

FIG. 10-11 Prayer hall of the Great Mosque, Córdoba, Spain, eighth to tenth centuries. (page 285)

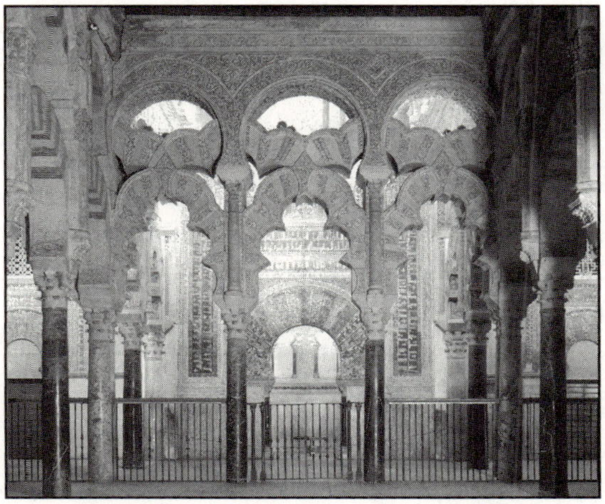

FIG. 10-12 Maqsura of the Great Mosque, Córdoba, Spain, 961–965. (page 285)

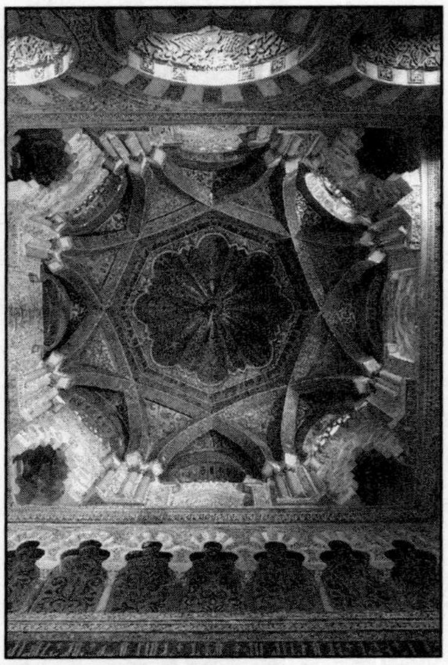

FIG. 10-13 Dome in front of the mihrab of the Great Mosque, Córdoba, Spain, 961–965. (page 286)

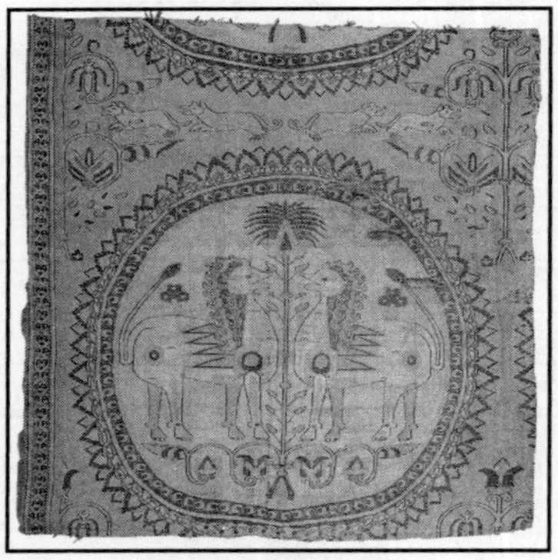

FIG. 10-14 Confronting lions and palm tree, fragment of a textile said to be from Zandana, near Bukhara, Uzbekistan, eighth century. Silk compound twill, 2′ 11″ × 2′ 9 1/2″. Musée Historique de Lorraine, Nancy. (page 286)

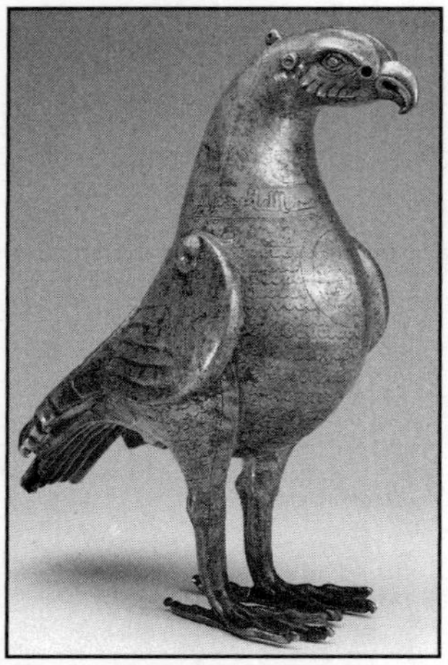

FIG. 10-15 SULAYMAN, Ewer in the form of a bird, 796. Brass with silver and copper inlay, 1′ 3″ high. Hermitage, Saint Petersburg. (page 287)

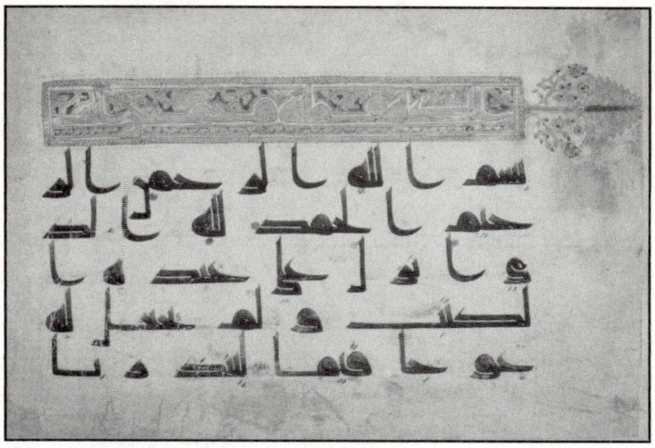

FIG. 10-16 Koran page with beginning of surah 18, *al-Kahf (The Cave),* ninth or early tenth century. Ink and gold on vellum, 7 1/4″ × 10 1/4″. Chester Beatty Library and Oriental Art Gallery, Dublin. (page 288)

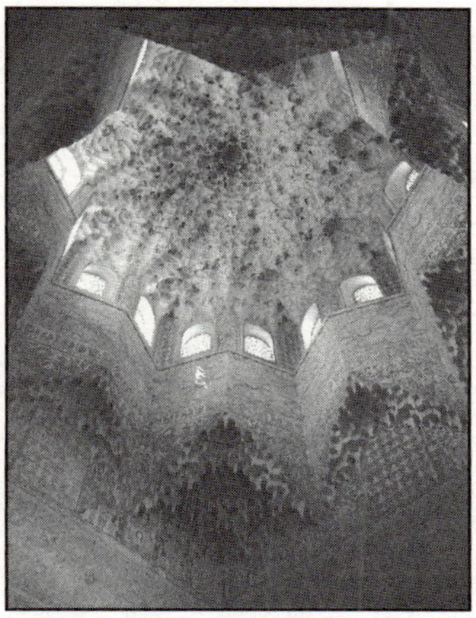

FIG. 10-17 Muqarnas dome, Hall of the Two Sisters, Alhambra palace, Granada, Spain, 1354–1391. (page 288)

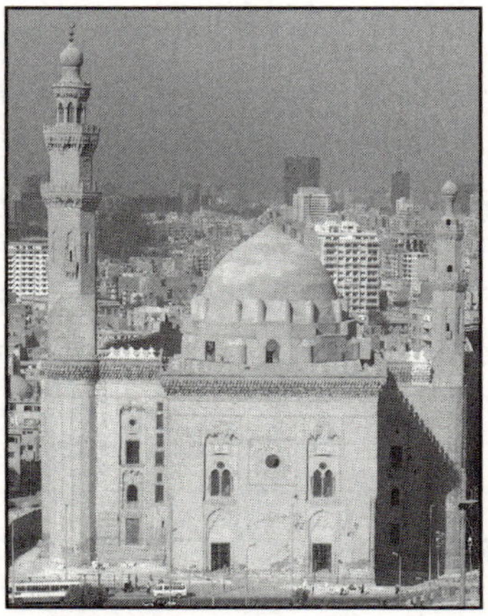

FIG. 10-18 Madrasa-mosque-mausoleum complex of Sultan Hasan (view from the south with the mausoleum in the foreground), Cairo, Egypt, begun 1356. (page 289)

FIG. 10-19 Plan of the madrasa-mosque-mausoleum complex of Sultan Hasan, Cairo, Egypt, begun 1356. (page 289)

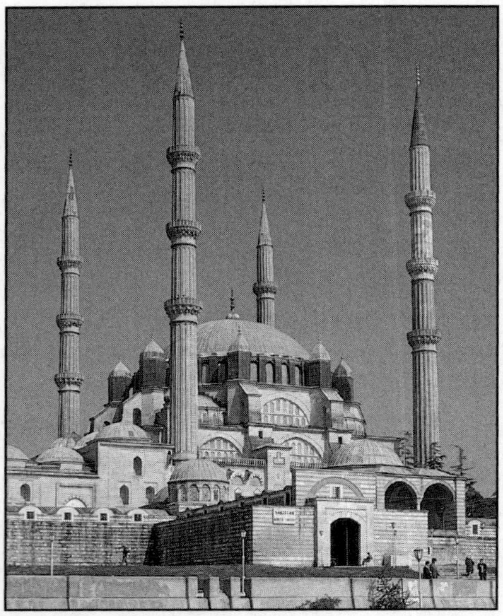

FIG. 10-20 SINAN, Mosque of Selim II, Edirne, Turkey, 1568–1575. (page 290)

FIG. 10-21 SINAN, plan of the Mosque of Selim II, Edirne, Turkey, 1568–1575. (page 290)

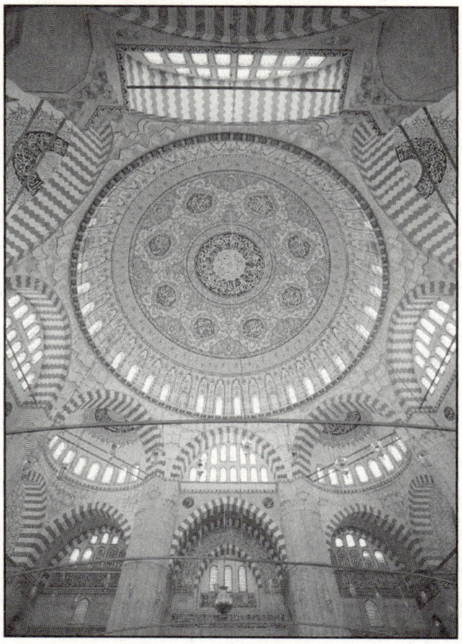

FIG. 10-22 SINAN, interior of the Mosque of Selim II, Edirne, Turkey, 1568–1575. (page 291)

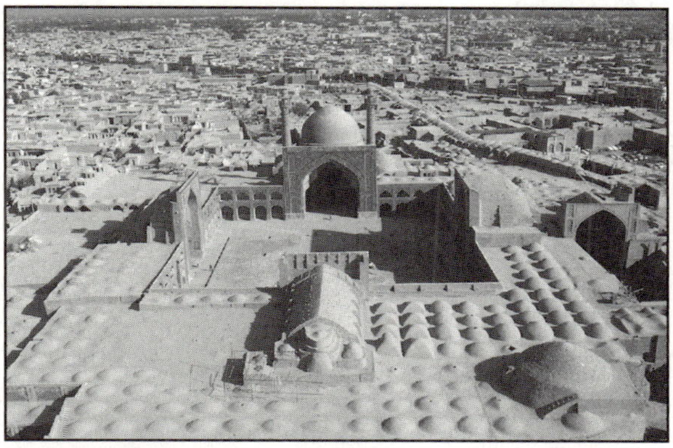

FIG. 10-23 Aerial view of the Great Mosque (looking southwest), Isfahan, Iran, eleventh to seventeenth centuries. (page 292)

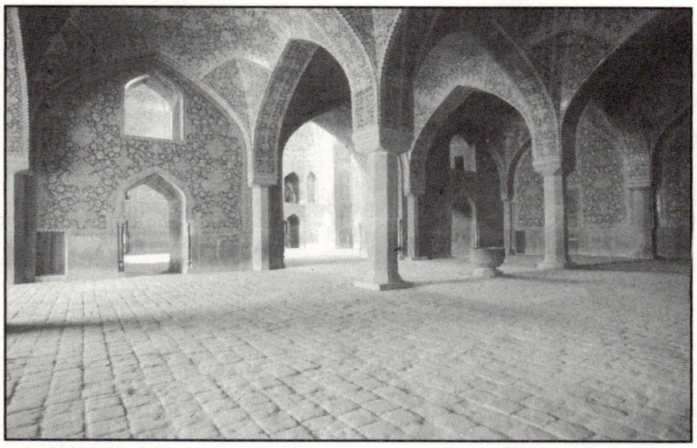

FIG. 10-24 Winter prayer hall of the Shahi (Imam) Mosque, Isfahan, Iran, 1611–1638. (page 292)

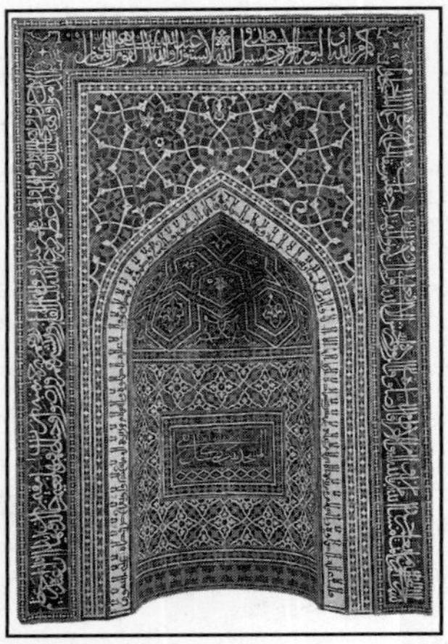

FIG. 10-25 Mihrab from the Madrasa Imami, Isfahan, Iran, ca. 1354. Glazed mosaic tilework, 11′ 3″ × 7′ 6″. Metropolitan Museum of Art, New York. (page 293)

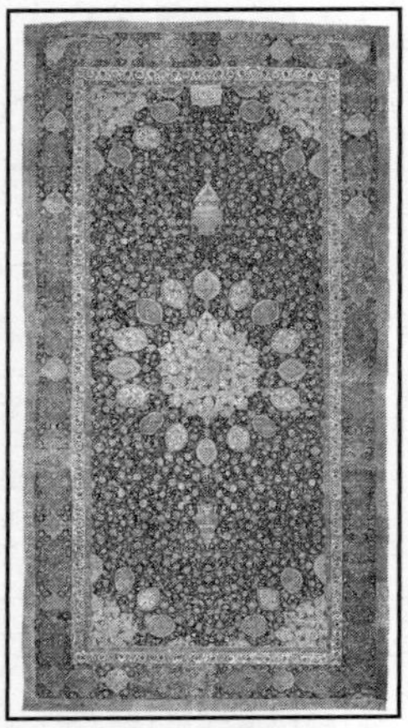

FIG. 10-26 MAQSUD OF KASHAN, carpet from the funerary mosque of Shaykh Safi al-Din, Ardabil, Iran, 1540. Knotted pile of wool and silk, 34′ 6″ × 17′ 7″. Victoria & Albert Museum, London. (page 295)

FIG. 10-27 SULTAN-MUHAMMAD, the court of Gayumars, detail of folio 20 verso of the *Shahnama* of Shah Tahmasp, from Tabriz, Iran, ca. 1525–1535. Ink, watercolor, and gold on paper, full page approx. 1′ 1″ × 9″. Prince Sadruddin Aga Khan Collection, Geneva. (page 295)

FIG. 10-28 Ottoman royal ceremonial caftan, from Istanbul, Turkey, ca. 1550. Polychrome silk and gilt-metal thread, 4′ 9″ high. Topkapi Palace Museum, Istanbul. (page 296)

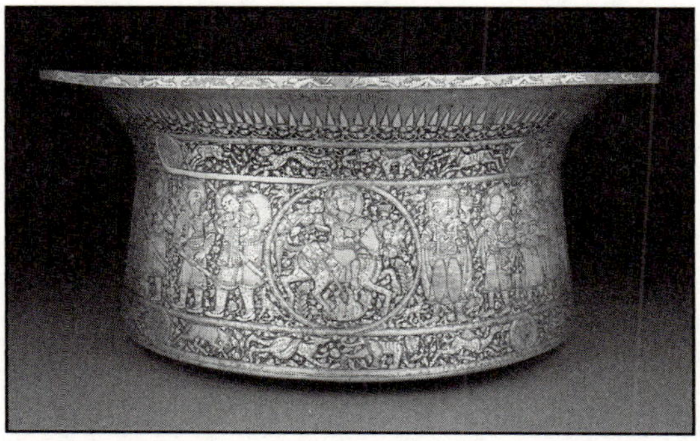

FIG. 10-29 MUHAMMAD IBN AL-ZAYN, basin *(Baptistère de Saint Louis),* from Egypt, ca. 1300. Brass, inlaid with gold and silver, 8 3/4″ high. Louvre, Paris. (page 297)

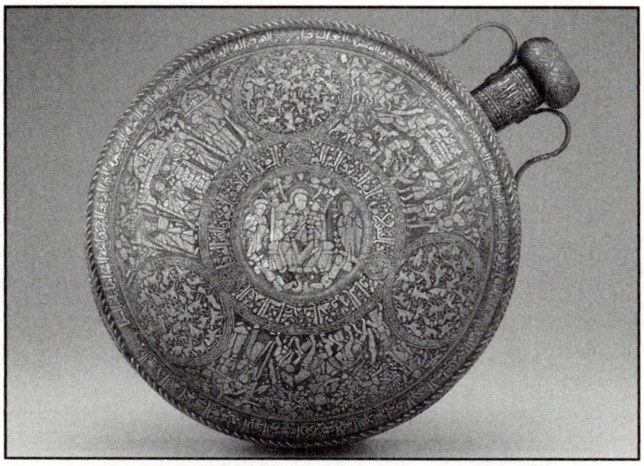

FIG. 10-30 Canteen with episodes from the life of Christ, from Syria, ca. 1240–1250. Brass, inlaid with silver, 1′ 2 1/2″ diameter. Freer Gallery of Art, Washington, D.C. (page 298)

Chapter 11

Europe after the Fall of Rome:
Early Medieval Art in the West

Goals

- Understand the distinctive artistic traditions of the European peoples beyond the Roman Empire.
- Know the different types of art, media, and their respective cultures.
- Trace influences of medieval art styles.
- Examine the secular and religious architectural forms in the early middle ages.

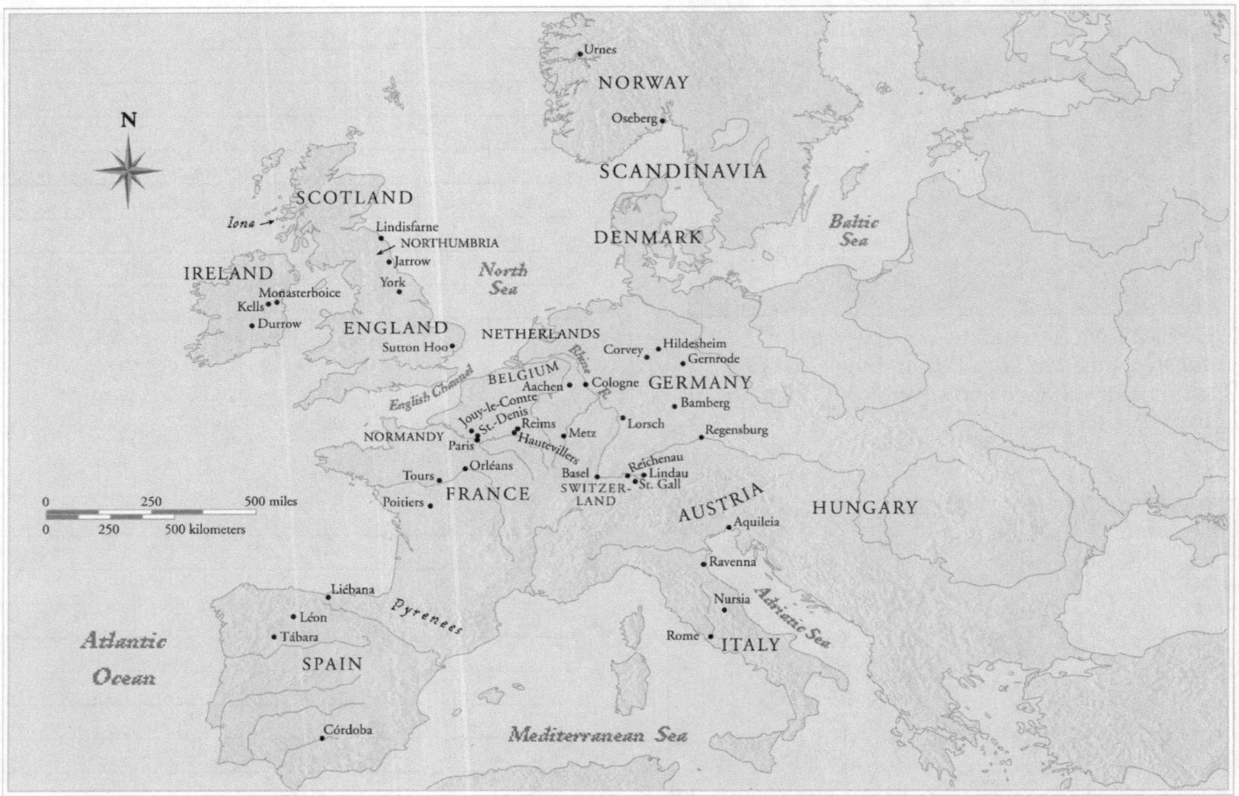

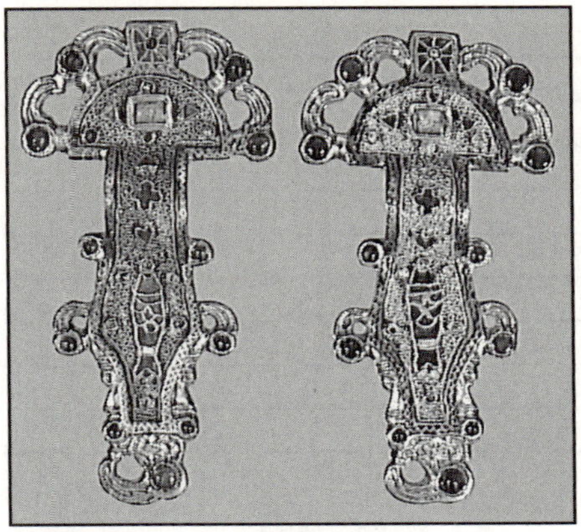

FIG. 11-01 Merovingian looped fibula, from Jouy-le-Comte, France, mid-sixth century. Silver gilt worked in filigree, with inlays of garnets and other stones, 4″ long. Musée des Antiquités Nationales, Saint-Germain-en-Laye. (page 303)

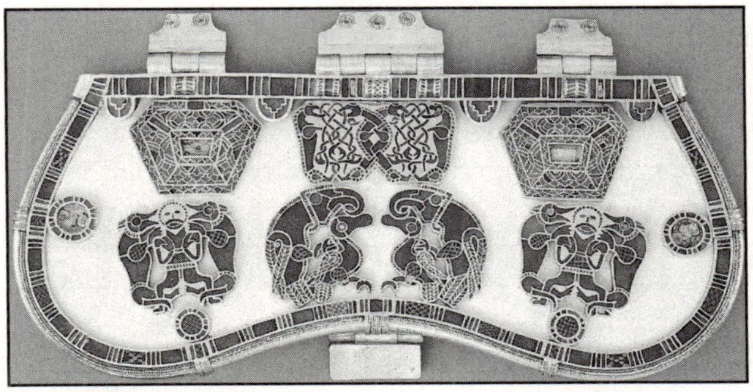

FIG. 11-02 Purse cover, from the Sutton Hoo ship burial in Suffolk, England, ca. 625. Gold, glass, and enamel cloisonné with garnets and emeralds, 7 1/2″ long. British Museum, London. (page 303)

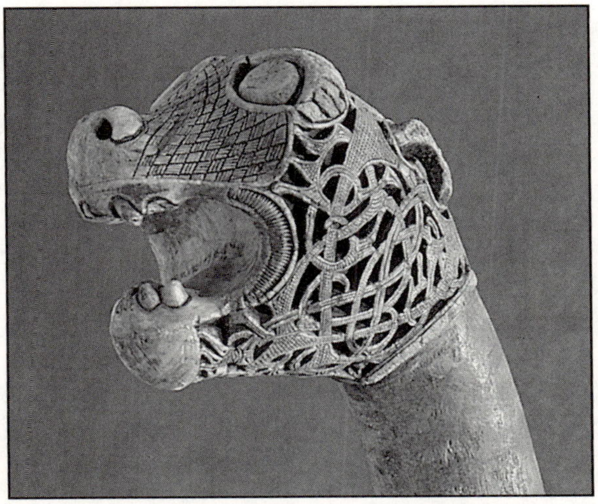

FIG. 11-03 Animal-head post, from the Viking ship burial, Oseberg, Norway, ca. 825. Wood, head approx. 5″ high. University Museum of National Antiquities, Oslo. (page 304)

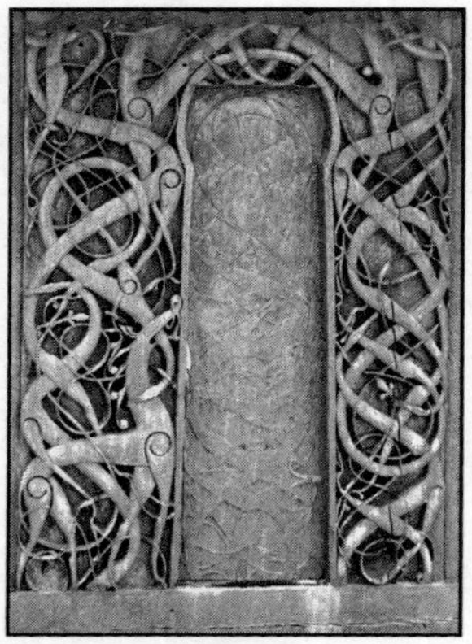

FIG. 11-04 Wooden portal of the stave church at Urnes, Norway, ca. 1050–1070. (page 305)

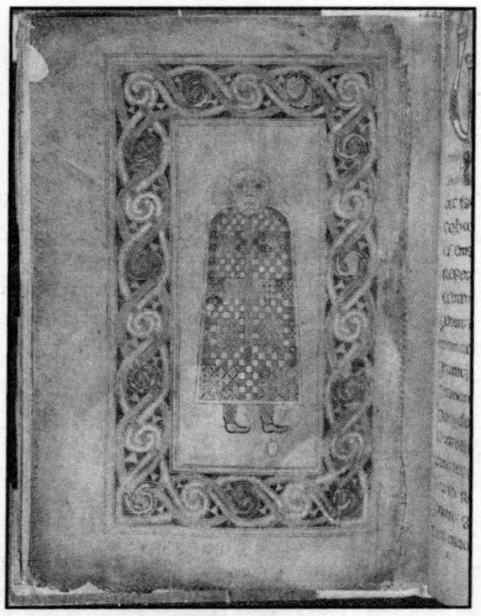

FIG. 11-05 Man (symbol of Saint Matthew), folio 21 verso of the *Book of Durrow,* possibly from Iona, Scotland, ca. 660–680. Ink and tempera on parchment, 9 5/8″ × 6 1/8″. Trinity College Library, Dublin. (page 306)

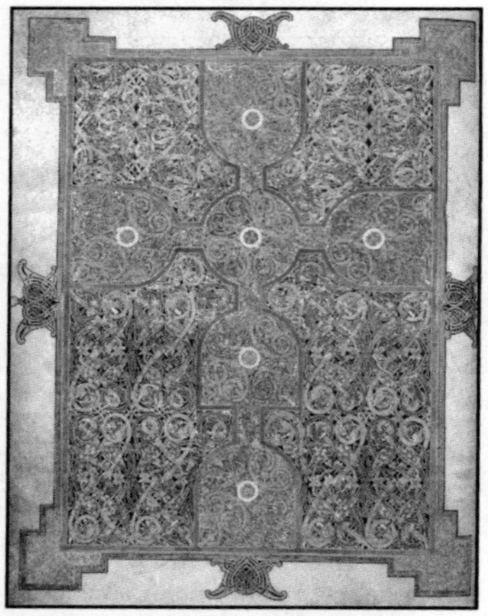

FIG. 11-06 Cross and carpet page, folio 26 verso of the *Lindisfarne Gospels,* from Northumbria, England, ca. 698–721. Tempera on vellum, 1′ 1 1/2″ × 9 1/4″. British Library, London. (page 307)

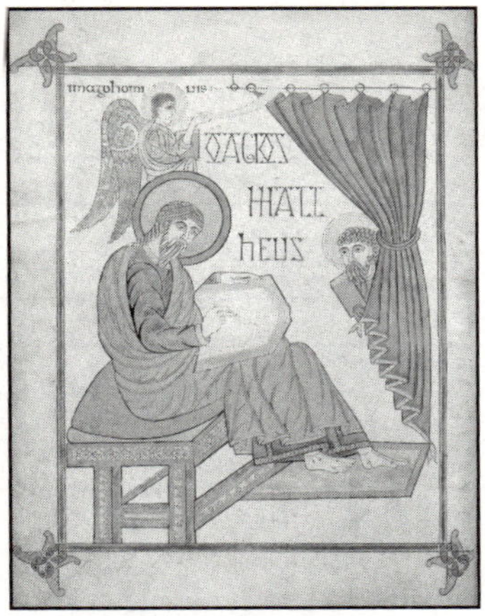

FIG. 11-07 Saint Matthew, folio 25 verso of the *Lindisfarne Gospels,* from Northumbria, England, ca. 698–721. Tempera on vellum, 1′ 1 1/2″ × 9 1/4″. British Library, London. (page 307)

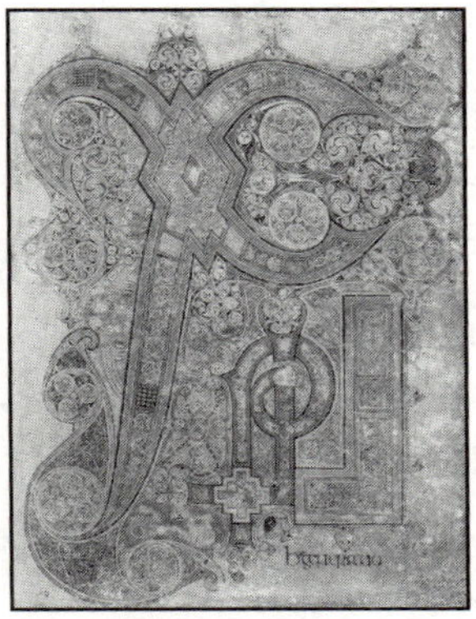

FIG. 11-08 Chi-rho-iota page, folio 34 recto of the *Book of Kells,* probably from Iona, Scotland, late eighth or early ninth century. Tempera on vellum, 1′ 1″ × 9 1/2″. Trinity College Library, Dublin. (page 308)

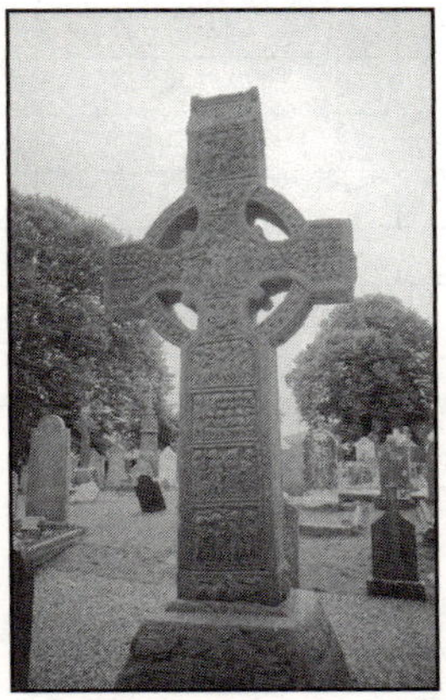

FIG. 11-09 *High Cross of Muiredach* (east face), Monasterboice, Ireland, 923. Sandstone, approx. 18′ high. (page 309)

FIG. 11-10 EMETERIUS, the tower and scriptorium of San Salvador de Tábara, colophon (folio 168) of the *Commentary on the Apocalypse* by Beatus, from Tábara, Spain, 970. Tempera on parchment, 1′2 1/8″ × 10″. Archivo Histórico Nacional, Madrid. (page 309)

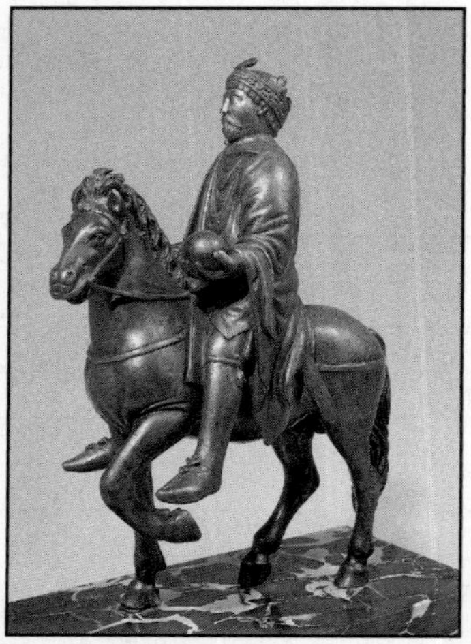

FIG. 11-11 Equestrian portrait of Charlemagne or Charles the Bald, from Metz, France, ninth century. Bronze, originally gilt, 9 1/2″ high. Louvre, Paris. (page 310)

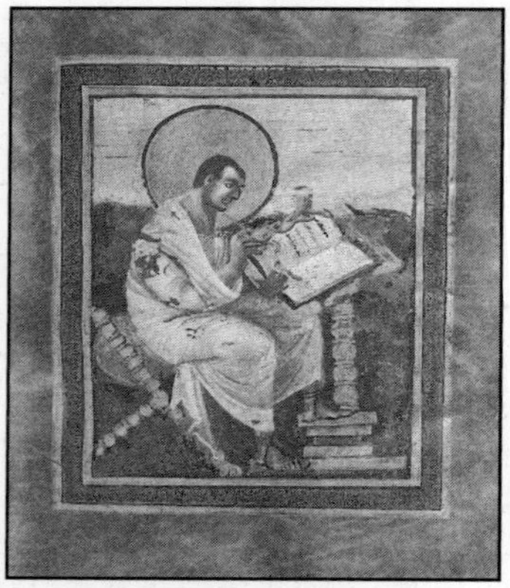

FIG. 11-12 Saint Matthew, folio 15 recto of the *Coronation Gospels (Gospel Book of Charlemagne),* from Aachen, Germany, ca. 800–810. Ink and tempera on vellum, 1′ 3/4″ × 10″. Schatzkammer, Kunsthistorisches Museum, Vienna. (page 311)

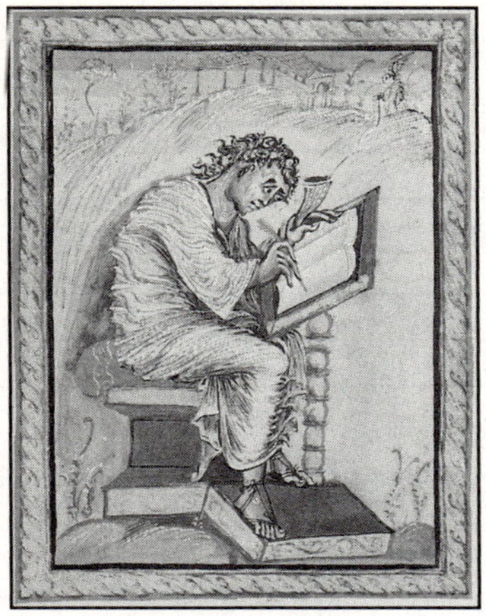

FIG. 11-13 Saint Matthew, folio 18 verso of the *Ebbo Gospels (Gospel Book of Archbishop Ebbo of Reims),* from Hautvillers (near Reims), France, ca. 816–835. Ink and tempera on vellum, 10 1/4″ × 8 3/4″ . Bibliothèque Municipale, Épernay. (page 311)

FIG. 11-14 Psalm 44, detail of folio 25 recto of the *Utrecht Psalter,* from Hautvillers (near Reims), France, ca. 820–835. Ink on vellum, full page, 1′ 1″ × 9 7/8″. University Library, Utrecht. (page 312)

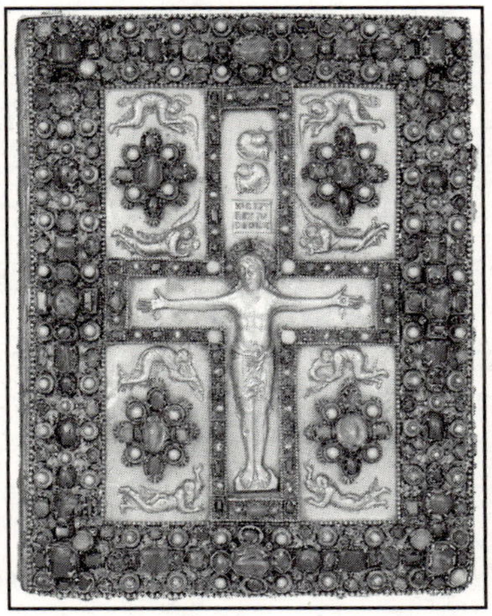

FIG. 11-15 Crucifixion, front cover of the *Lindau Gospels,* from Saint Gall, Switzerland, ca. 870. Gold, precious stones, and pearls, 1′ 1 3/8″ × 10 3/8″. Pierpont Morgan Library, New York. (page 313)

FIG. 11-16 Restored plan of the Palatine Chapel of Charlemagne, Aachen, Germany, 792–805. (page 313)

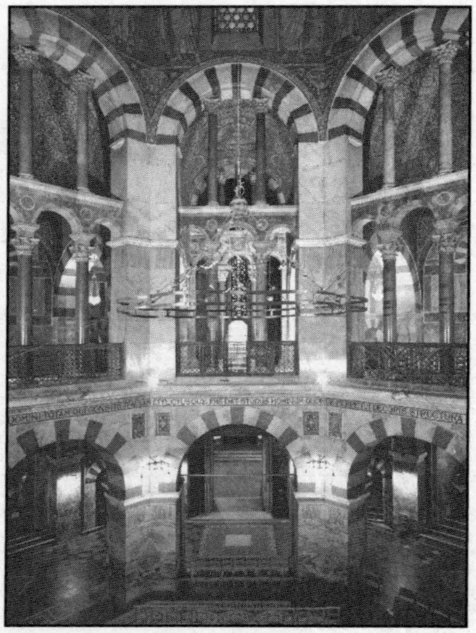

FIG. 11-17 Interior of the Palatine Chapel of Charlemagne, Aachen, Germany, 792–805. (page 313)

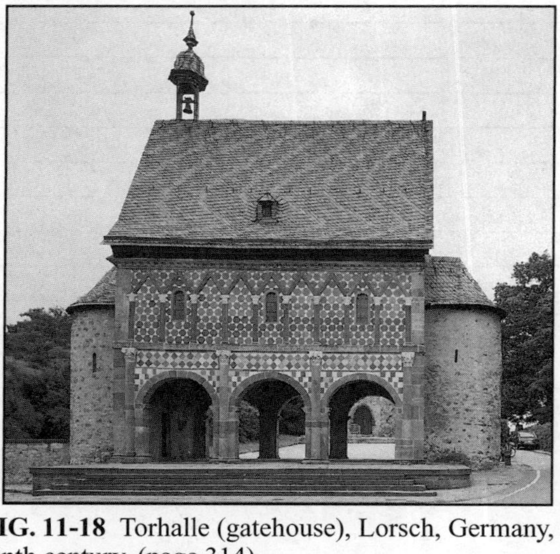

FIG. 11-18 Torhalle (gatehouse), Lorsch, Germany, ninth century. (page 314)

FIG. 11-19 Schematic plan for a monastery at Saint Gall, Switzerland, ca. 819. (Redrawn after a ninth-century manuscript; original in red ink on parchment, 2′ 4″ × 3′ 8 1/8″. Stiftsbibliothek, Saint Gall.) (page 315)

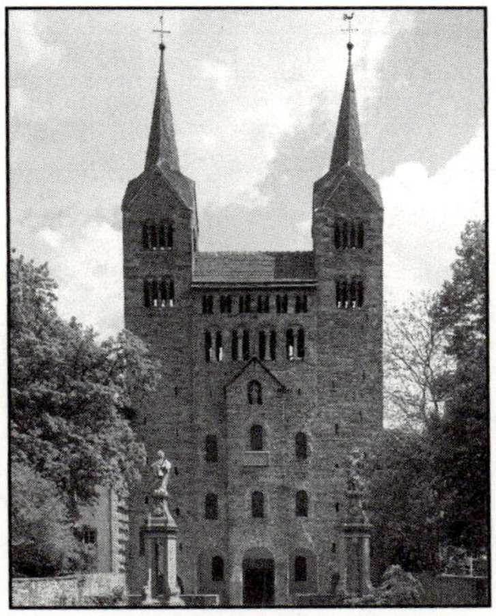

FIG. 11-20 Westwork of the abbey church, Corvey, Germany, 873–885. (page 316)

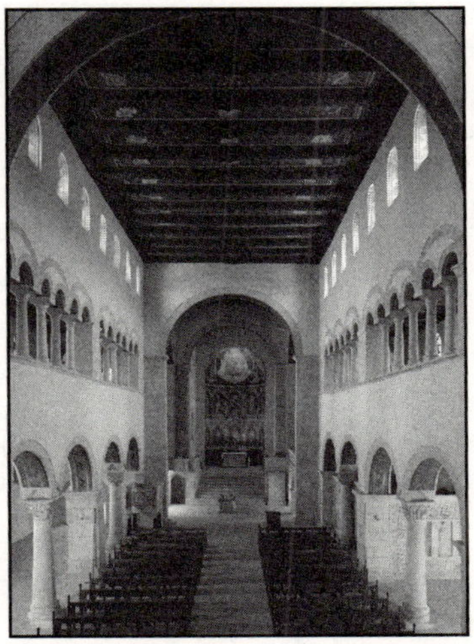

FIG. 11-21 Nave of the church of Saint Cyriakus, Gernrode, Germany, 961–973. (page 317)

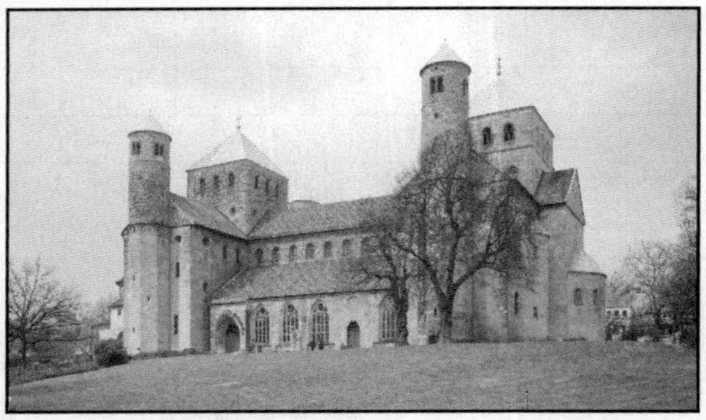

FIG. 11-22 Saint Michael's, Hildesheim, Germany, 1001–1031. (page 318)

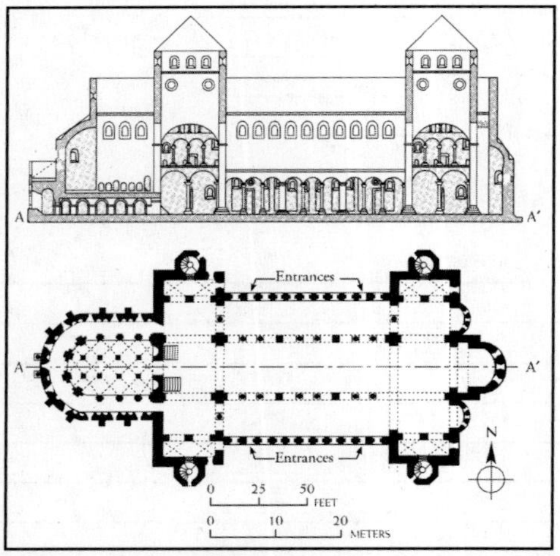

FIG. 11-23 Longitudinal section *(top)* and plan *(bottom)* of the abbey church of Saint Michael's, Hildesheim, Germany, 1001–1031. (page 318)

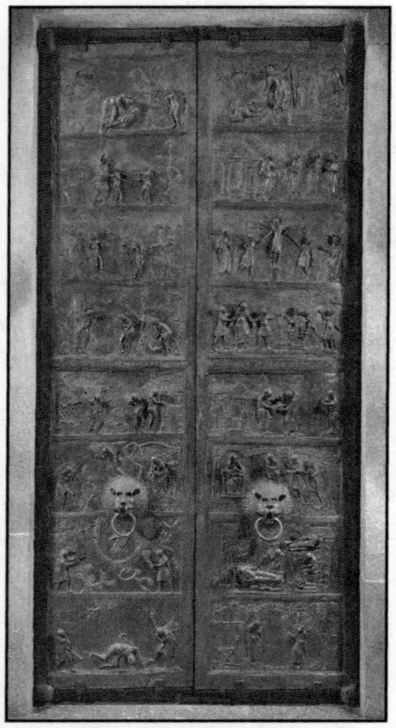

FIG. 11-24 Doors with relief panels (Genesis, left door; life of Christ, right door), commissioned by Bishop Bernward for Saint Michael's, Hildesheim, Germany, 1015. Bronze, 16′ 6″ high. (page 319)

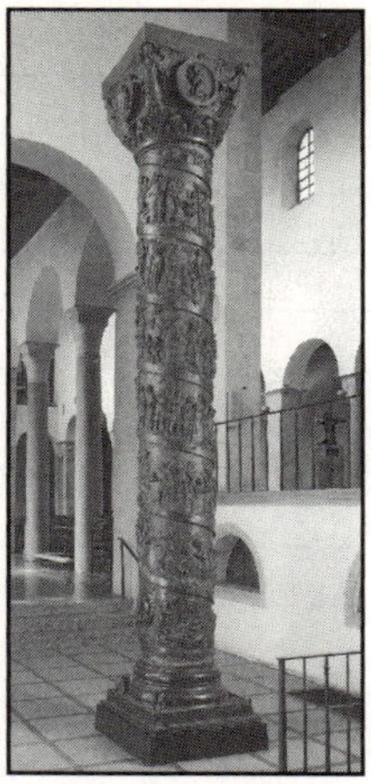

FIG. 11-25 Column with reliefs illustrating the life of Christ, commissioned by Bishop Bernward for Saint Michael's, Hildesheim, Germany, ca. 1015–1022. Bronze, 12′ 6″ tall. (page 320)

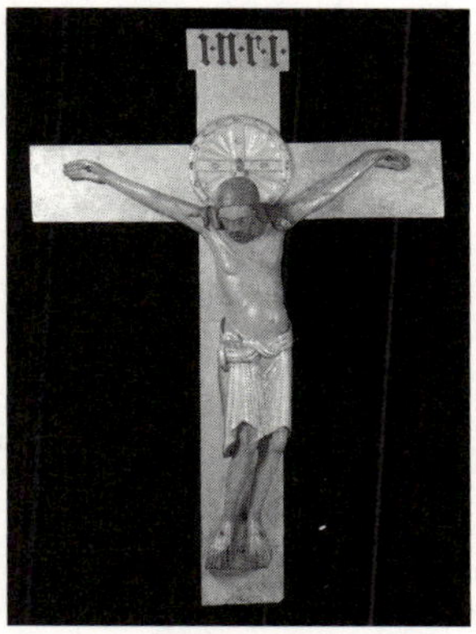

FIG. 11-26 Crucifix commissioned by Archbishop Gero for Cologne Cathedral, Cologne, Germany, ca. 970. Painted wood, height of figure 6′ 2″. Cathedral, Cologne. (page 321)

FIG. 11-27 Abbess Uta dedicating her codex to the Virgin, folio 2 recto of the *Uta Codex,* from Regensburg, Germany, ca. 1025. Tempera on parchment, approx. 9 5/8″ × 5 1/8″. Bayerische Staatsbibliothek, Munich. (page 322)

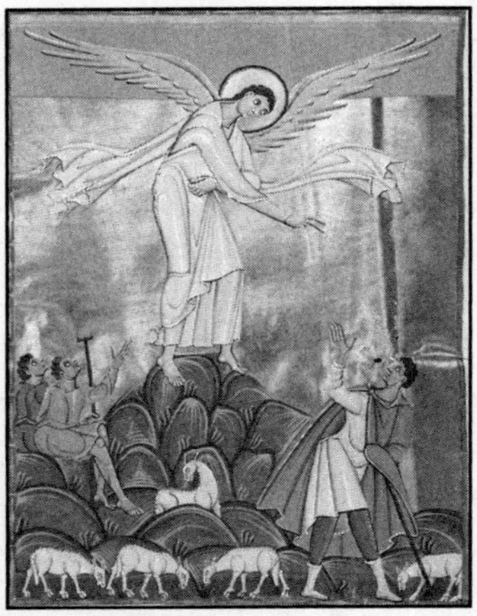

FIG. 11-28 Annunciation to the Shepherds, folio in the *Lectionary of Henry II,* from Reichenau, Germany, 1002–1014. Tempera on vellum, approx. 1′ 5″ × 1′ 1″. Bayerische Staatsbibliothek, Munich. (page 323)

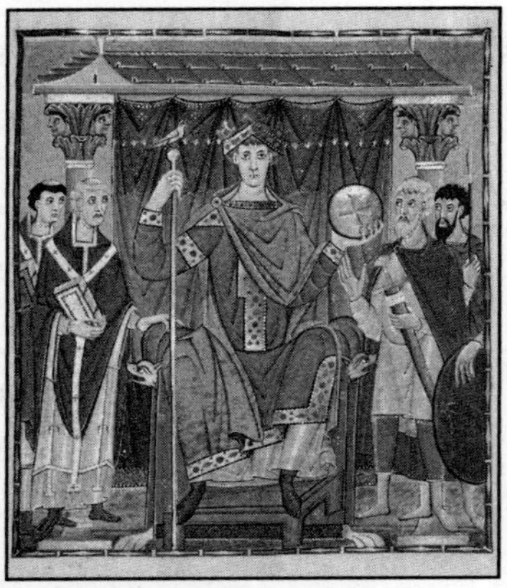

FIG. 11-29 Otto III enthroned, folio 24 recto of the *Gospel Book of Otto III,* from Reichenau, Germany, 997–1000. Tempera on vellum, 1′ 1″ × 9 3/8″. Bayerische Staatsbibliothek, Munich. (page 324)

Chapter 12

The Age of Pilgrimages:
Romanesque Art

Goals

- Understand the term "Romanesque" in designating the artistic style of a historic period.
- Examine the need for large-scale pilgrimage churches, the growth of architecture, and urban centers.
- Understand the "millennial" and apocalyptic mood of the Romanesque era and their impact on artistic themes.
- Recognize differences and similarities in regional Romanesque architecture and artistic styles.
- Understand the narrative function of the human figure in Romanesque sculpture.

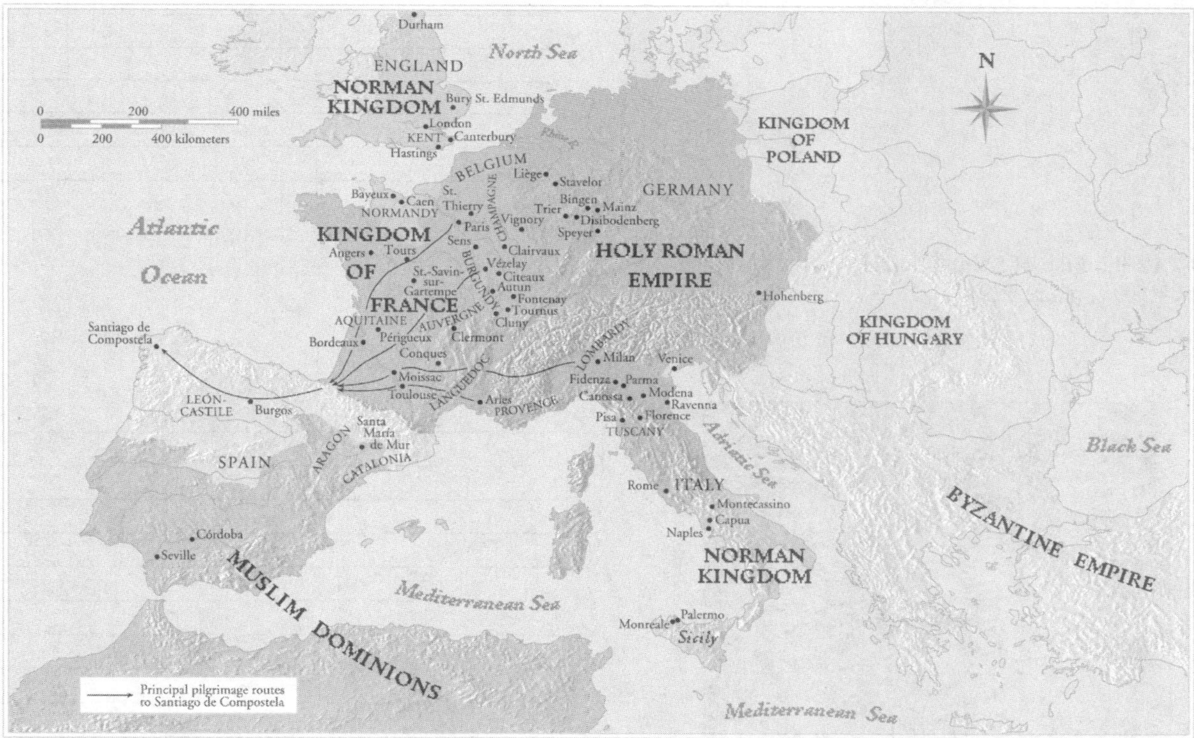

FIG. 12-01 Interior of Saint-Étienne, Vignory, France, 1050–1057. (page 329)

FIG. 12-02 Plan of Saint-Étienne, Vignory, France, 1050–1057. (page 329)

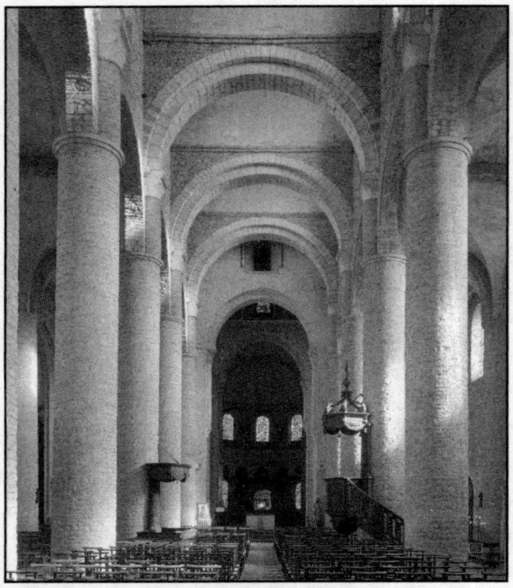

FIG. 12-03 Interior of Saint-Philibert, Tournus, France. Nave vaults, ca. 1060. (page 330)

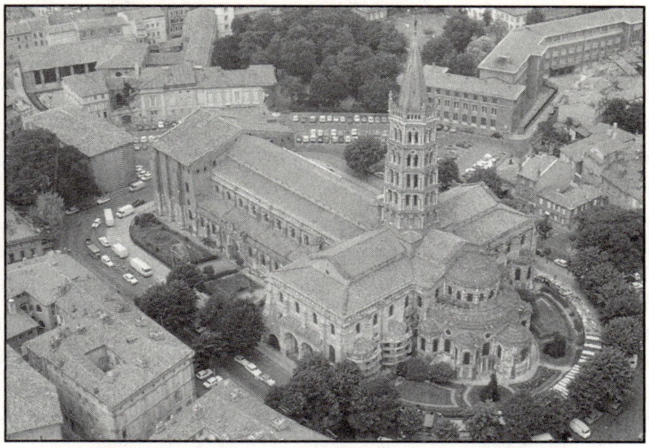

FIG. 12-04 Aerial view of Saint-Sernin (from the southeast), Toulouse, France, ca. 1070–1120. (page 332)

FIG. 12-05 Plan of Saint-Sernin, Toulouse, France, ca. 1070–1120 (after Kenneth John Conant). (page 332)

FIG. 12-06 Interior of Saint-Sernin, Toulouse, France, ca. 1070–1120. (page 333)

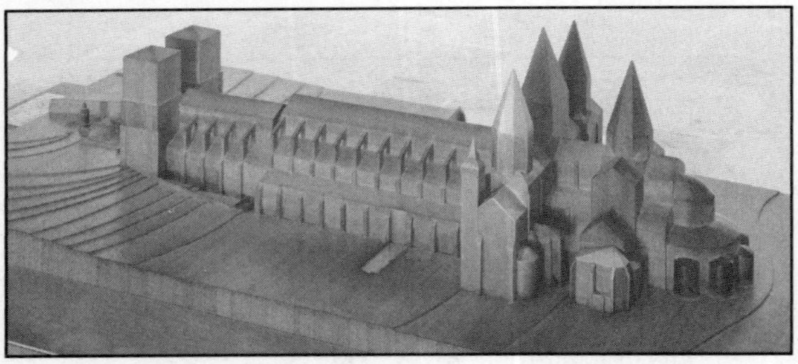

FIG. 12-07 Model of the third abbey church ("Cluny III"), Cluny, France, 1088–1130. Musée du Farinier, Cluny. (page 333)

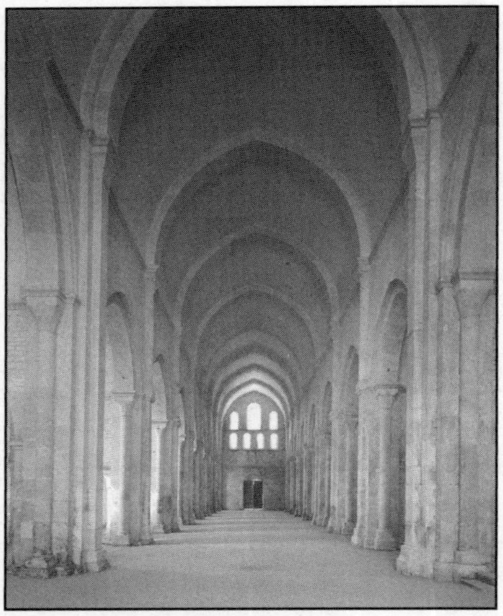

FIG. 12-08 Interior of abbey church of Notre-Dame, Fontenay, France, 1139–1147. (page 334)

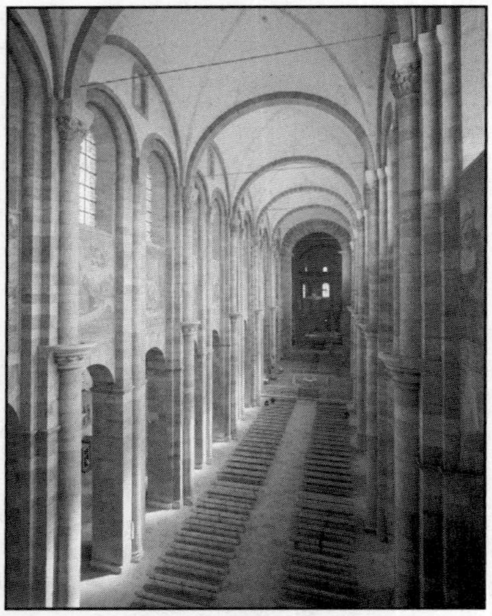

FIG. 12-09 Interior of Speyer Cathedral, Speyer, Germany, begun 1030; nave vaults, ca. 1082–1106. (page 334)

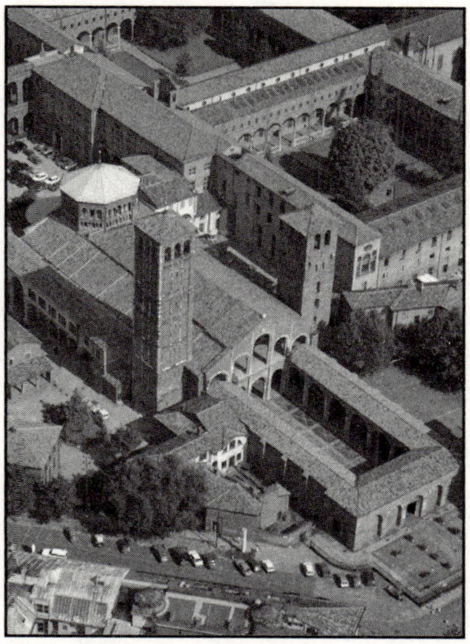

FIG. 12-10 Aerial view of Sant'Ambrogio, Milan, Italy, late eleventh to early twelfth century. (page 335)

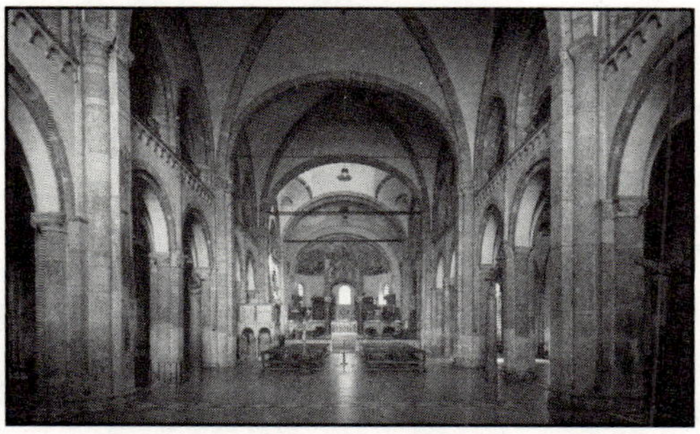

FIG. 12-11 Interior of Sant'Ambrogio, Milan, Italy, late eleventh to early twelfth century. (page 335)

FIG. 12-12 West facade of Saint-Étienne, Caen, France, begun 1067. (page 336)

FIG. 12-13 Interior of Saint-Étienne, Caen, France, vaulted ca. 1115–1120. (page 336)

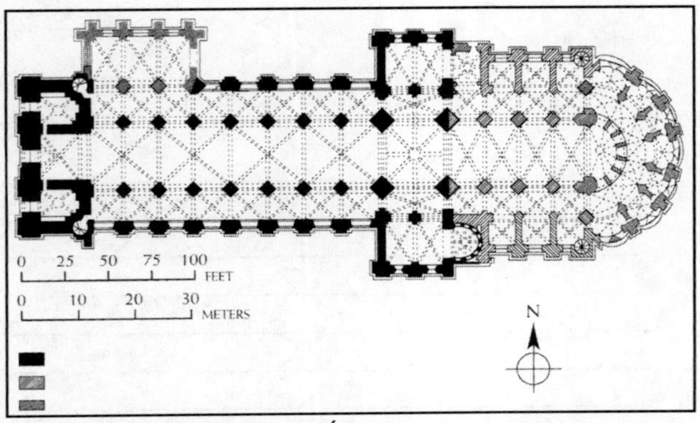

FIG. 12-14 Plan of Saint-Étienne, Caen, France. (page 336)

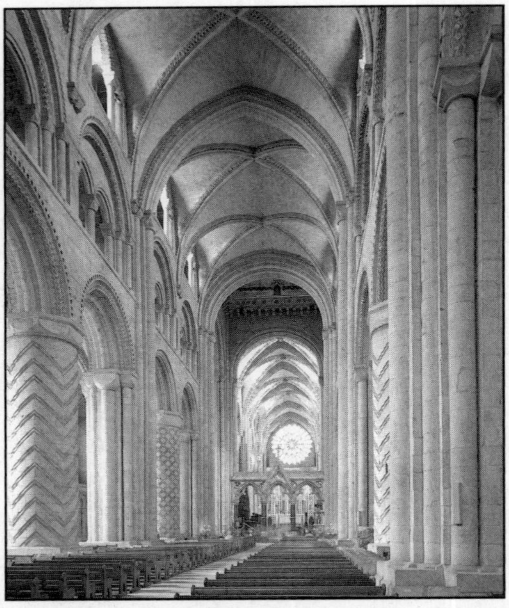

FIG. 12-15 Interior of Durham Cathedral, Durham, England, begun ca. 1093. (page 337)

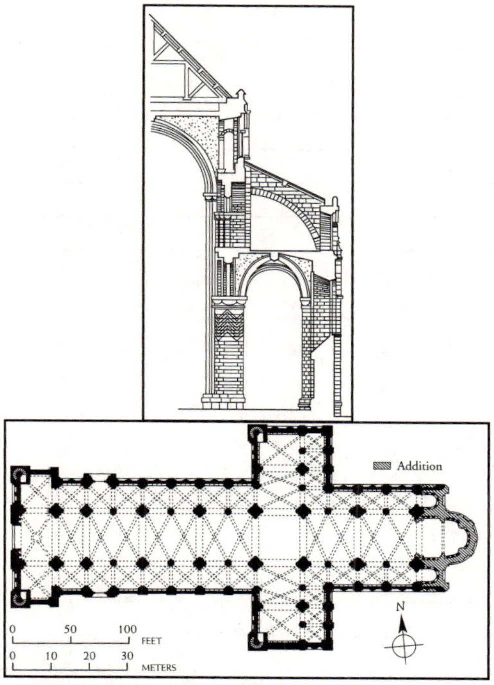

FIG. 12-16 Lateral section *(top)* and plan *(bottom)* of Durham Cathedral, Durham, England (after Kenneth John Conant). (page 337)

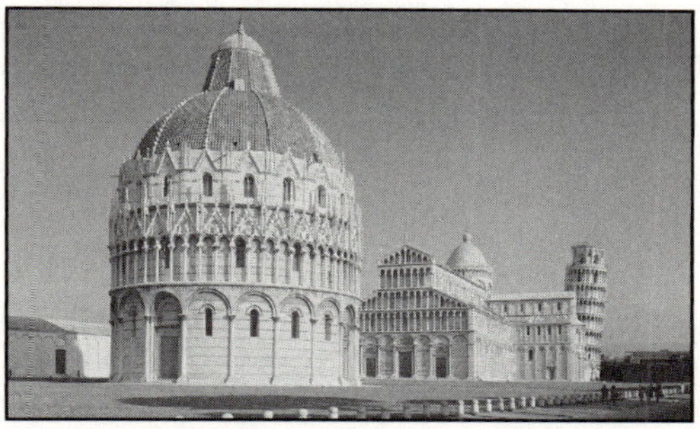

FIG. 12-17 Cathedral complex, Pisa, Italy; cathedral begun 1063; baptistery begun 1153; campanile begun 1174. (page 338)

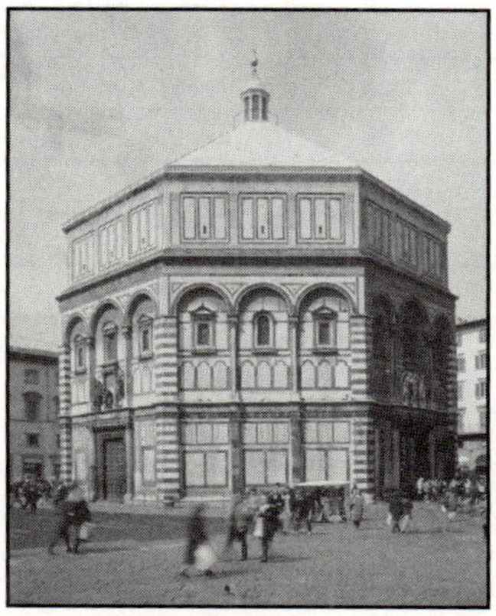

FIG. 12-18 Baptistery of San Giovanni, Florence, Italy, dedicated 1059. (page 339)

FIG. 12-19 Interior of San Miniato al Monte, Florence, Italy, ca. 1062–1090. (page 339)

FIG. 12-20 Cloister of Saint-Pierre, Moissac, France, ca. 1100–1115. Limestone with marble relief panels, piers approx. 6′ high. (page 340)

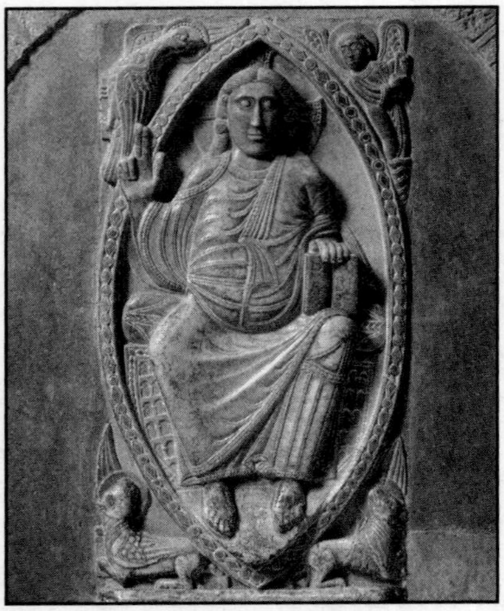

FIG. 12-21 BERNARDUS GELDUINUS, Christ in Majesty, relief in the ambulatory of Saint-Sernin, Toulouse, France, ca. 1096. Marble, 4′ 2″ high. (page 341)

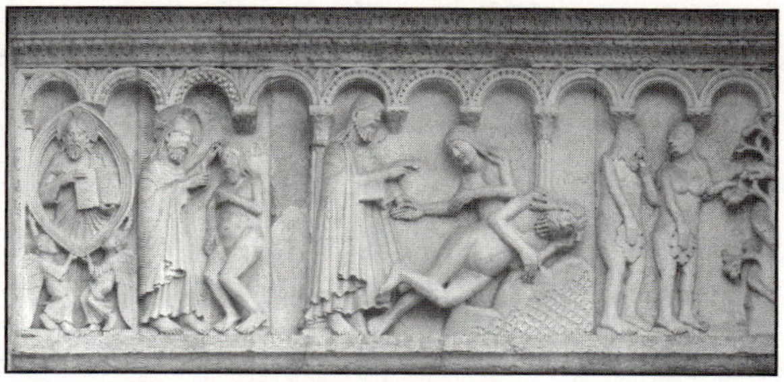

FIG. 12-22 WILIGELMO, creation and temptation of Adam and Eve, frieze on the west facade, Modena Cathedral, Modena, Italy, ca. 1110. Marble, approx. 3′ high. (page 342)

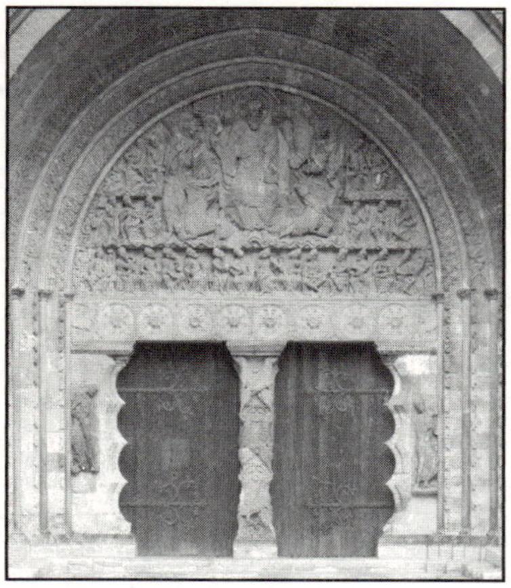

FIG. 12-23 South portal of Saint-Pierre, Moissac, France, ca. 1115–1135. (page 342)

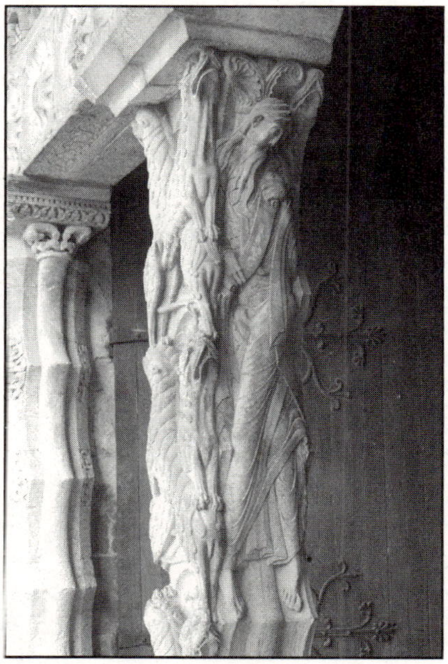

FIG. 12-24 Lions and Old Testament prophet (Jeremiah or Isaiah?), from the trumeau of the south portal of Saint-Pierre, Moissac, France, ca. 1115–1130. Marble, approx. life-size. (page 344)

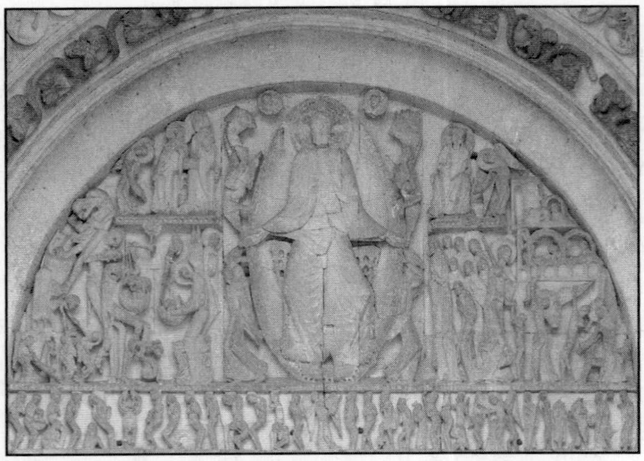

FIG. 12-25 GISLEBERTUS, Last Judgment, west tympanum of Saint-Lazare, Autun, France, ca. 1120–1135. Marble, approx. 21′ wide at base. (page 344)

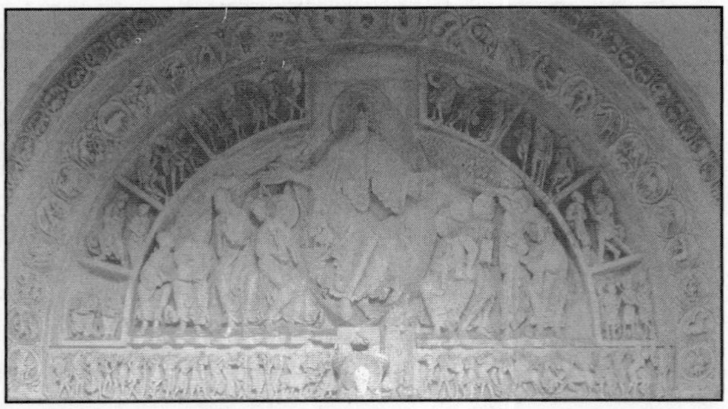

FIG. 12-26 Ascension of Christ and Mission of the Apostles, tympanum of the center portal of the narthex of La Madeleine, Vézelay, France, 1120–1132. (page 345)

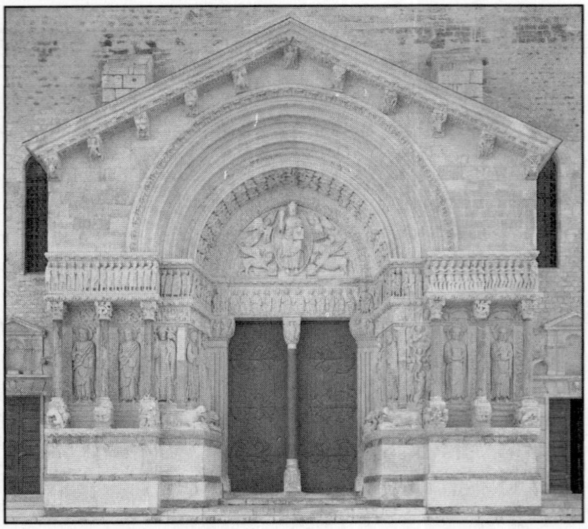

FIG. 12-27 Central portal, west facade, Saint-Trophîme, Arles, France, mid-12th century. (page 346)

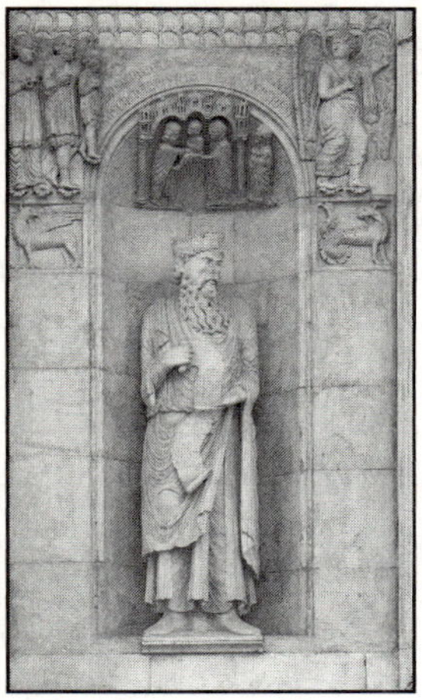

FIG. 12-28 BENEDETTO ANTELAMI, King David, statue in a niche on the west facade of Fidenza Cathedral, Fidenza, Italy, ca. 1180–1190. Marble, approx. life-size. (page 347)

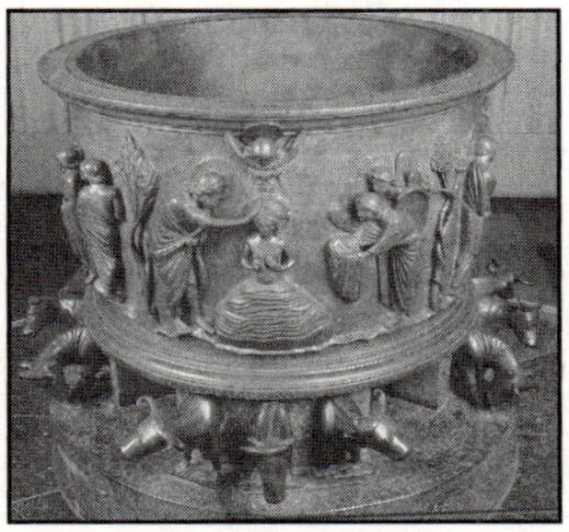

FIG. 12-29 RAINER OF HUY, Baptism of Christ, baptismal font from Notre-Dame-des-Fonts, Liège, Belgium, 1107–1118. Bronze, 2′ 1″ high. Saint-Barthélémy, Liège. (page 347)

FIG. 12-30 Virgin and Child *(Morgan Madonna)*, from the Auvergne, France, second half of 12th century. Painted wood, 2′ 7″ high. Metropolitan Museum of Art, New York (gift of J. Pierpont Morgan, 1916). (page 348)

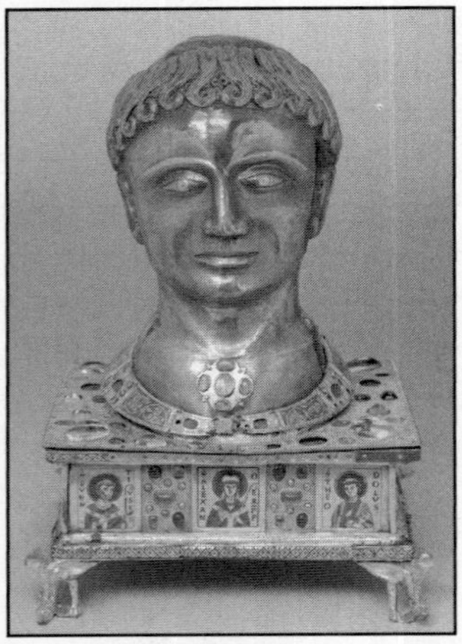

FIG. 12-31 Head reliquary of Saint Alexander, from Stavelot Abbey, Belgium, 1145. Silver repoussé (partly gilt), gilt bronze, gems, pearls, and enamel, approx. 1′ 5 1/2″ high. Musées Royaux d'Art et d'Histoire, Brussels. (page 349)

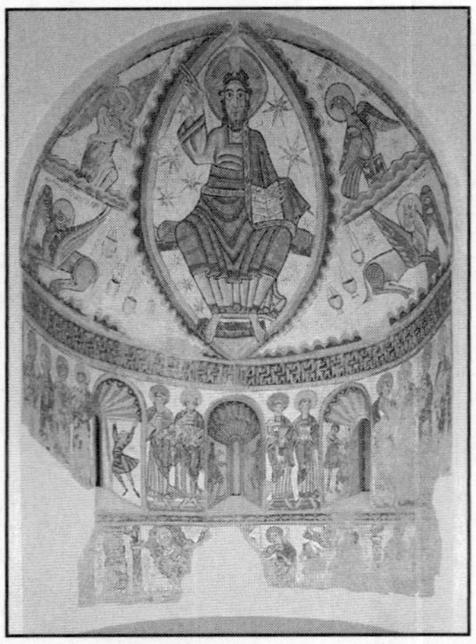

FIG. 12-32 Christ in Majesty, apse fresco from Santa María de Mur, near Lérida, Spain, mid-twelfth century. 24′ × 22′. Museum of Fine Arts, Boston. (page 350)

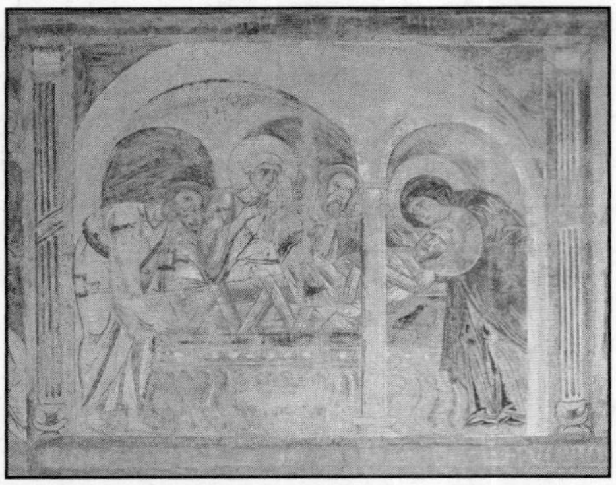

FIG. 12-33 Entombment of Christ, fresco above the nave arcade, Sant'Angelo in Formis, near Capua, Italy, ca. 1085. (page 351)

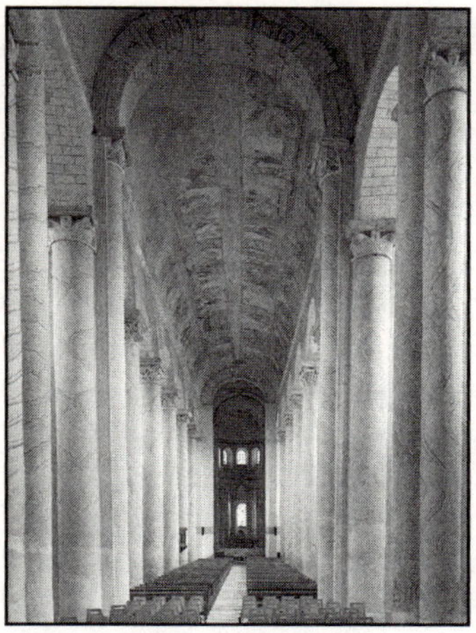

FIG. 12-34 Nave of the abbey church, Saint-Savin-sur-Gartempe, France. Painted barrel vault, ca. 1100. (page 351)

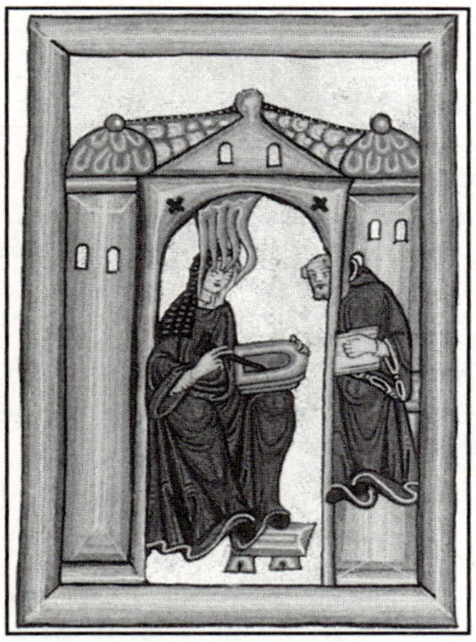

FIG. 12-35 The vision of Hildegard of Bingen, detail of a facsimile of a lost folio in the *Scivias* by Hildegard of Bingen, from Trier or Bingen, Germany, ca. 1150–1179. Formerly in Hessische Landesbibliothek, Wiesbaden. (page 352)

FIG. 12-36 Initial *R* with knight fighting a dragon, folio 4 verso of the *Moralia in Job,* from Cîteaux, France, ca. 1115–1125. Ink and tempera on vellum, 1′ 1 3/4″ × 9 1/4″. Bibliothèque Municipale, Dijon. (page 352)

FIG. 12-37 Master Hugo, Moses expounding the Law, folio 94 recto of the *Bury Bible,* from Bury Saint Edmunds, England, ca. 1135. Ink and tempera on vellum, approx. 1′ 8″ × 1′ 2″. Corpus Christi College, Cambridge. (page 354)

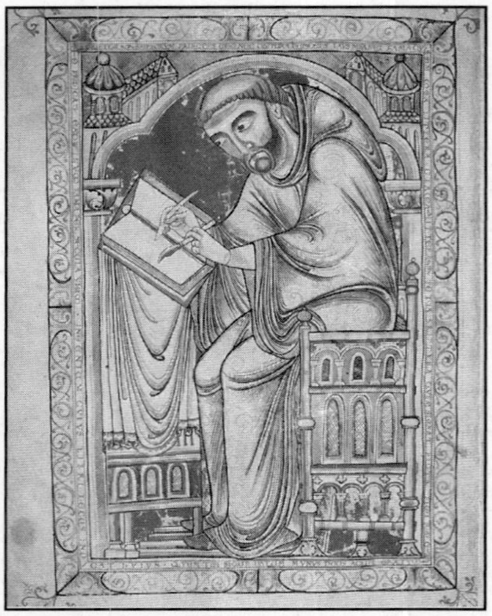

FIG. 12-38 Eadwine the Scribe(?), Eadwine the Scribe at work, folio 283 verso of the *Eadwine Psalter,* ca. 1160–1170. Ink and tempera on vellum. Trinity College, Cambridge. (page 354)

FIG. 12-39 Funeral procession to Westminster Abbey, detail of the *Bayeux Tapestry,* from Bayeux Cathedral, Bayeux, France, ca. 1070–1080. Embroidered wool on linen, 1′ 8″ high (entire length of fabric 229′ 8″). Centre Guillaume le Conquérant, Bayeux. (page 355)

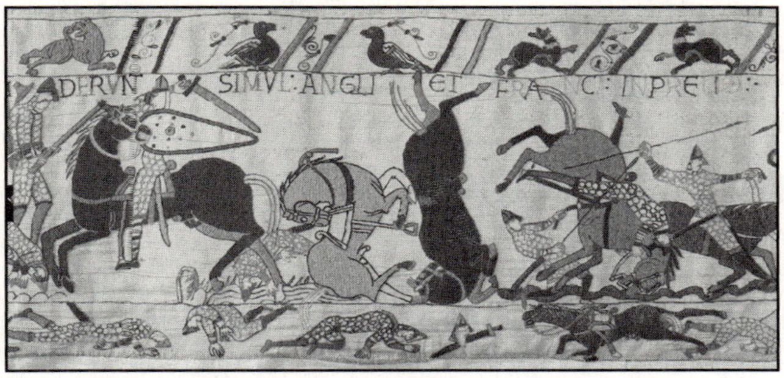

FIG. 12-40 Battle of Hastings, detail of the *Bayeux Tapestry,* from Bayeux Cathedral, Bayeux, France, ca. 1070–1080. Embroidered wool on linen, 1′ 8″ high (entire length of fabric 229′ 8″). Centre Guillaume le Conquérant, Bayeux. (page 355)

Chapter 13

The Age of Great Cathedrals:
Gothic Art

Goals

- Understand the origins and spread of the Gothic style.
- Understand the changes in European religious concepts that made Gothic art and architecture possible.
- Understand the art, architecture, and architectural decoration of the Gothic style in France.
- Examine the variations of the Gothic Style in England, Germany, and Italy.
- Examine the development of sculpture, book arts, and other media in the Gothic era.
- Name and identify important Gothic cathedrals.

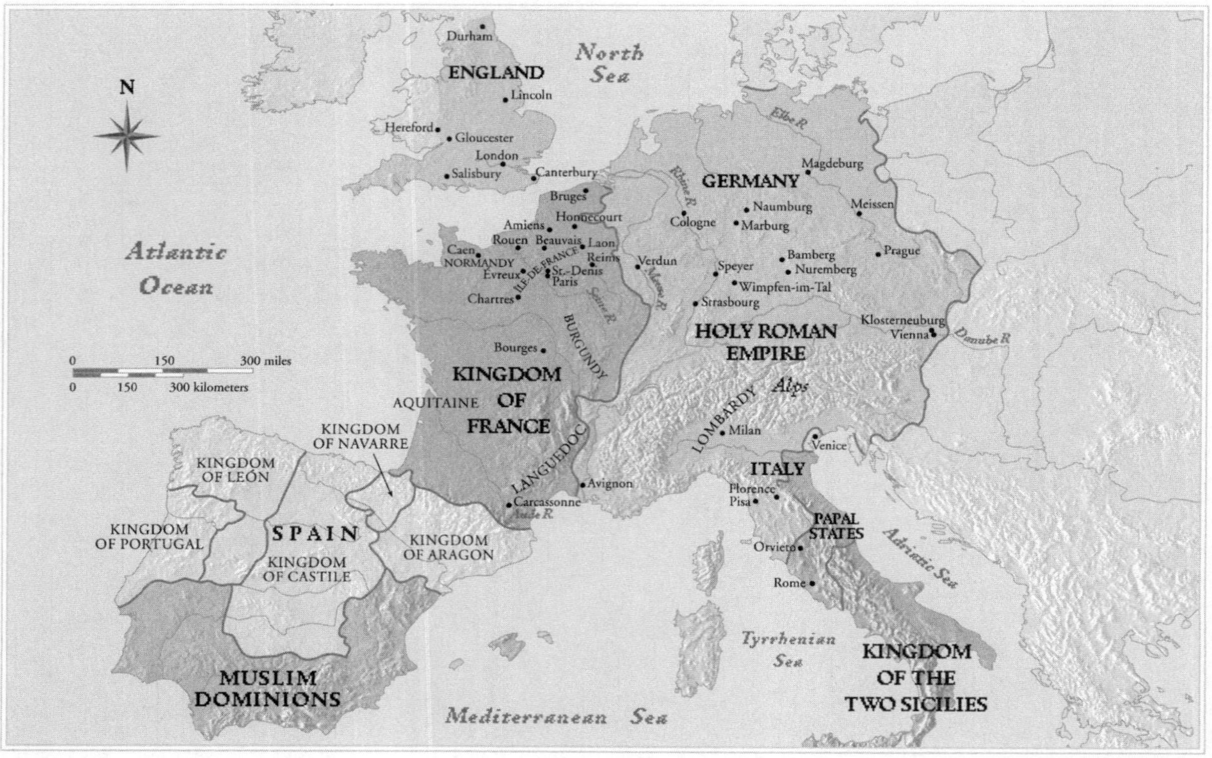

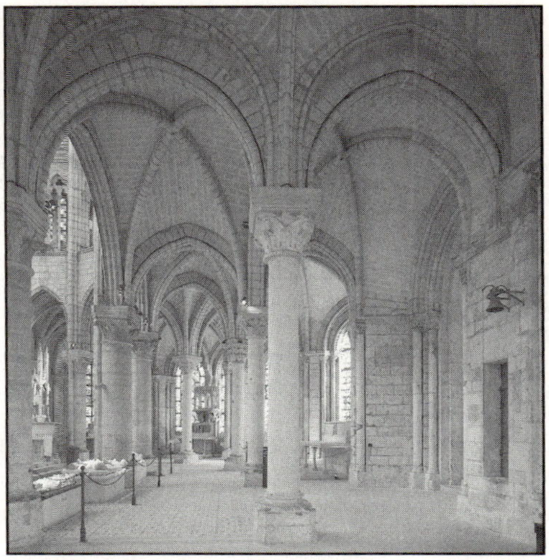

FIG. 13-01 Ambulatory and radiating chapels, abbey church, Saint-Denis, France, 1140–1144. (page 361)

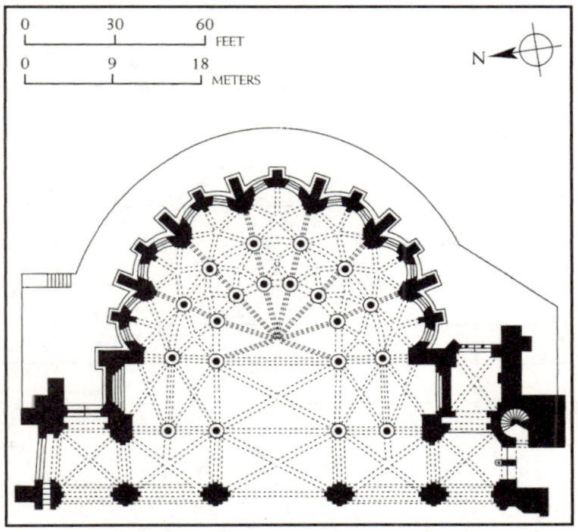

FIG. 13-02 Plan of the east end, abbey church, Saint-Denis, France, 1140–1144 (after Sumner Crosby). (page 361)

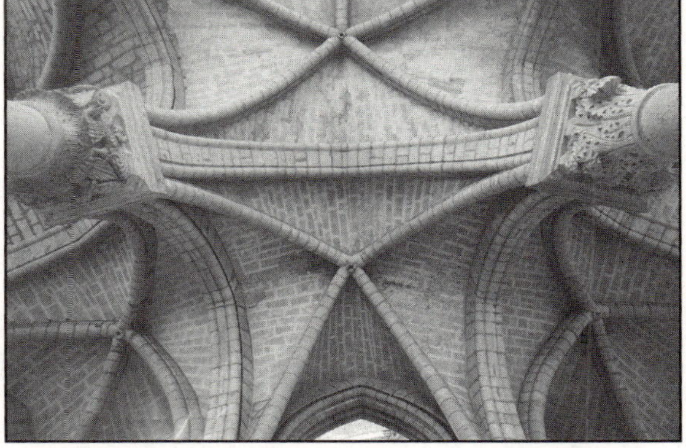

FIG. 13-03 Vaults of the ambulatory and radiating chapels of the choir, abbey church, Saint-Denis, France, 1140–1144. (page 362)

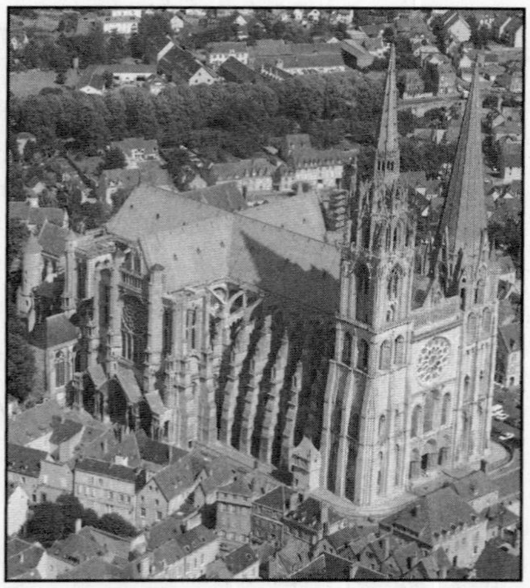

FIG. 13-04 Aerial view of Chartres Cathedral (from the northwest), Chartres, France, begun 1134; rebuilt after 1194. (page 363)

FIG. 13-05 Royal Portal, west facade, Chartres Cathedral, Chartres, France, ca. 1145–1155. (page 364)

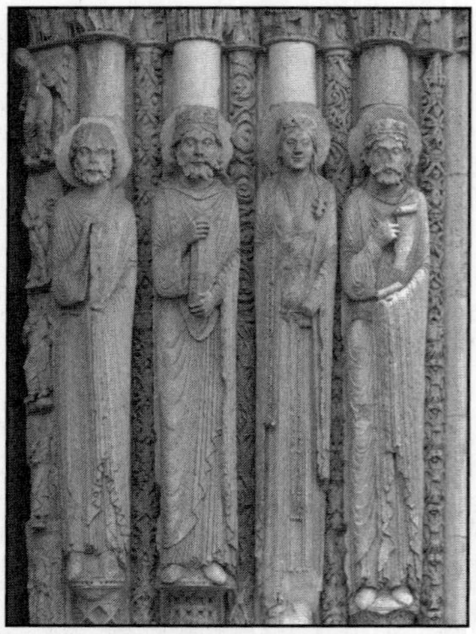

FIG. 13-06 Old Testament kings and queen, jamb statues, central doorway of Royal Portal, Chartres Cathedral, Chartres, France, ca. 1145–1155. (page 364)

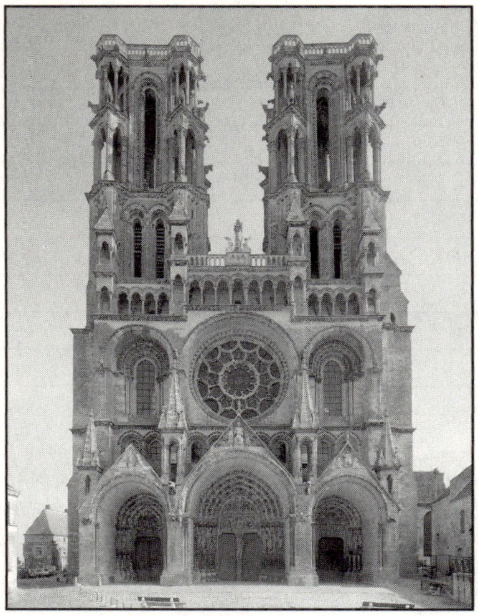

FIG. 13-07 West facade of Laon Cathedral, Laon, France, begun ca. 1190. (page 365)

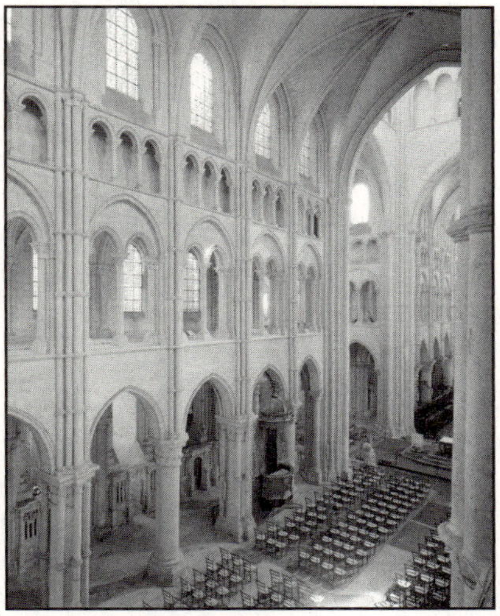

FIG. 13-08 Interior of Laon Cathedral (view facing northeast), Laon, France, begun ca. 1190. (page 365)

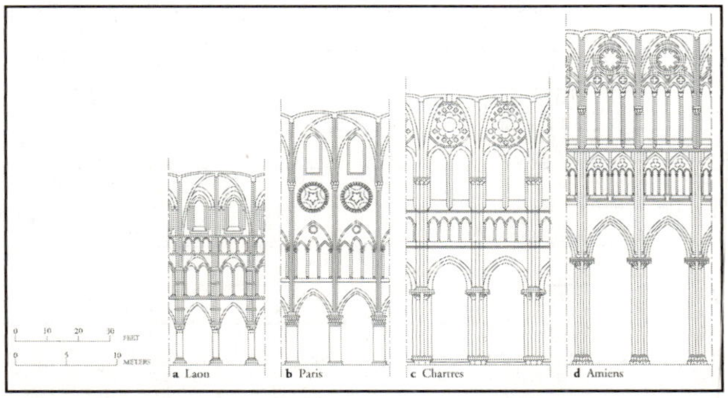

FIG. 13-09 Nave elevations of four French Gothic cathedrals at the same scale (after Louis Grodecki). (page 366)

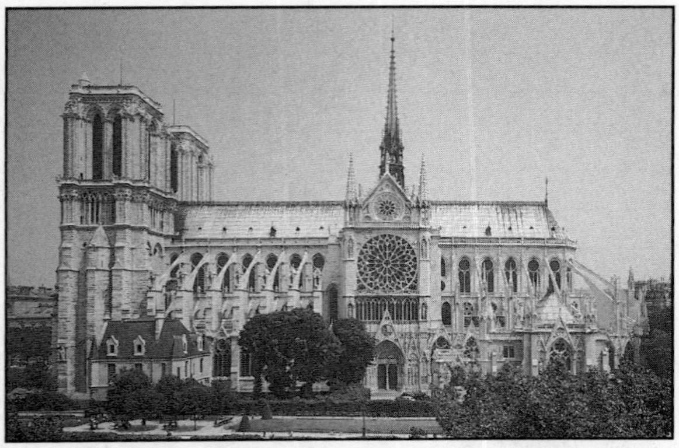

FIG. 13-10 Notre-Dame (view from the south), Paris, France, begun 1163; nave and flying buttresses, ca. 1180–1200; remodeled after 1225. (page 366)

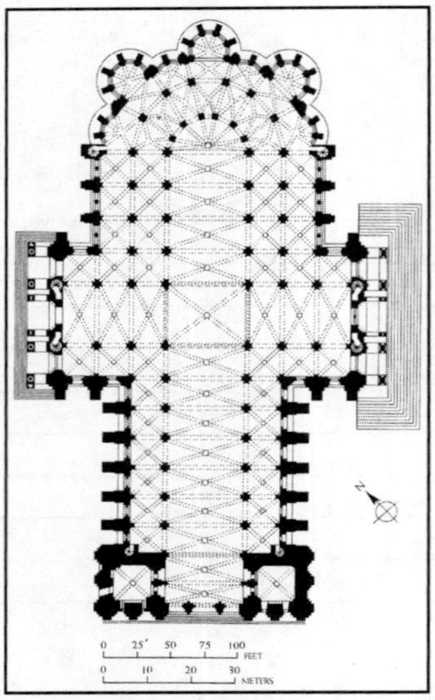

FIG. 13-11 Plan of Chartres Cathedral, Chartres, France, as rebuilt after 1194 (after Paul Frankl). (page 369)

FIG. 13-12 Interior of Chartres Cathedral (view facing east), Chartres, France, begun 1194. (page 369)

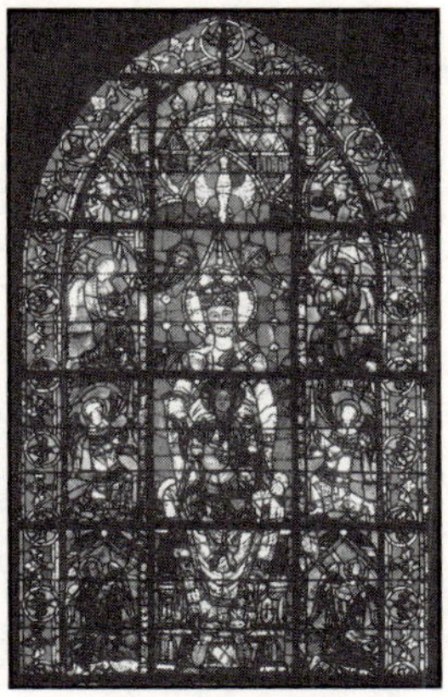

FIG. 13-13 Virgin and Child and angels *(Notre Dame de la Belle Verrière),* window in the choir of Chartres Cathedral, Chartres, France, ca. 1170, with 13th-century side panels. Stained glass, 16′ × 7′ × 8″. (page 370)

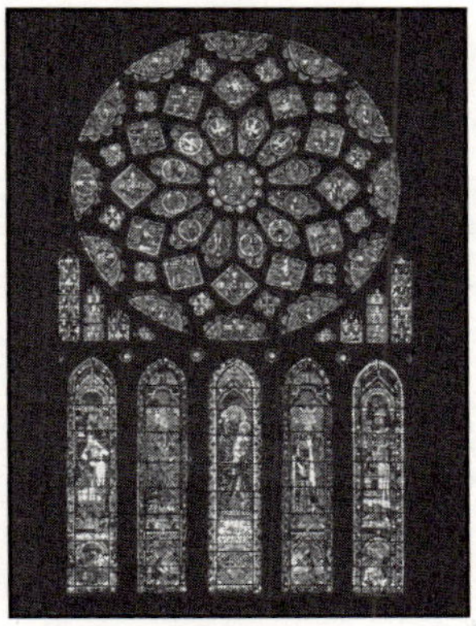

FIG. 13-14 Rose window and lancets, north transept, Chartres Cathedral, Chartres, France, ca. 1220. Stained glass, rose window approx. 43′ in diameter. (page 371)

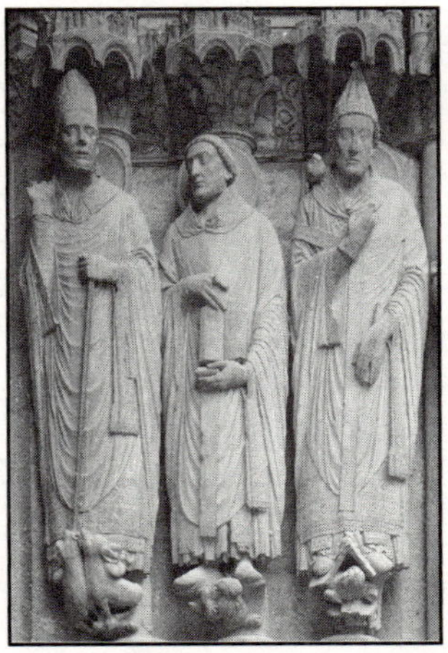

FIG. 13-15 Saints Martin, Jerome, and Gregory, jamb statues, Porch of the Confessors (right doorway), south transept, Chartres Cathedral, Chartres, France, ca. 1220–1230. (page 373)

FIG. 13-16 Saint Theodore, jamb statue, Porch of the Martyrs (left doorway), south transept, Chartres Cathedral, Chartres, France, ca. 1230. (page 373)

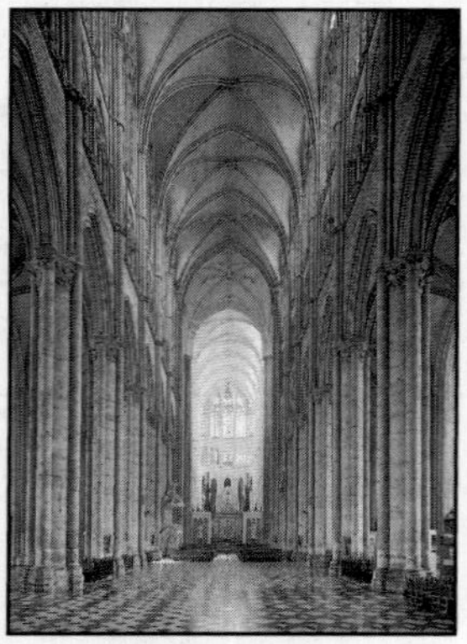

FIG. 13-17 ROBERT DE LUZARCHES, THOMAS DE CORMONT, and RENAUD DE CORMONT, interior of Amiens Cathedral (view facing east), Amiens, France, begun 1220. (page 374)

FIG. 13-18 ROBERT DE LUZARCHES, THOMAS DE CORMONT, and RENAUD DE CORMONT, vaults, clerestory, and triforium of the choir of Amiens Cathedral, Amiens, France, begun 1220. (page 374)

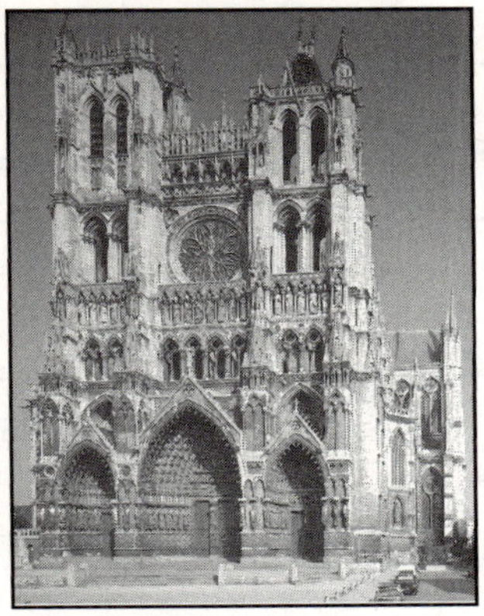

FIG. 13-19 ROBERT DE LUZARCHES, THOMAS DE CORMONT, and RENAUD DE CORMONT, west facade of Amiens Cathedral, Amiens, France, begun 1220. (page 375)

FIG. 13-20 Christ *(Beau Dieu),* trumeau statue of central doorway, west facade, Amiens Cathedral, Amiens, France, ca. 1220–1235. (page 375)

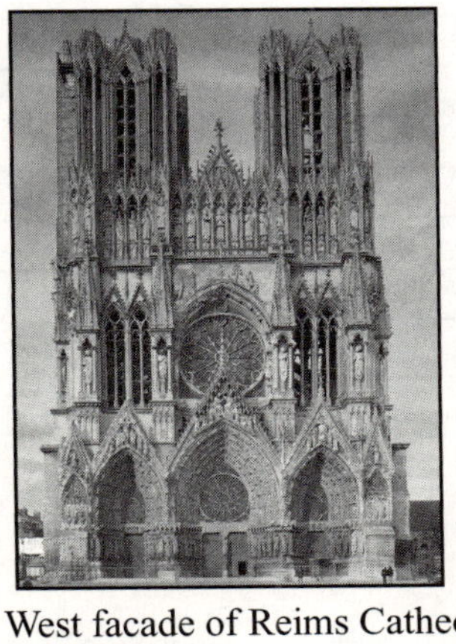

FIG. 13-21 West facade of Reims Cathedral, Reims, France, ca. 1225–1290. (page 376)

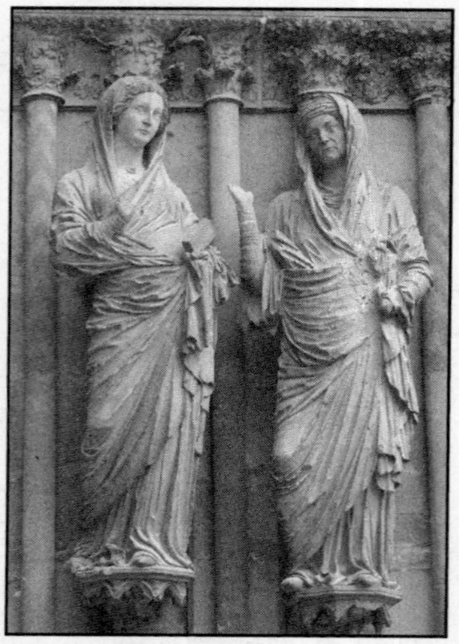

FIG. 13-22 Visitation, jamb statues of central doorway, west facade, Reims Cathedral, Reims, France, ca. 1230. (page 377)

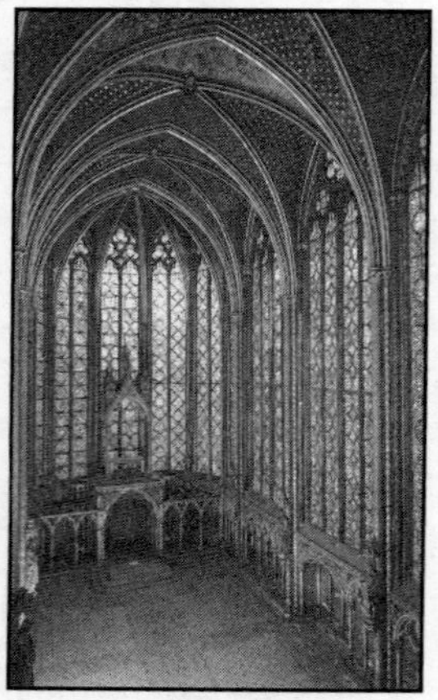

FIG. 13-23 Interior of the upper chapel, Sainte-Chapelle, Paris, France, 1243–1248. (page 378)

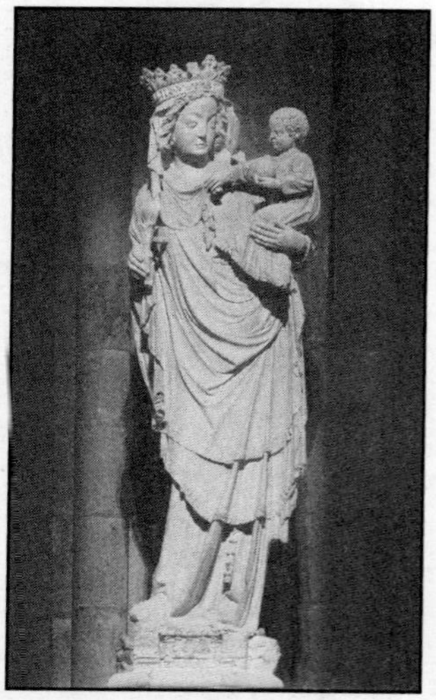

FIG. 13-24 Virgin and Child *(Virgin of Paris),* Notre-Dame, Paris, France, early 14th century. (page 378)

FIG. 13-25 West facade of Saint-Maclou, Rouen, France, ca. 1500–1514. (page 379)

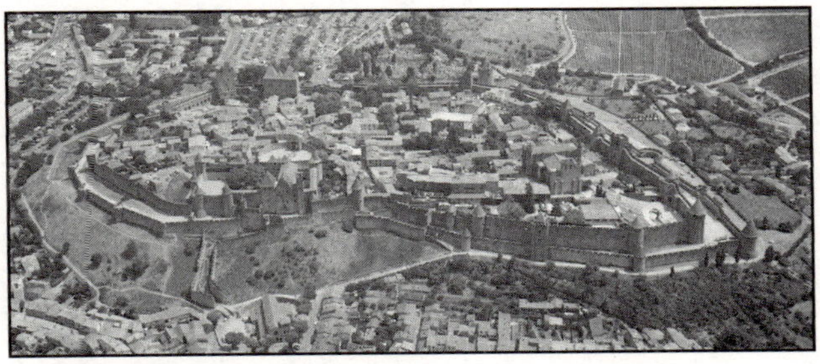

FIG. 13-26 Aerial view of the fortified town of Carcassonne, France. Bastions and towers, twelfth–thirteenth centuries, restored by EUGÈNE VIOLLET-LE-DUC in the nenteenth century. (page 380)

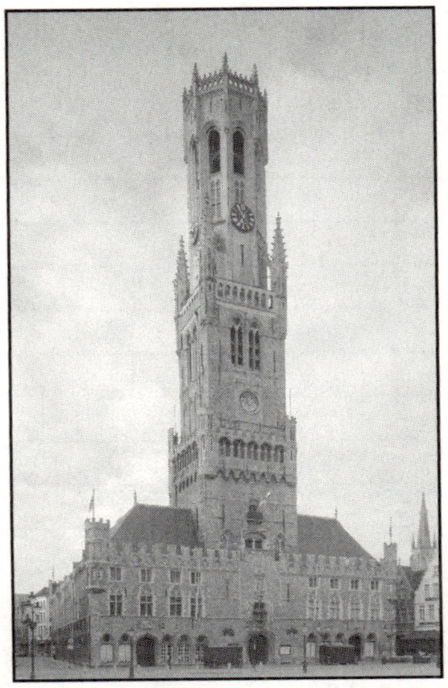

FIG. 13-27 Hall of the cloth guild, Bruges, Netherlands, begun 1230. (page 380)

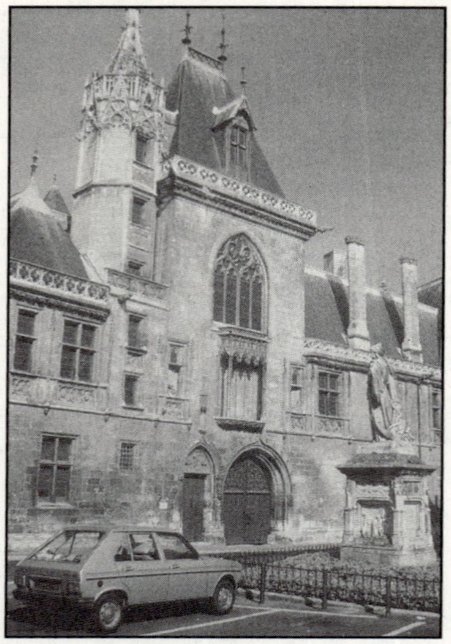

FIG. 13-28 House of Jacques Coeur, Bourges, France, 1443–1451. (page 381)

FIG. 13-29 VILLARD DE HONNECOURT, figures based on geometric shapes, folio 18 verso of a sketchbook, from Paris, France, ca. 1220–1235. Ink on vellum, 9 1/4″ × 6″ Bibliothèque Nationale, Paris. (page 381)

FIG. 13-30 God as architect of the world, folio 1 verso of a moralized Bible, from Paris, France, ca. 1220–1230. Ink, tempera, and gold leaf on vellum, 1′ 1 1/2″ × 8 1/4″. Österreichische National-bibliothek, Vienna. (page 382)

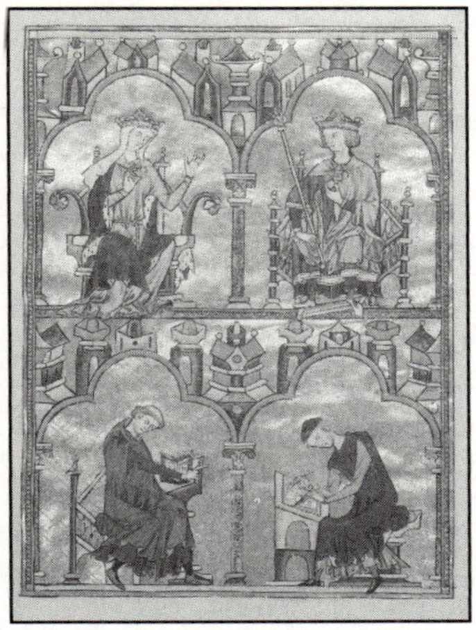

FIG. 13-31 Blanche of Castile, Louis IX, and two monks, dedication page (folio 8 recto) of a moralized Bible, from Paris, France, 1226–1234. Ink, tempera, and gold leaf on vellum, 1′ 3″ × 10 1/2″. Pierpont Morgan Library, New York. (page 383)

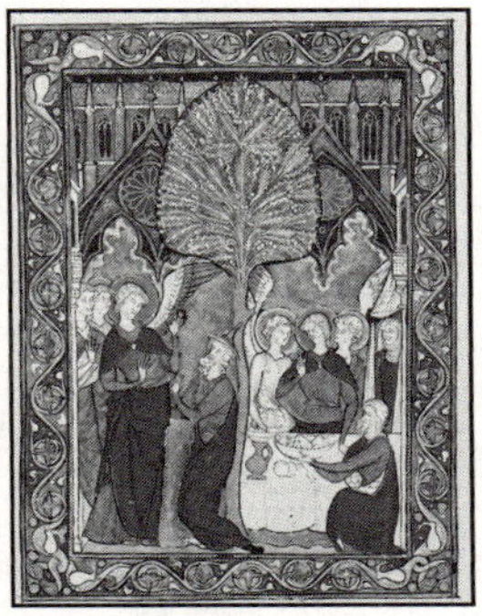

FIG. 13-32 Abraham and the three angels, folio 7 verso of the *Psalter of Saint Louis,* from Paris, France, 1253–1270. Ink, tempera, and gold leaf on vellum, 5″ × 3 1/2″. Bibliothèque Nationale, Paris. (page 383)

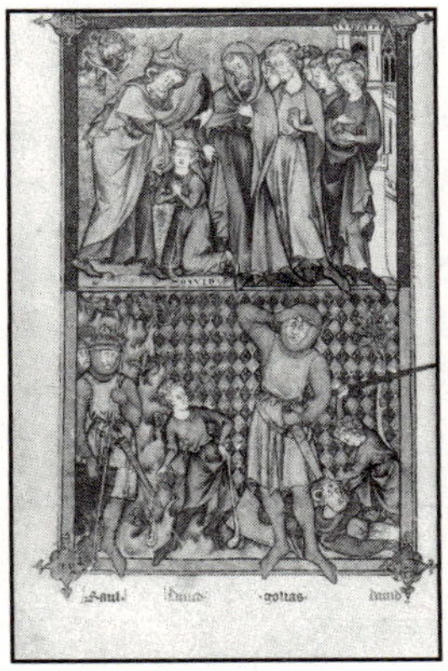

FIG. 13-33 MASTER HONORÉ, David anointed by Samuel and battle of David and Goliath, folio 7 verso of the *Breviary of Philippe le Bel,* from Paris, France, 1296. Ink and tempera on vellum, 7 7/8″ × 4 7/8″. Bibliothèque Nationale, Paris. (page 384)

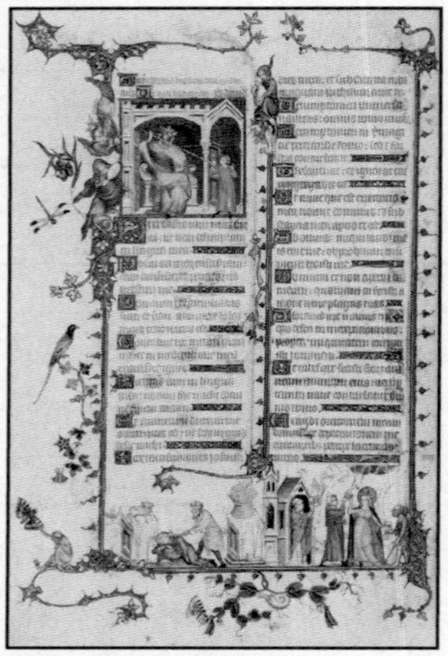

FIG. 13-34 JEAN PUCELLE, David before Saul, folio 24 verso of the *Belleville Breviary,* from Paris, France, ca. 1325. Ink and tempera on vellum, 9 1/2″ × 6 3/4″. Bibliothèque Nationale, Paris. (page 384)

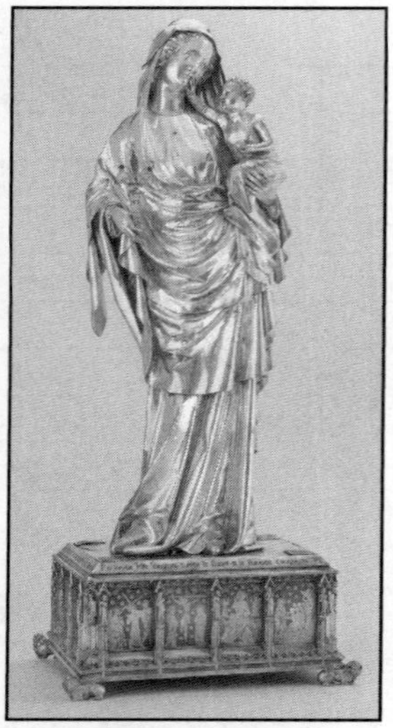

FIG. 13-35 *Virgin of Jeanne d'Evreux,* from the abbey church of Saint-Denis, France, 1339. Silver gilt and enamel, 2′ 3 1/2″ high. Louvre, Paris. (page 385)

FIG. 13-36 The Castle of Love and knights jousting, lid of a jewelry casket, from Paris, France, ca. 1330–1350. Ivory and iron, 4 1/2″ × 9 3/4″. Walters Art Museum, Baltimore. (page 386)

FIG. 13-37 Aerial view of Salisbury Cathedral, Salisbury, England, 1220–1258; west facade completed 1265; spire ca. 1320–1330. (page 387)

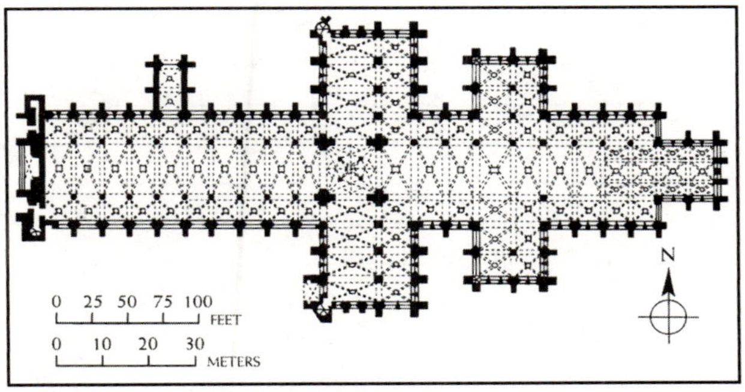

FIG. 13-38 Plan of Salisbury Cathedral, Salisbury, England, 1220–1258. (page 387)

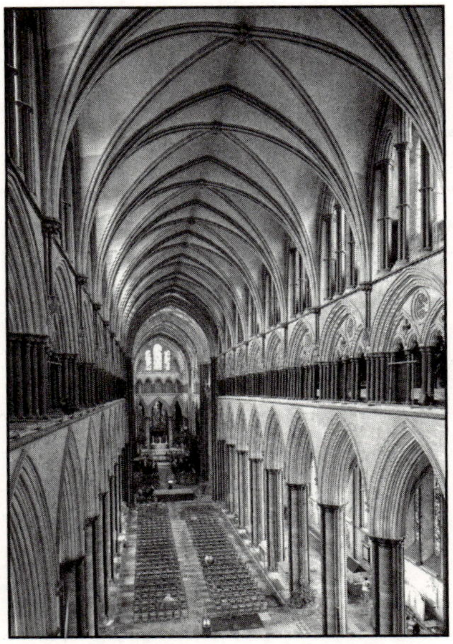

FIG. 13-39 Interior of Salisbury Cathedral (view facing east), Salisbury, England, 1220–1258. (page 387)

FIG. 13-40 Choir of Gloucester Cathedral (view facing east), Gloucester, England, 1332–1357. (page 388)

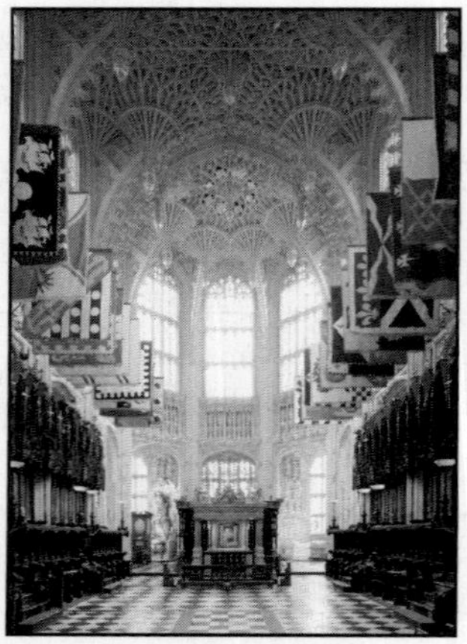

FIG. 13-41 ROBERT and WILLIAM VERTUE, Chapel of Henry VII, Westminster Abbey, London, England, 1503–1519. (page 388)

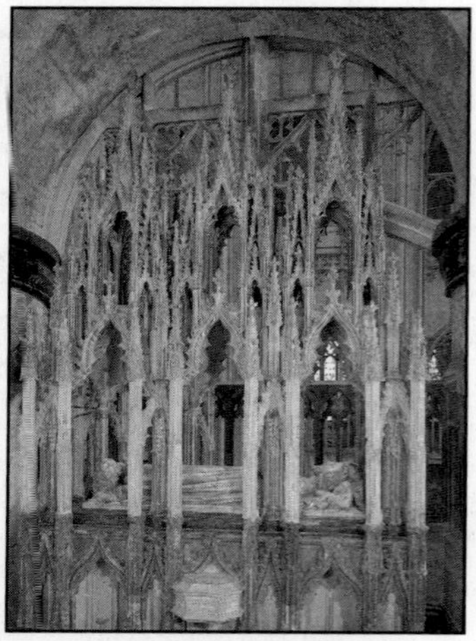

FIG. 13-42 Tomb of Edward II, Gloucester Cathedral, Gloucester, England, ca. 1330–1335. (page 389)

FIG. 13-43 RICHARD DE BELLO(?), *Mappa Mundi,* (world map) of Henry III, ca. 1277–1289. Tempera on vellum, approx. 5′ 2″ × 4′ 4″. Hereford Cathedral, Hereford, England. (page 389)

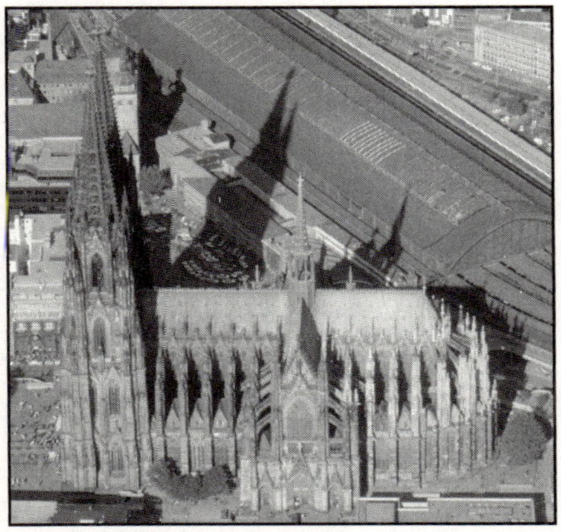

FIG. 13-44 GERHARD OF COLOGNE, aerial view of Cologne Cathedral (from the south), Cologne, Germany, begun 1248; nave, facade, and towers completed 1880. (page 390)

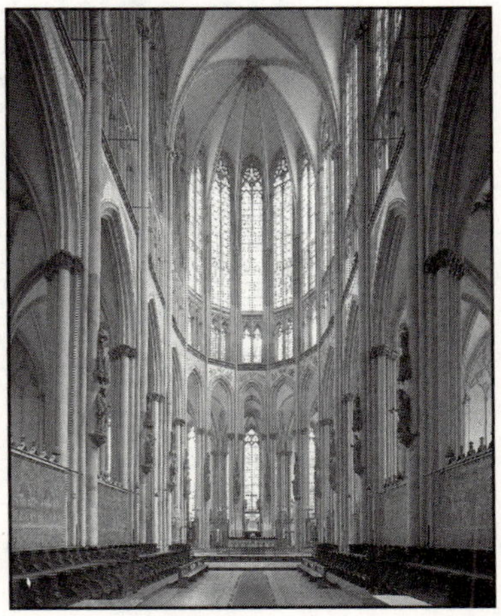

FIG. 13-45 GERHARD OF COLOGNE, Choir of Cologne Cathedral (view facing east), Cologne, Germany, completed 1322. (page 391)

FIG. 13-46 Saint Elizabeth (view facing northwest), Marburg, Germany, 1235–1283. (page 391)

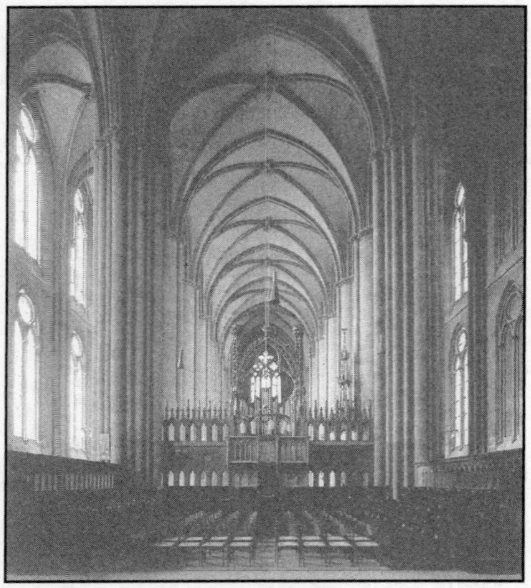

FIG. 13-47 Interior of Saint Elizabeth (view facing west), Marburg, Germany, 1235–1283. (page 391)

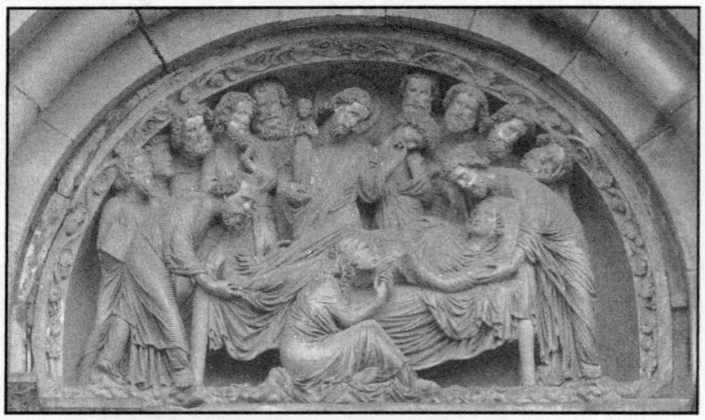

FIG. 13-48 Death of the Virgin, tympanum of left doorway, south transept, Strasbourg Cathedral, Strasbourg, France, ca. 1230. (page 392)

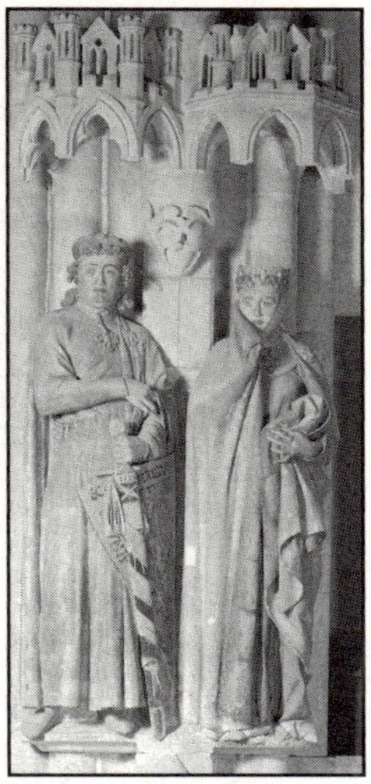

FIG. 13-49 Ekkehard and Uta, statues in the west choir, Naumburg Cathedral, Naumburg, Germany, ca. 1249–1255. Painted limestone, approx. 6′ 2″ high. (page 393)

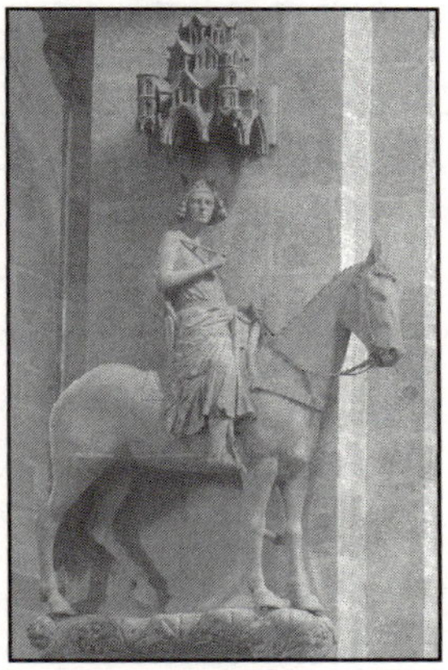

FIG. 13-50 Equestrian portrait *(Bamberg Rider),* statue in the east choir, Bamberg Cathedral, Germany, ca. 1235–1240. Sandstone, 7′ 9″ high. (page 393)

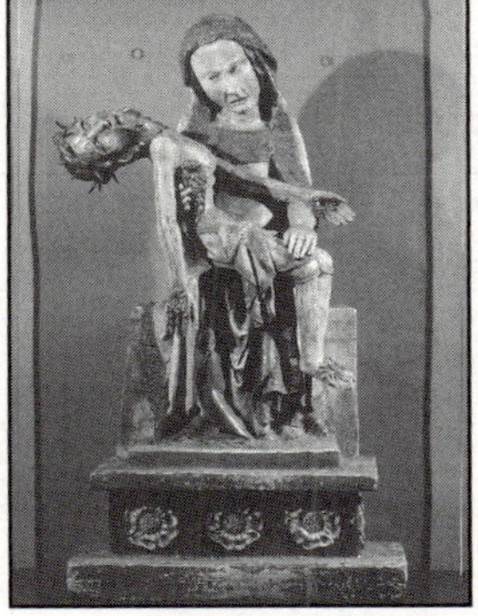

FIG. 13-51 Virgin with the Dead Christ *(Röttgen Pietà),* from the Rhineland, Germany, ca. 1300–1325. Painted wood, 2′ 10 1/2″ high. Rheinisches Landemuseum, Bonn. (page 394)

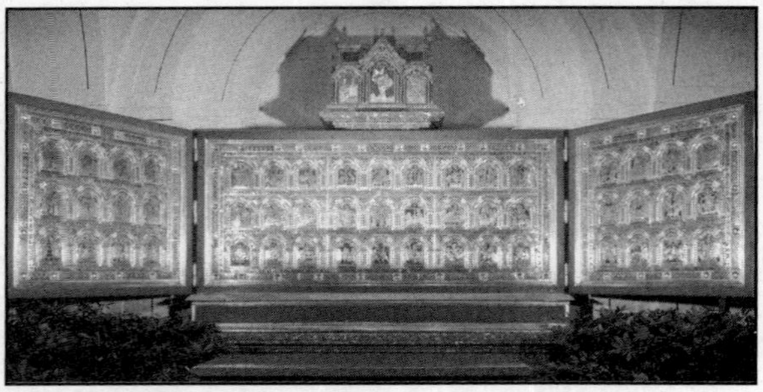

FIG. 13-52 NICHOLAS OF VERDUN, the *Klosterneuburg Altar,* from the abbey church at Klosterneuburg, Austria, 1181. Gilded copper and enamel, 3′ 6 3/4″ high. Stiftsmuseum, Klosterneuburg. (page 394)

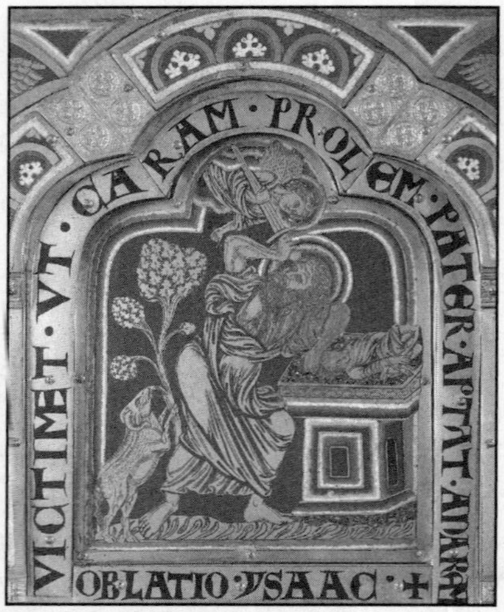

FIG. 13-53 NICHOLAS OF VERDUN, Sacrifice of Isaac, detail of the *Klosterneuburg Altar,* from the abbey church at Klosterneuburg, Austria, 1181. Gilded copper and enamel, 5 1/2″ high. Stiftsmuseum, Klosterneuburg. (page 395)

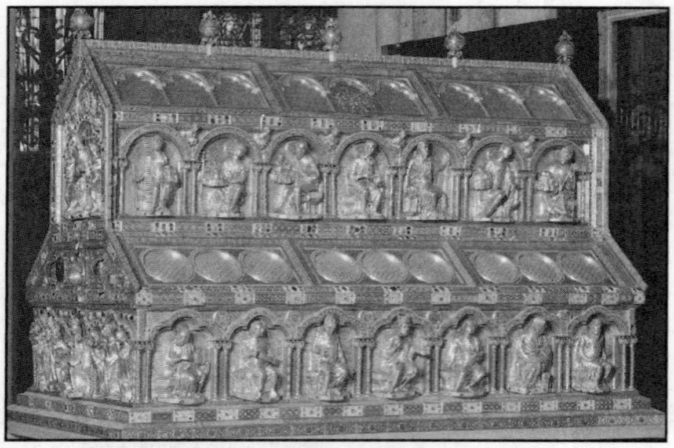

FIG. 13-54 NICHOLAS OF VERDUN, *Shrine of the Three Kings,* from Cologne Cathedral, Cologne, Germany, begun ca. 1190. Silver, bronze, enamel, and gemstones, 5′ 8″ × 6′ × 3′ 8″. Cathedral Treasury, Cologne. (page 395)

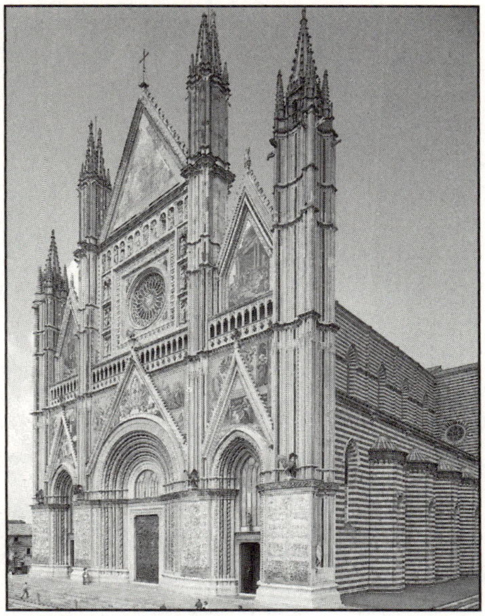

FIG. 13-55 Lorenzo Maitani, west facade of Orvieto Cathedral, Orvieto, Italy, begun 1310. (page 396)

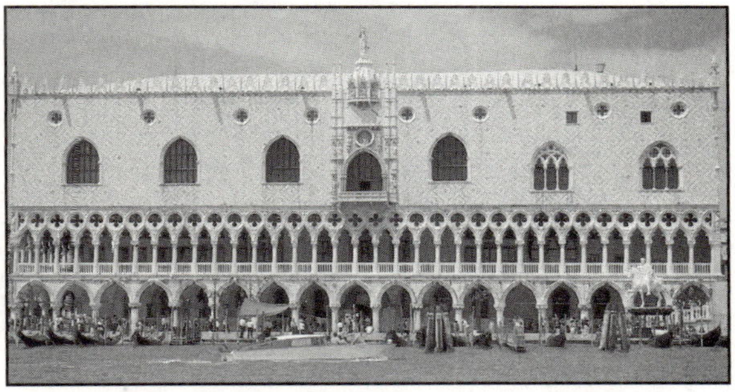

FIG. 13-56 Doge's Palace, Venice, Italy, begun ca. 1340–1345; expanded and remodeled, 1424–1438. (page 397)

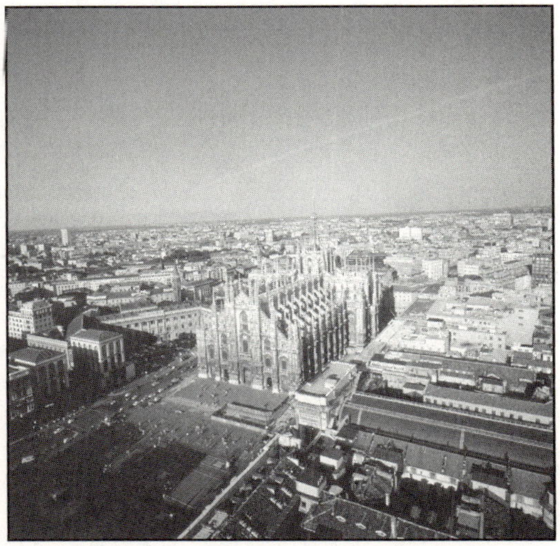

FIG. 13-57 Aerial view of Milan Cathedral (from the southwest), Milan, Italy, begun 1386. (page 398)